ScottForesman

WORLD ATLAS

 **ScottForesman**

A Division of HarperCollinsPublishers

Editorial Office: Glenview, Illinois
Regional Offices: Sunnyvale, California • Atlanta, Georgia
Glenview, Illinois • Oakland, New Jersey • Dallas, Texas

Maps prepared by

Bartholomew, a division of HarperCollins/*Publishers*

Picture credits

Cover

Imtek Imagineering/MASTERFILE

Title Page

NASA

Photographs

J. Allan Cash Photolibrary
The Hutchison Library
London Docklands Development Corporation
Meteorological Department, National Centre for Atmospheric
  Research/National Science Foundation, US
Panos Pictures
Science Photo Library
Sefton Photo Library
Tropix Photographic Library
United States Environment Programme

Scott Foresman Staff

Scott Foresman gratefully acknowledges the contributions
of the following individuals:

Editorial

Barbara Flynn, Mary Chase

Design

Barbara Schneider, Virginia Pierce, Ron Stachowiak

Production

Fran Simon, Derrick Everett

ISBN: 0-673-35171-8

789—PT—989796

Contents

How to Use This Atlas

An atlas is a book of maps. It may also contain photographs, charts, diagrams, graphs, and tables. You can use an atlas as a reference tool to find the location of countries, cities, towns, roads, rivers, mountains and to compare land and water areas.

The *Scott, Foresman World Atlas* is divided into six parts. The first part is introductory. It includes tips on how to use this atlas.

Parts 2, 3, and 4 cover three content areas. The three content areas are Space and Place, Environment and Society, and Spatial Dynamics and Connections. These content areas were established by the National Assessment of Educational Progress in Geography. They draw from the five basic geographic themes. These themes are location, place (physical and human characteristics), human/environment interaction (relationships within places), movement, and regions. Having the atlas organized in this manner will help you gain a better understanding of the world.

Part 2 (Space and Place) will help you develop an understanding of distributions on the Earth's surface and the processes that shape them. This part of the atlas begins with a glossary of geographical terms that provides you with a basic geography vocabulary. The part also contains basic information about the patterns on the earth's surface.

World thematic maps focus on special subjects or themes—such as physical features, climate regions, and natural vegetation. For example, look at the map of natural vegetation on pages 16-17. Suppose you want to know where Africa's deserts are located. Using the color-coded map key, you can see that a huge desert stretches across northern Africa and a much smaller desert runs along the coast of southwestern Africa. Use the map scale to estimate the size of these deserts. You will find that the desert in northern Africa—the Sahara—is more than 3,500 miles from west to east and 1,500 miles from north to south. This desert is larger than the entire United States.

Many of the thematic maps in this atlas use colors to represent a certain quantity. See, for example, the world population distribution map on pages 24-25.

Here each color is used to represent a certain number of people. You can see at a glance which parts of the world are most densely populated (northwest Europe, south Asia, and east Asia).

Also in this part of the atlas, some pages focus on natural forces—such as earthquakes, volcanoes, floods, and tropical storms. By studying the maps and the related visuals and text, you can discover how these natural forces continually change the earth's surface.

Part 3 (Environment and Society) examines the Earth as a human habitat . This part will help you understand how people depend on, adapt to, are affected by, and modify the physical or natural environment. The maps, diagrams, and photographs focus on topics such as deforestation, desertification, pollution, and resources. You will see that many modifications that people make, such as planting trees to reduce erosion from winds, may have positive consequences. However, other modifications people make, such as locating a landfill over a ground water source, may have negative consequences.

Part 4 (Spatial Dynamics and Connections) will help you understand the dynamics of the connections among people and places. These connections include trade relationships, economic diversity, and migration and travel.

The fifth and largest part of this atlas (Regions) contains detailed physical and political maps. Look at the table of contents on pages 3-4. You will see that this part is divided into six regions—North America, South America, Europe, Asia, Africa, and Oceania and Polar Regions.

You will use the maps in this part most often to find states, cities, mountains, lakes, and rivers, and so forth. The easiest way to locate a place is to use the index on pages 123-135 inclusive. The index lists hundreds of place names in alphabetical order. The page on which a place name can be found is listed in bold (dark) type before the name. The numbers following the place name show its particular latitude and longitude.

Let's assume that you want to locate the city of Baghdad which is the capital of Iraq. What steps should you take? First, turn to the index and look up Baghdad. The number in bold type, 95, is the atlas page that you should turn to. Use the geographical coordinates provided (latitude 33°20′N and longitude 44°26′E), to help you find Baghdad on page 95. If you want to see where Iraq is located in relation to other countries, refer to the world political map on pages 48-49.

Note that smaller towns generally appear only on large scale maps, such as the United States regional maps (pages 58-63). In densely populated areas, many smaller towns are omitted in order to make the map easier to read.

Many maps in this part have small black and white locator maps in the upper right-hand margin. For example, look at the map of Central America and the West Indies on pages 66-67. The locator map shows you where this area is located in relation to the rest of the Americas.

Some pages in this part have small maps called inset maps. For example, the map of southern South America on pages 72-73 has an inset map of the Buenos Aires. The inset map shows details of this important urbanized area.

The sixth part of this atlas includes a handy reference table as well as the index described above. Here you will find the flags, capital cities, area and population statistics, major or official languages, and lists of important products for all the world's independent countries.

The Basic Skills of Map Reading
Basically, every map needs to have a title, a scale, a latitude-longitude grid, symbols, and a map projection.

Title. No good map is complete without a map title. It allows you to identify the map's subject matter at first glance. In this atlas, the map titles are in the top margins. Each title identifies the part of the atlas, the area of the world it covers, and the purpose of the map. For example, the title of the map on pages 14-15 is: "Space and Place/The World: Climatic Regions and Graphs."

Scale. Scale refers to the relationship between a map and the part of the earth it represents. It allows you to compare distances on the map to distances on the earth's surface. Scale may be shown in one of three ways. First, it may be shown as a ratio, such as 1:40,000,000. Such a ratio appears on the North America map on page 50. The ratio means that one inch on the map equals 40,000,000 inches on the ground. Second, a map's scale may also be stated in words, such as "One inch equals 631 miles." This statement means that one inch on the map equals 631 miles on the earth's surface. To arrive at this figure, divide 40,000,000 inches by 63,360 inches (the number of inches in a mile). The answer is 631 miles. Third, scale may be shown with a bar scale. This scale is a straight line with distances marked out on it, with each mark representing a set number of miles or kilometers on the earth's surface. Using the bar scale on the map of the Netherlands, Belgium and Luxembourg on page 80, estimate the distance between Amsterdam and Rotterdam. You will see that the distance is about 38 miles.

On most maps in this atlas, scale is shown both as a ratio and by means of a bar scale. These guides will help you estimate distances between places on the map.

The scale on the atlas maps varies from map to map. One inch might equal 100 miles on one map and 500 miles on another. For example, compare the scale of the British Isles (1:4,000,000) on page 79 to that of North America (1:40,000,000) on page 50. The map of the British Isles has the larger scale: one inch on the map represents 63 miles on the ground. The scale of the North American map is smaller: one inch equals 631 miles. Keep in mind that a larger scale map shows a smaller area in greater detail.

Latitude and Longitude. Cartographers use a grid system to locate places on Earth. The system, as shown in the latitude and longitude diagram on page 7, makes use of imaginary criss-crossing lines called parallels and meridians. The parallels run east and west around the earth. They measure latitude—the distance measured in degrees (°) north and south of the Equator. The distance between each degree of latitude is about 70 miles. The Equator is 0° latitude and divides the Earth into two hemispheres: the

Latitude and Longitude Diagram

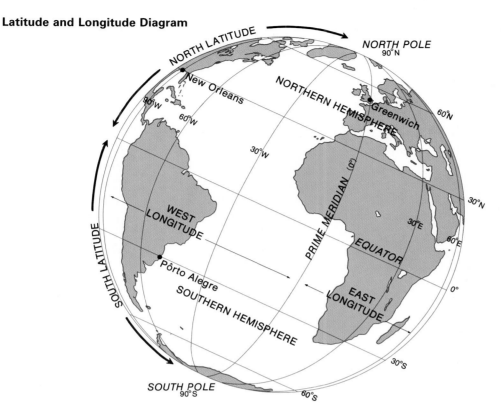

Northern Hemisphere and the Southern Hemisphere. All degrees of latitude are either north of the Equator or south of it. The North Pole is 90°N, and the South Pole is 90°S.

Look at the line representing 30°N latitude on the diagram. You can see that the city of New Orleans is located on this parallel. Because it is north of the Equator, New Orleans has a north latitude position. Pôrto Alegre, located at 30°S latitude, is in the southern latitudes. Now turn to the United States map on pages 54-55 and locate New Orleans. Find 30°N latitude along the margin of either page and move your finger across the parallel until you come to New Orleans. Use the same method to locate the Brazilian city of Pôrto Alegre on pages 72-73.

Meridians are the lines that run north and south from pole to pole. They are not parallel; rather, they meet at the poles. The Prime Meridian, which is shown on the diagram, passes through Greenwich, England. It is located at 0° longitude. The Prime Meridian divides the earth into Eastern and Western hemispheres. Every location to the east, up to 180°, is east longitude. Every place to the west, up to 180°, is west longitude. As you can see on the map on pages 112-113, the 180° meridian passes through the country of Fiji in the South Pacific.

Turn again to the map on pages 54-55. You will see that longitude 90°W intersects New Orleans. Now turn to the map on pages 72-73 and estimate the longitude of Pôrto Alegre. It is about 50°W. Thus, the latitude and longitude of this city is approximately 30°S and 50°W.

Degrees of latitude and longitude are further divided into small units called minutes. There are 60 minutes in each degree, and they are marked by the symbol ('). New Orleans is actually located at 30°0'N and 90°5'W. Pôrto Alegre is actually located at 30°7'S and 50°55'W.

Symbols. Like the other essential elements of a map, the map key serves a special function. The one on page 8 shows various symbols used throughout this atlas. Symbols can stand for many different things. Dots, circles, squares, and larger symbols are used for settlements. These will vary with the size of the community. Larger communities tend to have larger symbols and larger and bolder printed names.

Bold magenta lines show international boundaries—the border lines that separate one country from another. Dot-dash-dot lines are used for internal boundaries, such as states in the United States and provinces in Canada.

Blue represents water, and blue lines indicate rivers. Swamps, marshes, and canals each have their own unique symbols. Notice, for example, the many swamp symbols found in the low-lying areas of southern Florida. (See pages 54-55.)

Color is also used to show varying elevations of land areas and depth of water bodies. As land increases in elevation, the colors change from green to yellow, to orange, to purple and white. As water increases in depth, the color changes from white to light blue to dark blue.

Map Projection. Most maps are not entirely accurate because of a basic property of the earth's surface—it is curved. Map projections are scientific attempts to solve or reduce the problem of distortion, which changes the shape and size of the continents. Many different types have been developed. Each one has some distinct advantages and disadvantages. You can read about the main kinds of projections on page 136.

In this atlas, many projections are used. You will find the name of the map projection below the bar scale on most maps.

Key to Symbols

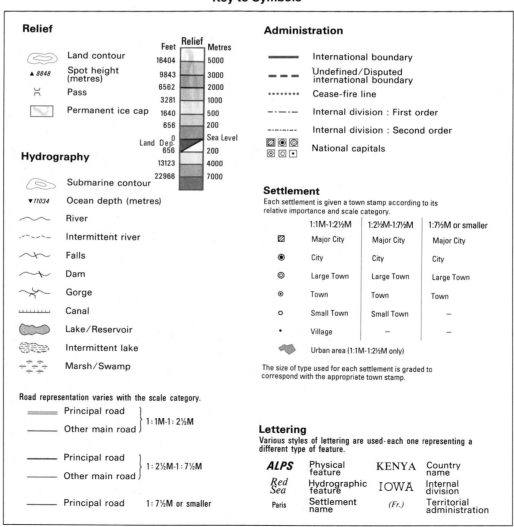

Glossary of Geographical Terms

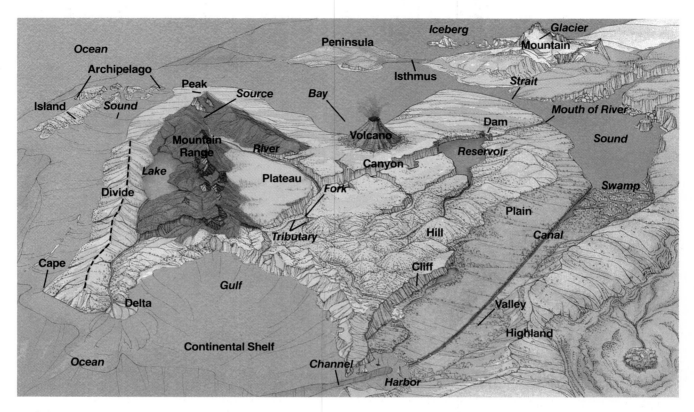

Landforms Diagram

agriculture   science, art, or occupation of cultivating the soil to produce crops, and also of raising live-stock.

altitude   height above the earth's surface. The altitude of a place is usually expressed in feet or meters above or below sea level.

archipelago (är′kə pel′ə gō)   a group of many islands *See diagram.* The Aleutian Islands form an archipelago.

atmosphere   the mass of gases that surrounds the earth and is held to it by the force of gravity.

atoll (at′ol)   a flat, circular-shaped coral island or group of islands enclosing or partly enclosing a body of water called a lagoon.

barrier   a wall built by people to break the impact of waves, often near the entrance to a harbor.

basin   **1** all the land drained by a river and the streams that flow into it. **2** land enclosed by higher land.

bauxite (bôk′sīt)   a claylike mineral from which aluminum is obtained; aluminum ore.

bay   part of an ocean or a lake extending into the land, having a wide opening. A bay is usually smaller than a gulf and larger than a cove. *See diagram.*

butte (byüt)   a steep, flat-topped hill that stands alone on a plain; found in the dry regions of the western United States. A large butte is called a mesa.

canal   a waterway dug across land for transportation, irrigation, or water supply. *See diagram.* The Panama Canal connects the Atlantic and Pacific oceans.

canyon   a long, narrow valley with high, steep sides, often with a river flowing through it. *See diagram.* The Grand Canyon in North America is one mile deep, and it contains the Colorado River.

cape   a point of land which projects out into a body of water. *See diagram.* Cape Horn is at the southern tip of South America.

channel   **1** the bed of a river or a stream. **2** a small body of water that joins two larger bodies of water, like the English Channel. *See diagram.*

cliff   a steep slope of rock or soil. *See diagram.*

climate   **1** the pattern of weather a place has over a long period of time. Climate includes conditions of heat and cold, moisture and dryness, clearness and cloudiness, wind and calm. **2** region with certain conditions of heat and cold, rainfall, wind, sunlight, etc.

consumer goods   products made to satisfy human wants directly, such as clothing and food.

continent   any one of the seven largest masses of land on the earth. The continents, in order of size, are Asia, Africa, North America, South America, Antarctica, Europe, and Australia. Sometimes Asia and Europe are considered to be a single continent called Eurasia.

Pronunciation Key

a hat	**i** it	**oi** oil		a in about	
ā age	**ī** ice	**ou** out		e in taken	
ä far	**o** hot	**u** cup	ə =	i in pencil	
e let	**ō** open	**ù** put		o in lemon	
ē equal	**ô** order	**ü** rule		u in circus	
ėr term					

continental drift according to the theory of plate tectonics, the movement of continents on huge plates that slide across the surface of the earth's mantle.

continental shelf the margin of the continent that extends underwater beyond the shoreline. *See diagram.*

copra (kō′prə) the dried meat of coconuts pressed for coconut oil—used for cooking, soap, shampoo, and margarine.

coral a limestone formation built on underwater rocks by colonies of polyps, small marine animals. Coral may form islands or reefs, sometimes developing on the tops of volcanoes to build atolls.

cordillera (kor′də lyer′ə) a system of mountain ranges, usually set in parallel ridges.

cove 1 a small, sheltered bay; inlet on the shore; mouth of a creek. 2 a sheltered place among hills or woods.

crater a bowl-shaped depression in the earth or around the opening of a volcano. The Greater Meteor Crater near Flagstaff, Arizona, probably resulted from the impact of a large meteorite. Crater Lake in Oregon occupies the crater of an extinct volcano.

dam a wall built across a stream or river to hold back water. *See diagram.*

delta a more or less triangular deposit of sand and soil that collects at the mouth of some rivers. *See diagram.* The Nile River has a large delta.

desert a region with sparse vegetation due to little or no rainfall. A desert may be hot or cold. Local words for desert are often used as place names, like Sahara and Gobi.

divide a ridge of land between two regions drained by different rivers. *See diagram.* The Continental Divide in western North America separates streams flowing toward the Pacific Ocean from those flowing toward the Atlantic Ocean.

downstream the direction toward which a river flows.

Equator imaginary circle around the middle of the earth, halfway between the Poles.

erosion the wearing away of the surface of the earth by all processes, including weathering.

estuary (es′chü er′ē) a broad river mouth into which the tide flows.

export article sent to another country for sale.

fiord or **fjord** a long, narrow inlet of the sea bordered by steep cliffs. Formed by glaciers, fiords can be found along the coasts of Norway, Alaska, and New Zealand.

fork the place where a stream or tributary joins a river. *See diagram.*

glacier a large mass of ice formed over many years from snow on high ground wherever winter snowfall exceeds summer melting. It moves very slowly down a mountain, through a valley, or over a wide stretch of land. *See diagram.*

gulf an arm of an ocean or sea extending into the land. It is usually larger than a bay. *See diagram.*

harbor a sheltered area of water where ships can anchor safely. *See diagram.*

highland an area of mountains, hills, or plateaus. *See diagram.*

hill a raised part of the earth's surface with sloping sides—smaller than a mountian. *See diagram.*

iceberg a large mass of ice floating in the ocean. *See diagram.*

import an article for sale brought in from another country.

island a body of land smaller than a continent and completely surrounded by water. *See diagram.* Greenland is the world's largest island. New Guinea is the second largest.

isthmus (is′məs) a narrow strip of land with water on both sides, connecting two larger bodies of land. *See diagram.* The Isthmus of Panama connects North America and South America.

jute (jüt) a strong fiber obtained from two tropical plants related to the linden, used for making rope and coarse fabrics such as burlap.

lake a large body of water completely surrounded by land. *See diagram.*

lowland a region that is lower and flatter than surrounding land. Broad regions of flat lowlands are called plains.

meridians imaginary lines running from Pole to Pole around the earth. They indicate degrees of longitude. The meridian at 0° longitude is called the Prime Meridian.

mesa (mā′sə) a large butte; a steep, flat-topped hill that stands alone on a plain.

metal any of a class of elements which usually have a shiny surface, conduct heat and electricity, and can be hammered into thin sheets.

mineral any natural substance obtained by mining or quarrying; a mineral may be a metal, such as gold, a liquid, such as petroleum, or a combination of various minerals, such as bauxite.

monsoon a seasonal wind of the Indian Ocean and southern Asia, blowing from the southwest from April to October and from the northeast during the rest of the year.

mountain a raised part of the earth's surface with a pointed or rounded top—higher than a hill. *See diagram.*

mountain range a row of connected mountains. *See diagram.*

mouth (of a river) the part of a river where its waters flow into another body of water. *See diagram.*

oasis (ō ā′sis) a fertile place in the desert where there is water and vegetation.

ocean 1 the great body of salt water that covers almost three-quarters of the earth's surface. *See diagram.* 2 any of its four main divisions: the Pacific, Atlantic, Indian, and Arctic oceans.

parallels imaginary circles running parallel to the Equator around the earth. They indicate degrees of latitude. The parallels at the Poles, 90°N and 90°S, are points not circles.

peak the pointed top of a mountain or hill. *See diagram.*

peninsula (pə nin'sə lə) a piece of land jutting out from the mainland and almost surrounded by water. *See diagram.* Florida and Italy are peninsulas.

plain a broad and flat or gently rolling area. *See diagram.*

plateau (pla tō') a plain at a height considerably above sea level. *See diagram.* The Plateau of Tibet is the highest in the world.

polder a tract of lowland reclaimed from the sea or other body of water and protected by dikes. The Netherlands has extensive polder areas along the North Sea.

population density number of people living per unit of the earth's surface.

prairie (prer'ē) a large area of flat or rolling land covered with grass and very few trees.

precipitation moisture in the form of rain, dew, snow, and so on.

Prime Meridian imaginary line from which longitude east and west is measured; it runs through Greenwich, England, and its longitude is 0°.

rainforest a dense forest in a region where rain is heavy throughout the year. Rainforests are usually in tropical areas, though some may also be found in marine west coast climate areas like the Pacific Northwest coast of North American.

range a row of mountains.

reef a narrow ridge of rocks, sand, or coral lying at or near the surface of the water. The Great Barrier Reef off the northeast coast of Australia is over 1,200 miles long.

relief the differences in elevation between high and low spots in a particular area.

reservoir a place where water is collected and stored. *See diagram.*

resources the actual and potential wealth of a country; supplies that will meet a need, such as farmland or minerals.

rift valley a long, narrow depression with steep walls caused by the shifting of the earth's crust. The Great Rift Valley extends from Israel and Jordan all the way to Mozambique. The Dead Sea, Red Sea, and Lake Nyasa are part of this valley.

river a natural stream of water that flows into a lake or an ocean. *See diagram.* Small rivers are called brooks, creeks, rills, or runs.

river valley depression cut by the action of flowing water in a river.

savanna (sə van'ə) tall grassland with scattered trees between equatorial rainforests and steppes. The length of grass depends on the total rainfall.

savanna climate a tropical climate in which rain falls during the high sun season; also known as the "tropical wet-and-dry climate."

sea any large body of salt water. The word may refer to the oceans as a whole, to a part of an ocean, or to a smaller body of salt water like the Caspian Sea.

sound **1** a narrow body of water separating a large island from the mainland. **2** an inlet of the ocean. *See diagram.*

source (of a river) the place where a river or stream begins. *See diagram.*

staple crops the most important or principal farm products grown in a place.

steppe like the savanna, a treeless grassland, but drier and with short grass. Gradually, as the area of dryness increases, it merges into the desert.

strait a narrow waterway connecting two larger bodies of water. *See diagram.* The Strait of Gibraltar connects the Mediterranean Sea with the Atlantic Ocean.

subsistence farming small-scale farming in which the final products are consumed by the grower's family.

swamp a piece of low-lying land in which water collects. *See diagram.*

taiga (tī'gə) the needleleaf forest that lies south of the tundra in North America, Scandinavia, and northern Eurasia.

topography the shape and elevation of an area's terrain.

tributary stream that flows into a larger stream or body of water; part of a river system. *See diagram.*

tropical rainforest a dense forest of trees, vines, ferns, and flowers near the Equator that receives abundant rainfall the year round.

tundra (tun'drə) area of land between timberline and polar regions on which only mosses, lichens, and a few shrubs grow. The ground just beneath the thin topsoil may remain frozen the year round, as permafrost. Tundra exists in high latitudes and high altitudes.

uplands a hilly region; contrasted with highlands, a mountainous region.

upstream the direction from which a river flows.

urbanization the growth of cities.

valley low land between hills or mountains. *See diagram.*

volcano an opening in the earth's crust through which steam, ashes, and molten rock are forced out. *See diagram.* A volcano may be active (capable of erupting at any time), dormant (not currently active), or extinct (no longer active and unlikely to be so again). The state of Hawaii is located on the tops of some of the world's highest volcanoes, which lie mainly beneath the Pacific Ocean.

weathering process which wears away the earth's surface by changes of temperature, by wind, rain, frost, and so on; the breakup of rocks into fragments.

Pronunciation Key

a	hat	**i**	it	**oi**	oil		a	in about
ā	age	**ī**	ice	**ou**	out		e	in taken
ä	far	**o**	hot	**u**	cup	ə =	i	in pencil
e	let	**ō**	open	**ú**	put		o	in lemon
ē	equal	**ô**	order	**ü**	rule		u	in circus
ėr	term							

Space and Place

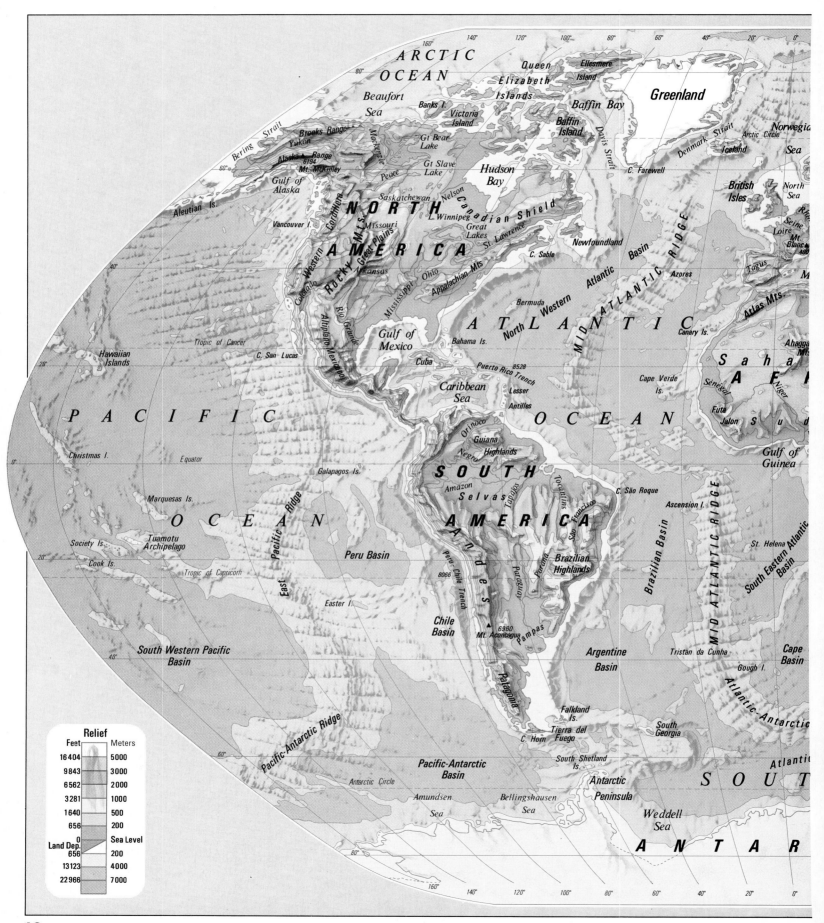

ARCTIC OCEAN

Queen
Elizabeth
Islands
Ellesmere
Island

Greenland

Beaufort
Sea
Banks I.
Victoria
Island
Baffin Bay
Baffin
Island
Davis Strait

Bering Strait
Brooks Range
Yukon
Mackenzie
Gt Bear
Lake
Hudson
Bay
Denmark Strait
Arctic Circle
Iceland
Norwegia
Sea

Alaska Range
6194
Mt. McKinley
Peace
Gt Slave
Lake
C. Farewell

Gulf of
Alaska
Saskatchewan
Nelson
Canadian Shield
British
Isles
North
Sea

Aleutian Is.
NORTH
L. Winnipeg
Great
Lakes
St. Lawrence
Newfoundland
Seine
Loire

Vancouver I.
AMERICA
Mts.
Missouri
Rocky
Cordillera
Western
Great Plains
Ohio
Appalachian Mts
C. Sable
Atlantic
Basin
Mt.
Blanc

Arkansas
Mississippi
Bermuda
North Western Atlantic
Azores
Tagus

Colorado
Rio Grande
Altiplano Mexicano
Tropic of Cancer
Gulf of
Mexico
Bahama Is.
A T L A N T I C
Canary Is.
Atlas Mts.

Hawaiian
Islands
C. San Lucas
Cuba
Puerto Rico Trench
8528
Lesser
Antilles
O C E A N
Cape Verde
Is.
Saha
AFI

P A C I F I C
Caribbean
Sea
Futa
Jalon
Sud

Christmas I.
Equator
Galapagos Is.
Orinoco
Guiana
Highlands
Gulf of
Guinea

Marquesas Is.
Negro
SOUTH
Amazon
Selvas
Tapajos
Tocantins
São Francisco
C. São Roque
Ascension I.
Brazilian Basin

O C E A N
Pacific Ridge
East
AMERICA
Andes
Brazilian
Highlands
Mid Atlantic Ridge
South Eastern Atlantic
Basin

Society Is.
Tuamotu
Archipelago
Peru Basin
Paraguay
Parana
St. Helena

Cook Is.
Tropic of Capricorn
8066
Peru Chile Trench
Easter I.

South Western Pacific
Basin
Chile
Basin
6960
Mt. Aconcagua
Pampas
Argentine
Basin
Tristan da Cunha
Gough I.
Cape
Basin

Patagonia
Falkland
Is.
Atlantic-Antarctic

Pacific-Antarctic Ridge
Tierra del
Fuego
C. Horn
South
Georgia

Pacific-Antarctic
Basin
South Shetland
Is.
Antarctic
Peninsula
S O U T

Antarctic Circle
Amundsen
Sea
Bellingshausen
Sea
Weddell
Sea
Atlantic

A N T A R

Relief	
Feet	Meters
16404	5000
9843	3000
6562	2000
3281	1000
1640	500
656	200
0 Land Dep.	Sea Level
656	200
13123	4000
22966	7000

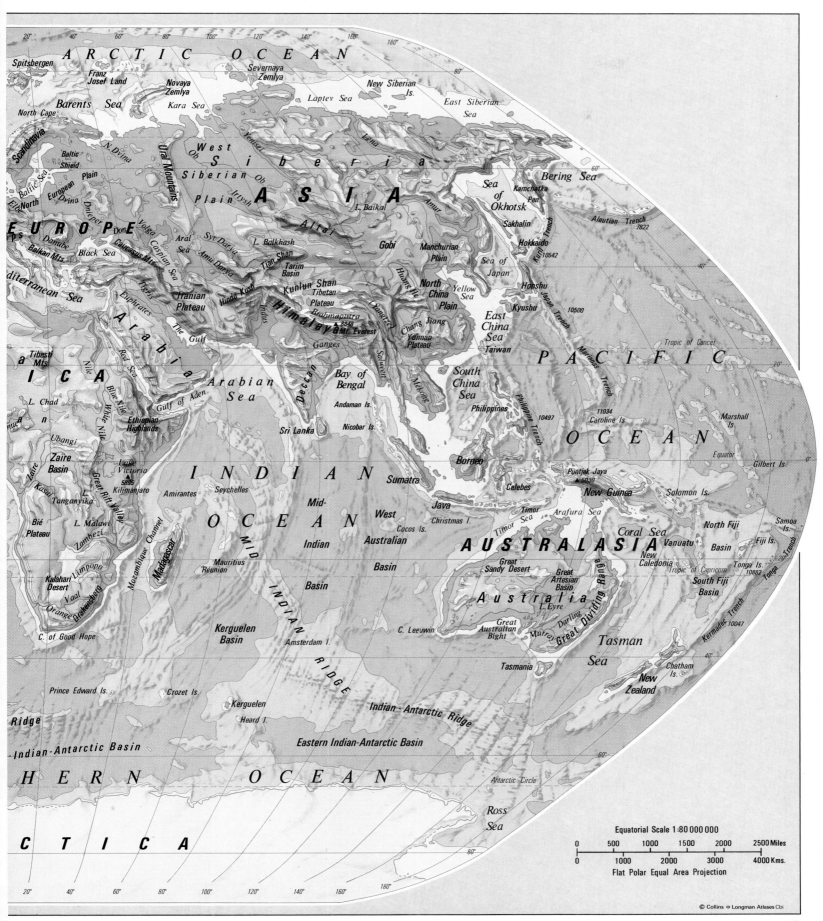

ARCTIC OCEAN

Spitsbergen
Franz Josef Land
Novaya Zemlya
Severnaya Zemlya
New Siberian Is.
Barents Sea
Kara Sea
Laptev Sea
East Siberian Sea
North Cape
Scandinavia
Baltic Shield
N. Dvina
Ural Mountains
West Siberian Plain
Ob
Siberian Plain
Ob
Irtysh
Yenisei
Lena
ASIA
Bering Sea
Kamchatka Pen.
60°
Baltic Sea
European Plain
Dnieper
Volga
Caspian Sea
L. Baikal
Amur
Sakhalin
Sea of Okhotsk
Aleutian Trench 7822
Elbe
North
Don
Aral Sea
Syr Darya
L. Balkhash
Altai
Gobi
Manchurian Plain
Hokkaido
Kuril Trench 10542
EUROPE
Danube
Balkan Mts
Black Sea
Caucasus Mts
Amu Darya
Tian Shan
Tarim Basin
Kunlun Shan
Manchurian Plain
Sea of Japan
Honshu
Japan Trench
Mediterranean Sea
Tigris
Euphrates
Iranian Plateau
Hindu Kush
Tibetan Plateau
Huang He
North China Plain
Yellow Sea
Kyushu
Japan Trench 10500
40°
Arabia
The Gulf
Indus
Himalaya
▲8848 Mt. Everest
Brahmaputra
Yangtze
Chang Jiang
East China Sea
PACIFIC
Tropic of Cancer
Tibesti Mts
Nile
Red Sea
Ganges
Deccan
Salween
Yunnan Plateau
Taiwan
20°
AFRICA
L. Chad
Blue Nile
White Nile
Gulf of Aden
Ethiopian Highlands
Arabian Sea
Bay of Bengal
Andaman Is.
Mekong
South China Sea
Philippines
Philippine Trench 10497
Caroline Is. 11034
Marshall Is.
OCEAN
Ubangi
Sri Lanka
Nicobar Is.
Equator
Zaire Basin
Kasai
Tanganyika
L. Victoria
Kilimanjaro ▲5895
Amirantes
Seychelles
INDIAN
Sumatra
Celebes
Puntjak Jaya ▲5030
New Guinea
Gilbert Is.
Solomon Is.
Bié Plateau
L. Malawi
Zambezi
OCEAN
Mid-
Java
Christmas I.
Timor Sea
Arafura Sea
North Fiji Basin
Samoa
Limpopo
Mozambique Channel
Madagascar
Mauritius
Réunion
West Indian Basin
Cocos Is.
Australian
Timor Sea
AUSTRALASIA
Vanuatu
Coral Sea
New Caledonia
Fiji Is.
Tonga Trench
Kalahari Desert
Vaal
Orange
Drakensberg
Great Sandy Desert
Great Artesian Basin
Tropic of Capricorn
Tonga Is. 10882
South Fiji Basin
C. of Good Hope
Kerguelen Basin
Amsterdam I.
C. Leeuwin
Australia
L. Eyre
Murray
Darling
Great Dividing Range
Kermadec Trench 10047
MID INDIAN RIDGE
Great Australian Bight
Tasman Sea
Tasmania
Chatham Is.
Prince Edward Is.
Crozet Is.
Kerguelen
Heard I.
Indian - Antarctic Ridge
New Zealand
Indian-Antarctic Basin
Eastern Indian-Antarctic Basin
SOUTHERN OCEAN
Ross Sea
ANTARCTICA

Equatorial Scale 1:80 000 000

| 0 | 500 | 1000 | 1500 | 2000 | 2500 Miles |

| 0 | 1000 | 2000 | 3000 | 4000 Kms. |

Flat Polar Equal Area Projection

© Collins ◇ Longman Atlases Cbi

13

Space and Place

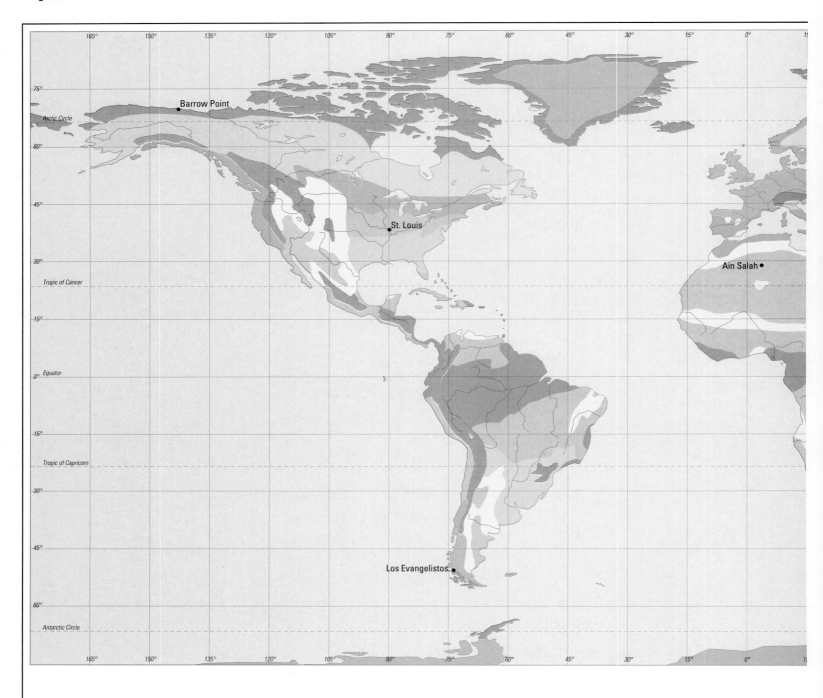

CLIMATIC GRAPHS

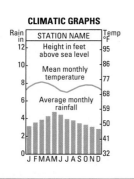

Rain in	STATION NAME	Temp °F
12	Height in feet above sea level	95
10		86
8	Mean monthly temperature	77
6		68
4	Average monthly rainfall	59
2		50
0		41
	J FMAM J J A SOND	32

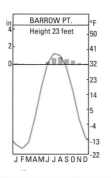

BARROW PT.
Height 23 feet

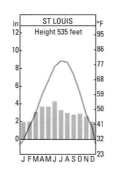

ST LOUIS
Height 535 feet

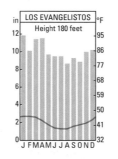

LOS EVANGELISTOS
Height 180 feet

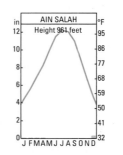

AIN SALAH
Height 961 feet

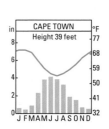

CAPE TOWN
Height 39 feet

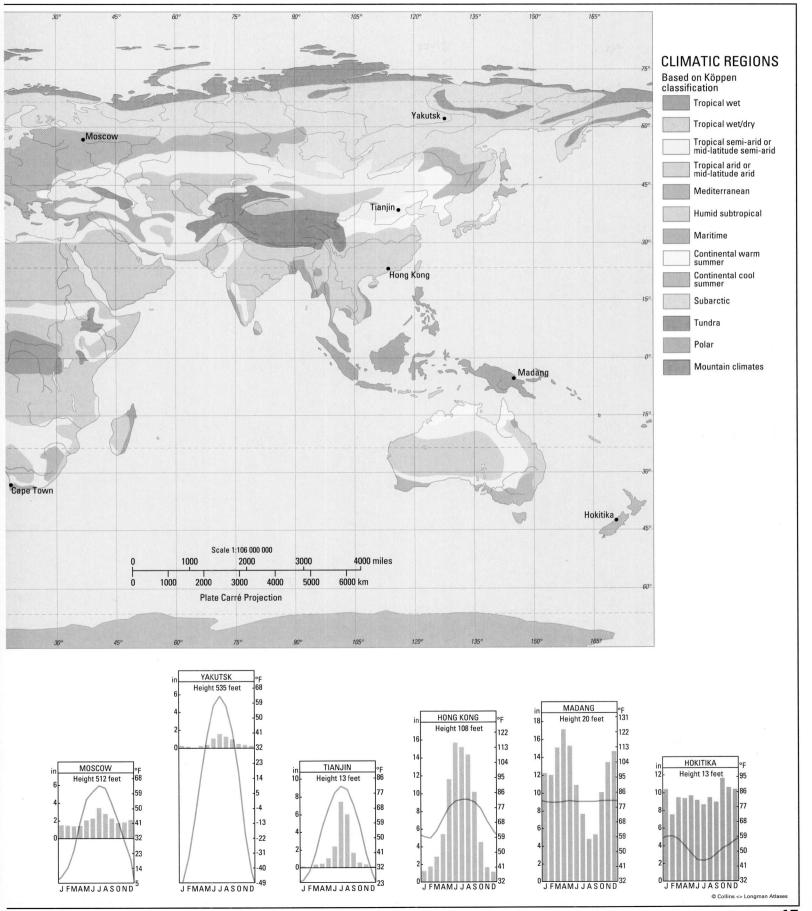

CLIMATIC REGIONS

Based on Köppen classification

- Tropical wet
- Tropical wet/dry
- Tropical semi-arid or mid-latitude semi-arid
- Tropical arid or mid-latitude arid
- Mediterranean
- Humid subtropical
- Maritime
- Continental warm summer
- Continental cool summer
- Subarctic
- Tundra
- Polar
- Mountain climates

Scale 1:106 000 000

Plate Carré Projection

YAKUTSK
Height 535 feet

MOSCOW
Height 512 feet

TIANJIN
Height 13 feet

HONG KONG
Height 108 feet

MADANG
Height 20 feet

HOKITIKA
Height 13 feet

© Collins <> Longman Atlases

Space and Place

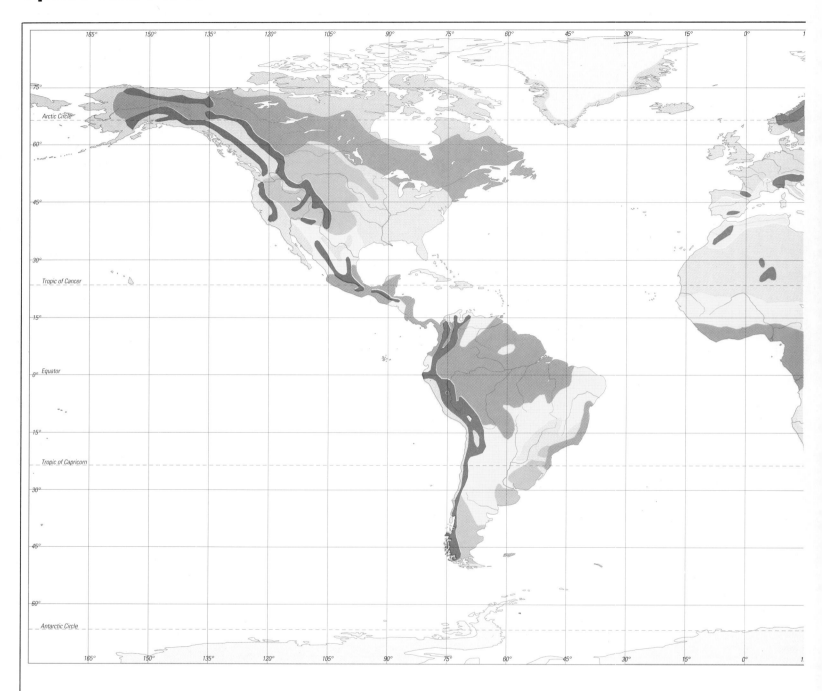

Ice cap, Antarctica

Tundra, Norway

Coniferous forest, Canada

Temperate deciduous forest, UK

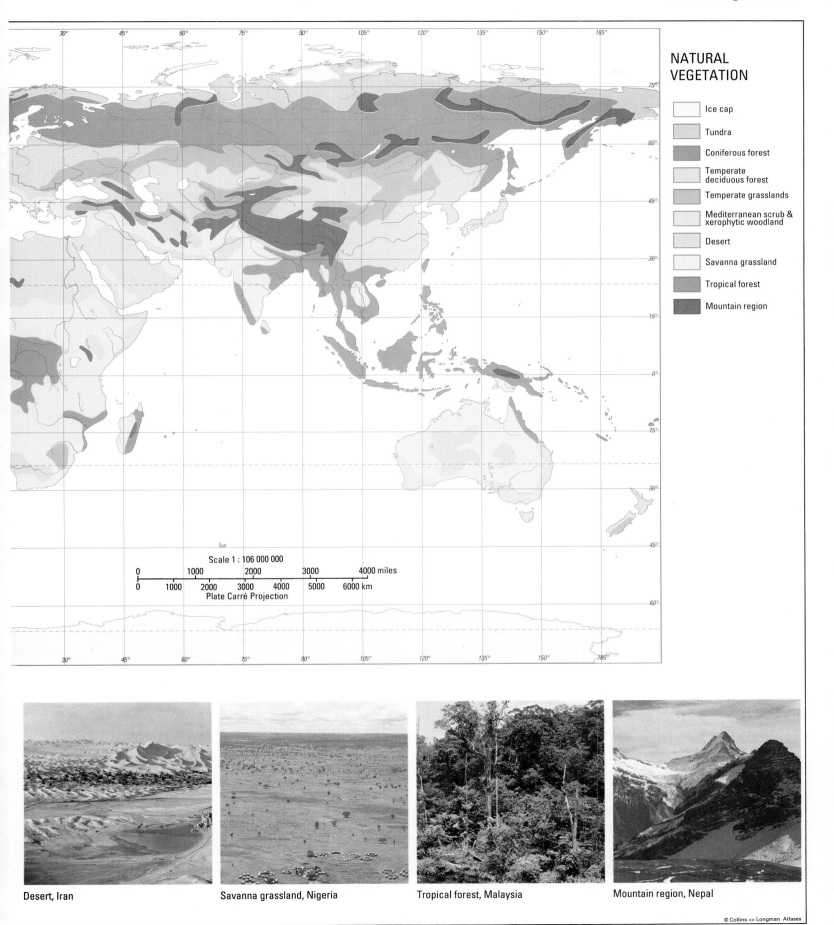

NATURAL VEGETATION

- Ice cap
- Tundra
- Coniferous forest
- Temperate deciduous forest
- Temperate grasslands
- Mediterranean scrub & xerophytic woodland
- Desert
- Savanna grassland
- Tropical forest
- Mountain region

Scale 1 : 106 000 000

| 0 | 1000 | 2000 | 3000 | 4000 miles |

| 0 | 1000 | 2000 | 3000 | 4000 | 5000 | 6000 km |

Plate Carré Projection

Desert, Iran

Savanna grassland, Nigeria

Tropical forest, Malaysia

Mountain region, Nepal

Space and Place

Plate boundaries, Earthquakes, and Volcanoes

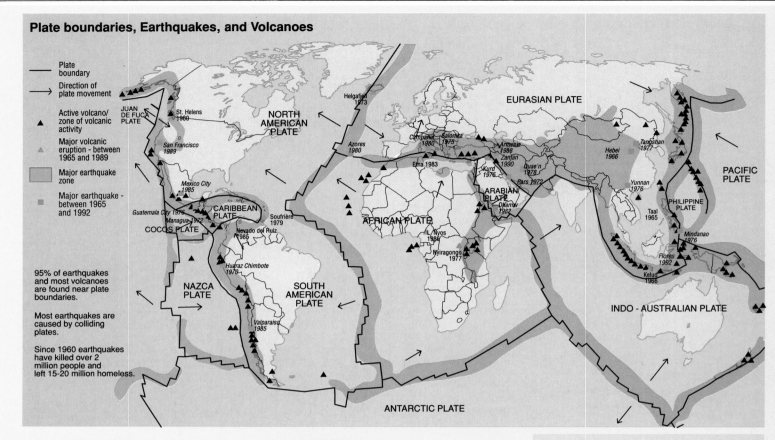

Legend:
- — Plate boundary
- → Direction of plate movement
- ▲ Active volcano/ zone of volcanic activity
- ▲ Major volcanic eruption - between 1965 and 1989
- Major earthquake zone
- ■ Major earthquake - between 1965 and 1992

95% of earthquakes and most volcanoes are found near plate boundaries.

Most earthquakes are caused by colliding plates.

Since 1960 earthquakes have killed over 2 million people and left 15-20 million homeless.

Plates labeled on map: JUAN DE FUCA PLATE, NORTH AMERICAN PLATE, EURASIAN PLATE, PACIFIC PLATE, CARIBBEAN PLATE, COCOS PLATE, AFRICAN PLATE, ARABIAN PLATE, PHILIPPINE PLATE, NAZCA PLATE, SOUTH AMERICAN PLATE, INDO - AUSTRALIAN PLATE, ANTARCTIC PLATE

Locations marked: St. Helens 1980, San Francisco 1989, Mexico City 1985, Guatemala City 1976, Managua 1972, Nevado del Ruiz 1985, Soufrière 1979, Huaraz Chimbote 1978, Valparaiso 1985, Helgafjell 1973, Azores 1980, Campania 1980, Salonika 1975, Etna 1983, Armenia 1988, Kurd 1976, Zanjan 1990, Quae'n 1978, Pars 1972, Dhamar 1982, L. Nyos 1986, Nyiragongo 1977, Hebei 1966, Tangshan 1977, Yunnan 1976, Taal 1965, Mindanao 1976, Flores 1992, Kelud 1966

The Structure of the Earth

The earth's surface or crust forms a rigid layer of rock which varies in thickness from 4 miles to 25 miles. Beneath the crust is a zone of semimolten rock known as the asthenosphere. Together with the upper mantle this reaches down to a depth of about 435 miles, below which there is the lower mantle and the core.

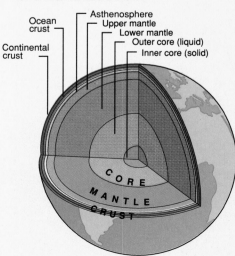

Labels: Ocean crust, Continental crust, Asthenosphere, Upper mantle, Lower mantle, Outer core (liquid), Inner core (solid), CORE, MANTLE, CRUST

The earth's interior consists of three layers - the crust on the surface, the mantle underneath and the core at the center.

Types of Plates

The crust is broken into huge plates which fit together like the parts of a giant jigsaw. These float on the semimolten rock below. The boundaries between the plates are the site of many volcanoes and earthquakes.

There are three types of boundaries:-
Diverging plates. When two plates move away from each other, molten rock wells up from the earth's core creating a ridge, e.g. the ridge in the Atlantic Ocean from Iceland to Antarctica.

Converging plates. When two plates move towards each other a trench is formed as one slides beneath the other. It was a movement of this kind which created the Himalayas.

Shearing plates. Sometimes neighboring plates move horizontally in opposite directions from one another, e.g. the San Andreas Fault in California.

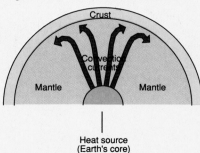

Labels: Crust, Convection currents, Mantle, Mantle, Heat source (Earth's core)

Convection and Plate Movement

Plate movements cause continents to drift at about 1 inch a year. They are carried by convection currents in the magma.

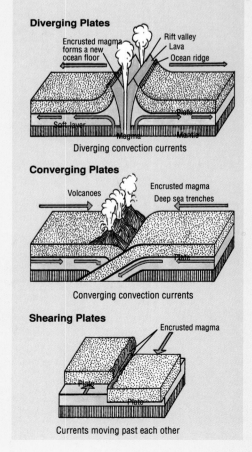

Diverging Plates

Labels: Encrusted magma forms a new ocean floor, Rift valley, Lava, Ocean ridge, Soft layer, Magma, Mantle, Plate

Diverging convection currents

Converging Plates

Labels: Volcanoes, Encrusted magma, Deep sea trenches, Plate

Converging convection currents

Shearing Plates

Labels: Encrusted magma, Plate, Plate

Currents moving past each other

Earthquakes

The shock from an earthquake spreads out from a point known as the epicenter. The amount of damage depends, among other things, on the depth of the epicenter.

The force of an earthquake is measured on a scale devised by an American, Dr Charles Richter in 1935. Each step on the scale represents a tenfold increase in intensity.

Parts of an earthquake

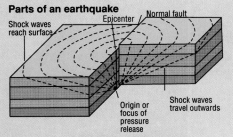

Major earthquakes since 1970

DATE	COUNTRY	FORCE (Richter scale)	DEATHS
31.5.70	Peru	7.7	66 800
23.12.72	Nicaragua	6.2	5 000
4.2.76	Guatemala	7.7	22 700
27.7.76	Tangshan, China	8.2	242 000
16.9.78	Iran	7.7	25 000
10.10.80	Algeria	7.5	2 600
23.11.80	Italy	6.8	3 000
13.12.82	Yemen	6.0	2 000
19.9.85	Mexico	8.1	25 000
7.12.88	Armenia	6.9	25 000
17.10.89	California, USA	6.9	300
21.6.90	Iran	7.5	40 000
12.12.92	Indonesia	7.5	2 000

Volcanoes

There are about 500 active volcanoes in the world. The majority of them are found in two main zones: a 'Ring of Fire' around the Pacific Ocean and an east-west belt from Europe to Indonesia.

Volcanic eruptions can cause terrible damage. Molten rock pours out of the vent over the surrounding area, and rock dust and gas are blown high into the atmosphere.

Mt. St. Helens Volcano

DATE: May 18, 1980

LOCATION: Washington, USA

EXTENT OF DEBRIS: 22,000 sq. miles

DEATHS: 60

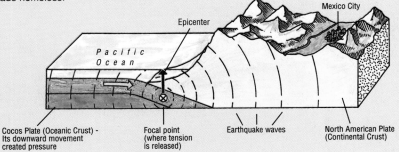

The Mexican Earthquake Disaster

Devastation in Mexico City. The photo shows a multi-story building which has completely collapsed.

Seven states were affected by the earthquake. There were thousands of deaths and injuries and over 30,000 people were made homeless.

Mount St. Helens Eruption

The eruption of the Mount St. Helens in the state of Washington was one of the most dramatic in recent years. The explosion blew out of the side of the cone, and reduced the height of the mountain by 1280 feet, creating a vast new crater. The blast also flattened half a million trees over a radius of 15 miles and blew dust high into the stratosphere across all of North America.

The volcano was in a remote area so only a small number of people were affected. It gave scientists an opportunity to find out more about what the early earth looked like. Plant life returned quickly to the devastated areas. It seems that pockets survived in gulleys and under rocks enabling life to regenerate quickly.

The Mexico City Earthquake

DATE:	September 19, 1985
EPICENTER:	40 miles west of the Pacific Ocean
FORCE:	8.1 (Richter scale)
AREA DEVASTATED:	310,000 sq. miles around Mexico City
DEATHS:	25,000
COSTS:	US $ 4 billion, including damage to buildings, public services and disruption of economic activity

STATES AFFECTED BY THE EARTHQUAKE

1. Jalisco
2. Colima
3. Michoacan
4. Guerrero
5. Mexico
6. Morelos
7. Veracruz

How the volcano blew

1. Build up of pressure
2. Landslide caused by stress
3. Eruption released magma

Results of the eruption

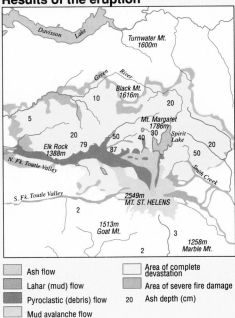

Ash flow
Lahar (mud) flow
Pyroclastic (debris) flow
Mud avalanche flow
Area of complete devastation
Area of severe fire damage
20 Ash depth (cm)

Space and Place

Many important towns and cities are built on rivers. The Nile, Indus, and Euphrates rivers supported some of the earliest civilizations. The needs of agriculture, communications, and trade have ensured that rivers remain important in the modern world. As population increases the demand on water resources is becoming greater. There is a pressing need for proper water management.

Major World Floods

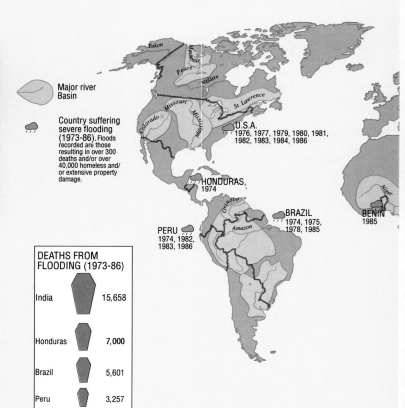

Major river Basin

Country suffering severe flooding (1973-86). Floods recorded are those resulting in over 300 deaths and/or over 40,000 homeless and/or extensive property damage.

U.S.A.
1976, 1977, 1979, 1980, 1981, 1982, 1983, 1984, 1986

HONDURAS 1974

BRAZIL 1974, 1975, 1978, 1985

BENIN 1985

PERU 1974, 1982, 1983, 1986

Deforestation and Floods

North & South Korea — Japan
Afghanistan — Pakistan — Nepal — China
USA
Mexico
Honduras
Brazil
Peru
Argentina
Kenya
India
Bangladesh
Indonesia
Mozambique
South Africa

Countries experiencing severe flooding (1963-85)
△ Flood(s) causing over 1,000 deaths in any one year
△ Flood(s) causing over 100 deaths in any one year

Annual rates of tropical forest clearance
- 1,250,000 - 2,500,000 acres
- 125,000 - 1,250,000 acres
- 0 - 125,000 acres

(Source UNEP Data)

Forests can delay the release of flood water by trapping it in their roots. When the trees are cut down the result is often soil erosion and flooding.

DEATHS FROM FLOODING (1973-86)

Country	Deaths
India	15,658
Honduras	7,000
Brazil	5,601
Peru	3,257
Pakistan	1,850
China	1,550
Indonesia	1,501
Bangladesh	403
Japan	335
USA	305
Mozambique	300

(Source UNEP Data)

The Effects of Deforestation

FORESTED AREA

Ⓐ Heavy rain and water from melting snow runs down slopes and becomes trapped in the roots of trees.

Ⓑ Some of the water evaporates, forms clouds, and is carried on the wind to arid regions.

Ⓒ The water flows on towards the sea in a fairly steady flow, free of silt.

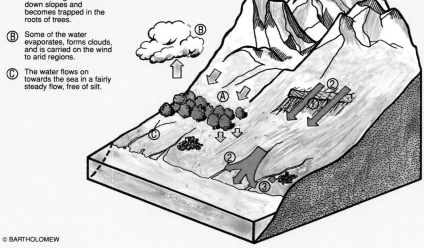

DEFORESTED AREA

① Without trees to hold it back, flood water rushes down mountain slopes.

② The swollen streams cut deep channels and carry away valuable top soil.

③ Further downstream the river channel becomes clogged with silt, causing floods.

Flooding in Bangladesh

In Bangladesh, the monsoon rains cause the rivers to flood each year. These floods are a normal part of life and help to renew the fertility of the soil. In recent years, however, the floods have become much more severe due to the clearance of forests in the Himalayas for fuel, farmland, and logging. These floods have caused serious damage and loss of life.

Severe flooding as a result of deforestation in the Himalayas is also a problem in India. Each year it spends over a million US$ on river defenses to control flooding.

SEPTEMBER 1987
671 dead
2 million homes washed away
4.3 million acres of land destroyed
3 million tons (10%) of rice and wheat crops lost

AUGUST 1988
Over 3,000 dead
75% of country flooded
250 bridges and 2,200 miles of road destroyed
3 million tons of rice and other crops destroyed

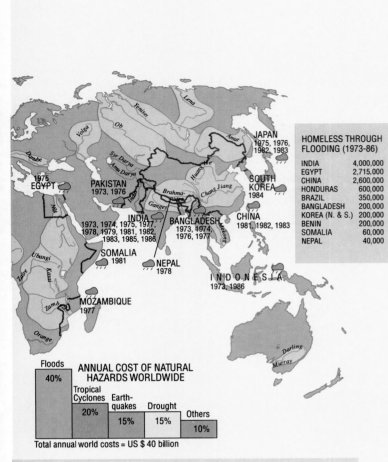

HOMELESS THROUGH FLOODING (1973-86)	
INDIA	4,000,000
EGYPT	2,715,000
CHINA	2,600,000
HONDURAS	600,000
BRAZIL	350,000
BANGLADESH	200,000
KOREA (N. & S.)	200,000
BENIN	200,000
SOMALIA	60,000
NEPAL	40,000

ANNUAL COST OF NATURAL HAZARDS WORLDWIDE

Floods	Tropical Cyclones	Earthquakes	Drought	Others
40%	20%	15%	15%	10%

Total annual world costs = US $ 40 billion

Flood Damage

Flooding causes more damage than any other environmental hazard.

While all countries in the world are affected by floods, the impact on people in developing countries is greater. The number of deaths and homes destroyed is often much higher. This is partly because they cannot afford to protect themselves, and partly because shortage of land forces them to live in vulnerable areas. In addition any loss of food crops, export crops, and employment can have a devastating effect.

Controlling Floods

Around the world there are plans for dams which will control floods and generate hydroelectric power.

Examples include:

Mekong dams on the Red River in Vietnam
Three Gorges Dam on the Chang Jiang in China
Narmada Dam in India

The problem with all these schemes is that they will flood large areas of land and attract industry which will put pressure on environmentally sensitive areas. Often local people do not benefit from them, foreign companies and banks taking most of the profits.

Many flood control measures only deal with the symptoms. The best solutions tackle the causes as well.

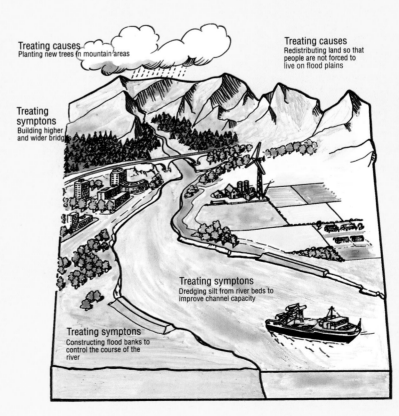

Space and Place

Tropical Storms

In tropical regions, intense storms form over the ocean in late summer and early autumn. The majority occur in the Northern Hemisphere. They are known as 'hurricanes' in either the North Atlantic Ocean or eastern Pacific Ocean, 'typhoons' in the western Pacific Ocean, and 'cyclones' in the Indian Ocean.

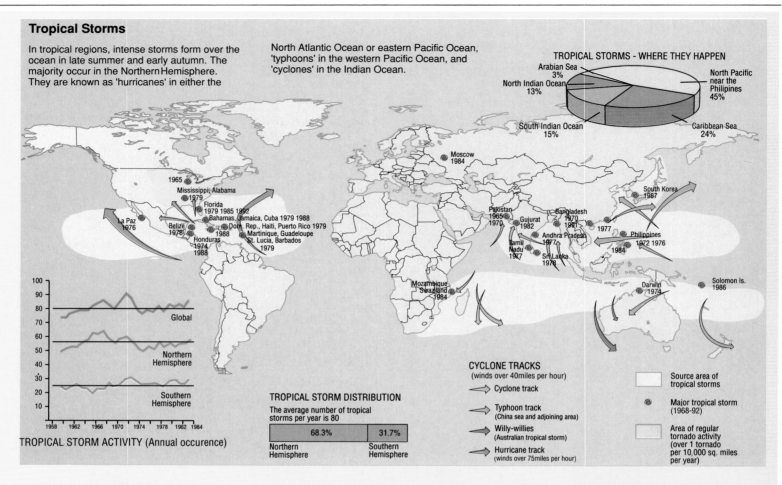

TROPICAL STORMS - WHERE THEY HAPPEN

- Arabian Sea 3%
- North Indian Ocean 13%
- North Pacific near the Philipines 45%
- South Indian Ocean 15%
- Caribbean Sea 24%

TROPICAL STORM ACTIVITY (Annual occurence)

TROPICAL STORM DISTRIBUTION
The average number of tropical storms per year is 80

Northern Hemisphere	Southern Hemisphere
68.3%	31.7%

CYCLONE TRACKS
(winds over 40miles per hour)

- Cyclone track
- Typhoon track (China sea and adjoining area)
- Willy-willies (Australian tropical storm)
- Hurricane track (winds over 75miles per hour)

- Source area of tropical storms
- Major tropical storm (1968-92)
- Area of regular tornado activity (over 1 tornado per 10,000 sq. miles per year)

The Life of a Tropical Storm

Tropical storms can only begin if sea temperatures rise to 80°F or more. This allows large quantities of moisture to evaporate into the atmosphere creating unsettled weather conditions. As the pressure drops, the storm begins to spin violently and is carried along by the trade winds. The storm sucks in more moisture as it passes over the warm ocean and becomes more intense. Eventually the storm moves to cooler areas, or passes over land, loses energy, and breaks up.

Structure of a Tropical Storm

At the center of a tropical storm there is an 'eye' of calm and cloudless skies. Around it, violent winds, often in excess of 100miles per hour, bring torrential rain that may last for several days.

Naming Tropical Storms

Since the Second World War, tropical storms have been named in alphabetical order during each year. This means you can tell from the initial letter how many there have been in a season. Typhoons often use the full range of the alphabet. Hurricanes, being less frequent, tend to only use the first half.

Structure of a Hurricane

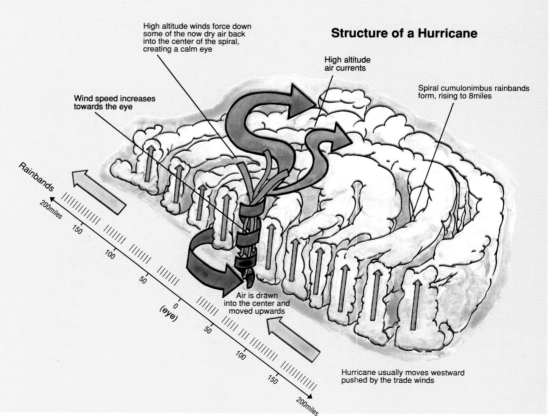

High altitude winds force down some of the now dry air back into the center of the spiral, creating a calm eye

High altitude air currents

Spiral cumulonimbus rainbands form, rising to 8miles

Wind speed increases towards the eye

Air is drawn into the center and moved upwards

Hurricane usually moves westward pushed by the trade winds

NORTH CAROLINA

SOUTH CAROLINA

GEORGIA

ATLANTIC OCEAN

Hurricane Hugo

First detected on September 9 as a cluster of storms off the west African coast, Hurricane Hugo developed into the strongest hurricane of 1989, sustaining wind speeds of 160 miles per hour. Hurricane Hugo left a trail of destruction across a number of Caribbean islands and in both the states of North and South Carolina. The cost of the storm damage was estimated at 10 billion US dollars and 49 lives were lost.

False color satellite image showing Hurricane Hugo as it struck the eastern coast of the United States at South Carolina on September 22, 1989.

The Effect of Hurricanes in the Caribbean

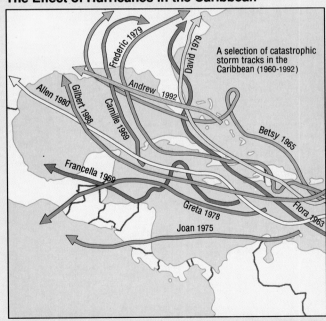

A selection of catastrophic storm tracks in the Caribbean (1960-1992)

Frederic 1979
David 1979
Andrew 1992
Allen 1980
Gilbert 1988
Camille 1969
Betsy 1965
Francella 1969
Greta 1978
Flora 1963
Joan 1975

Vehicles, caught in a hurricane in Houston, Texas, dodge live power lines.

Hurricane Camille caused severe flooding in the USA. More than 300 people were killed.

In 1988, Gilbert, the most powerful hurricane ever recorded, led to a national disaster being declared in Jamaica.

Hurricane David in 1979 caused widespread damage in Dominica. 1,300 people died and 100,000 were left homeless.

Hurricane Allen crossed Barbados and Jamaica causing death and destruction.

Hurricanes

Tropical storms can do terrible damage. Not only do the fierce winds tear buildings apart, but the low pressure can create a surge of seawater that floods coastal areas. The torrential rain adds to these problems.

In some parts of the world, special emergency services and hurricane warning systems have been set up. It is in poorer countries that most lives are lost and the damage is worst. Here many buildings are badly constructed and people can not afford to take precautions.

Tornadoes

Tornadoes are powerful, twisting wind storms associated with rain and thunderstorms. Usually about 100 yards in width, and with only the most violent lasting longer than an hour. They are rotating funnel clouds that extend downward from a mass of dark clouds. Wind speeds at the center can reach over 180 mph. At such high speed, tornadoes can cause loss of life and severe damage to property.

Tornadoes are particularly common in the United States especially in the Midwestern and Southern states where the warm humid air from the Gulf of Mexico meets the cool dry air from the north. They also occur, less frequently, in other parts of the world, including Australia and India.

Space and Place

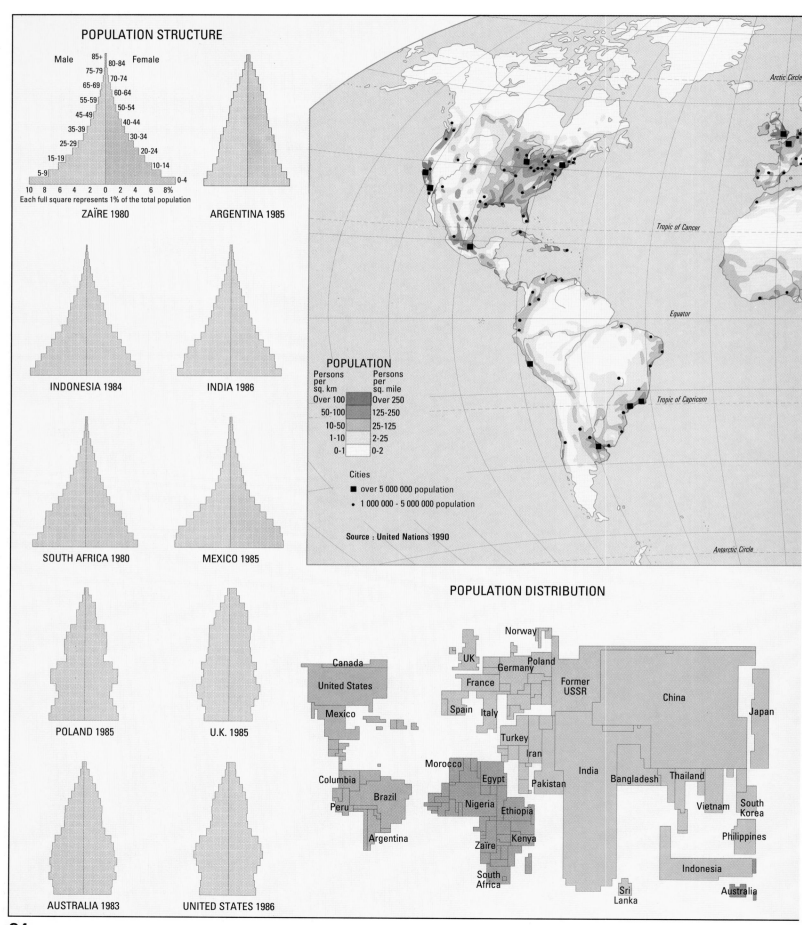

POPULATION STRUCTURE

Male | 85+ | Female
75-79 | 80-84
65-69 | 70-74
55-59 | 60-64
45-49 | 50-54
35-39 | 40-44
25-29 | 30-34
15-19 | 20-24
5-9 | 10-14
| 0-4

10 8 6 4 2 0 2 4 6 8%

Each full square represents 1% of the total population

ZAÏRE 1980

ARGENTINA 1985

INDONESIA 1984

INDIA 1986

SOUTH AFRICA 1980

MEXICO 1985

POLAND 1985

U.K. 1985

AUSTRALIA 1983

UNITED STATES 1986

POPULATION

Persons per sq. km	Persons per sq. mile
Over 100	Over 250
50-100	125-250
10-50	25-125
1-10	2-25
0-1	0-2

Cities

■ over 5 000 000 population

• 1 000 000 - 5 000 000 population

Source : United Nations 1990

Arctic Circle

Tropic of Cancer

Equator

Tropic of Capricorn

Antarctic Circle

POPULATION DISTRIBUTION

Norway
Canada
UK
Poland
Germany
United States
France
Former USSR
China
Japan
Mexico
Spain
Italy
Turkey
Iran
Morocco
Egypt
Pakistan
India
Bangladesh
Thailand
Columbia
Nigeria
Ethiopia
Vietnam
South Korea
Peru
Brazil
Zaïre
Kenya
Philippines
Argentina
South Africa
Indonesia
Sri Lanka
Australia

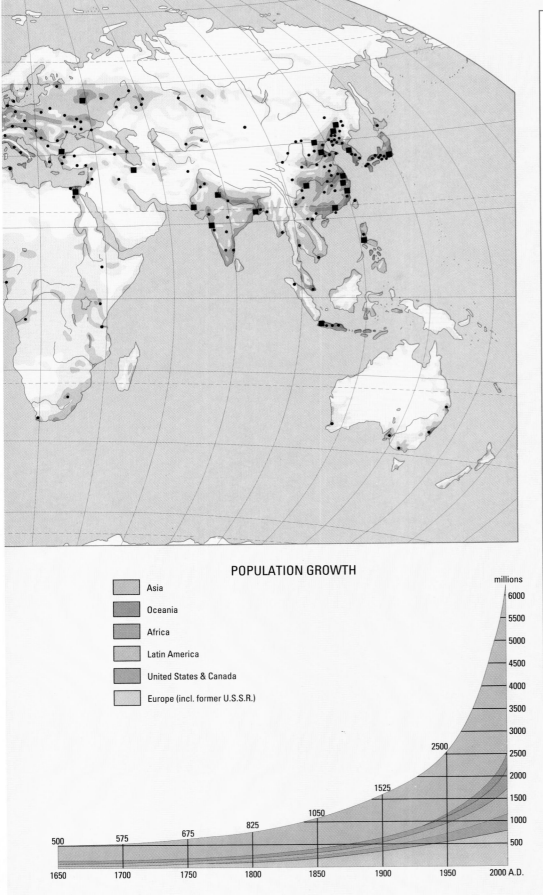

POPULATION GROWTH

- Asia
- Oceania
- Africa
- Latin America
- United States & Canada
- Europe (incl. former U.S.S.R.)

FACTfile — Largest Cities
Population figures in millions

AFRICA
City	Country	Pop.
Cairo	Egypt	9.0
Lagos	Nigeria	7.7
Alexandria	Egypt	3.7
Kinshasa	Zaïre	3.5
Casablanca	Morocco	3.2
Algiers	Algeria	3.0
Cape Town	South Africa	2.3
Abidjan	Côte d'Ivoire	2.2
Tripoli	Libya	2.1
Khartoum	Sudan	1.9

ASIA
City	Country	Pop.
Tokyo	Japan	18.1
Shanghai	China	13.4
Calcutta	India	11.8
Bombay	India	11.2
Seoul	South Korea	11.0
Beijing	China	10.8
Tianjin	China	9.4
Jakarta	Indonesia	9.3
Delhi	India	8.8
Manila	Philippines	8.5

EUROPE
City	Country	Pop.
Moscow	Russian Federation	8.8
Paris	France	8.5
London	United Kingdom	7.5
Milan	Italy	5.3
Madrid	Spain	5.2
St. Petersburg	Russian Federation	5.1
Naples	Italy	3.6
Barcelona	Spain	3.4
Athens	Greece	3.4
Katowice	Poland	3.4

NORTH AMERICA
City	Country	Pop.
Mexico City	Mexico	20.2
New York	United States	16.2
Los Angeles	United States	11.9
Chicago	United States	7.0
Philadelphia	United States	4.3
Detroit	United States	3.7
San Francisco	United States	3.7
Toronto	Canada	3.5
Dallas	United States	3.4
Guadalajara	Mexico	3.2

SOUTH AMERICA
City	Country	Pop.
São Paulo	Brazil	17.4
Buenos Aires	Argentina	11.5
Rio de Janeiro	Brazil	10.7
Lima	Peru	6.2
Santiago	Chile	4.7
Caracas	Venezuela	4.1
Belo Horizonte	Brazil	3.6
Porto Alegre	Brazil	3.1
Recife	Brazil	2.5
Salvador	Brazil	2.4

OCEANIA
City	Country	Pop.
Sydney	Australia	3.4
Melbourne	Australia	2.8
Brisbane	Australia	1.2
Perth	Australia	1.1

Note: Figures refer to urban agglomerations as defined by the U. N.

© Collins <> Longman Atlases

Environment and Society

Forests cover about one third of the world's land surface. Temperate and coniferous forests spread across areas of Europe, Asia, and North America. Further south, a band of tropical rain forests extending about ten degrees in latitude north and south of the equator, forms the richest habitat on earth.

Temperate and coniferous forests are generally carefully managed and are quick to regrow. Rain forests take longer to grow and occupy a more fragile environment. They are being destroyed at an alarming rate as people sell the wood and clear land for housing, crops, and industry.

Shrinking Forests

1950

Rest of the earth

Temperate and coniferous forest   Tropical forest

1975

2000

Tropical Rain Forest Under Threat

CENTRAL AMERICA
Between 33% and 50% destroyed

WEST AFRICA
Forest almost completely gone

INDIAN SUB-CONTINENT
Complete deforestation

PHILIPPINES

COLOMBIAN CHOCO

ECUADOR

WESTERN AMAZONIA

BRAZIL
10% of forest destroyed

CAMEROON

PENINSULAR MALAYSIA

NORTHWEST BORNEO

SOUTHEAST ASIA
Nearly 50% destroyed

MADAGASCAR

QUEENSLAND

Tropical rain forest

Edge of rain forest undergoing the most rapid removal

Threatened areas with large concentrations of endemic species

Half the world's rain forest has already been destroyed and an area the size of the United Kingdom is cleared each year. If this is allowed to continue only Brazil and Zaïre will be left with significant areas of rain forest by 2010.

Where the Wood Goes

1.6

North South

3.5

2.2

1.3

12.8

17.3

THE TOP TEN PRODUCERS OF HARDWOOD TIMBER

HARDWOOD TIMBER PRODUCTION (1988)
Roundwood production in million cubic yards

INDIA | UNITED STATES | INDONESIA | BRAZIL | CHINA | NIGERIA | FORMER USSR | MALAYSIA | PHILIPPINES | ETHIOPIA

Much of the woodwork in our homes comes from the rain forests. Tropical timber (hardwood) is also used by the construction industry for railway sleepers, harbor piles, jetties, and wharfs. In addition, a proportion is turned into logs and pulp for paper products.

Developing countries, burdened by debts, are under enormous pressure to exploit their forests. The problem with unrestrained logging is that it causes widespread devastation and opens up untouched areas for development. Carefully managed plantations could preserve the forests and earn money.

TROPICAL TIMBER TRADE

Hardwood exports

Figures in million cubic yards show the major trade flows in sawnwood, sawlogs and veneer logs (1988)

North South

The demand for hardwood production is growing rapidly. Some pressure to increase logging comes from the main importers in the "north" but timber is also in demand in the "south". In India, most of the 318 million yd³ produced is for domestic use as fuel.

The Real Costs of Rain Forest Destruction

What we are losing?

People
In South America the rain forest is the home for tribal groups like the Yanomani. Rubber tappers also operate in many areas.

Plants
Many crops and medicines come from rain forest plants which are a unique and extremely valuable resource.

Creatures
The rain forests are the richest and densest habitat on earth. They contain over half the world's insects, birds, and animals.

The rain forests generally grow on very poor soils. The trees protect the soil from tropical storms and help to keep it moist during the dry season. Once the trees are cleared, the earth quickly washes away and the land, exposed to the hot sun, turns to desert.

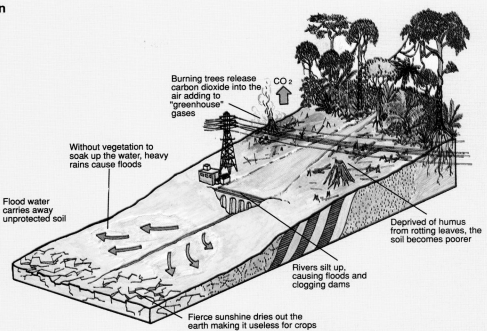

Burning trees release carbon dioxide into the air adding to "greenhouse" gases CO_2

Without vegetation to soak up the water, heavy rains cause floods

Flood water carries away unprotected soil

Deprived of humus from rotting leaves, the soil becomes poorer

Rivers silt up, causing floods and clogging dams

Fierce sunshine dries out the earth making it useless for crops

Deforestation in Amazonia

About a third of the world's rain forest is in Amazonia. This area mostly belongs to Brazil, but also covers parts of neighboring countries.

Many Brazilians want to open up Amazonia and exploit its riches. They see this as a way of developing industry and paying off debts. However, many projects take little account of the destruction which causes priceless areas of rain forest to literally go up in smoke.

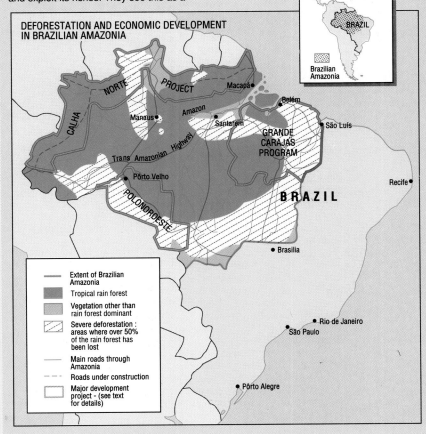

DEFORESTATION AND ECONOMIC DEVELOPMENT IN BRAZILIAN AMAZONIA

CALHA NORTE PROJECT

Macapá
Belém
Manaus
Amazon
Santarém
São Luís
GRANDE CARAJÁS PROGRAM
Trans Amazonian Highway
Pôrto Velho
Recife
POLONOROESTE
B R A Z I L
Brasília
Rio de Janeiro
São Paulo
Pôrto Alegre

BRAZIL
Brazilian Amazonia

Legend:
- Extent of Brazilian Amazonia
- Tropical rain forest
- Vegetation other than rain forest dominant
- Severe deforestation : areas where over 50% of the rain forest has been lost
- Main roads through Amazonia
- Roads under construction
- Major development project - (see text for details)

A huge area along the northern border of Brazil has been set aside for the Calha Norte Project. Here companies have been granted mining concessions and permission to explore for oil. Hydroelectric power stations are being built to provide power for industrial development. The dams for these schemes will flood large areas of land, threatening the homes of fifty thousand Indians.

Further south, the Grand Carajás Program involves a massive iron ore mine which will be linked by rail to a special port. Huge tracts of forest will also be cleared for a bauxite mine, cash crop plantations, and cattle ranches.

In the west, the Polonoroeste Development Project has allowed thouisands of immigrants to move into the area. Originally it was intended to open up the area for agriculture, but the soil is so poor it cannot sustain crops.

DEMANDS ON LAND IN BRAZILIAN AMAZONIA

	10^3 miles^2	% total
Already cleared	130	10%
Area to be flooded for HEP development	60	4.4%
Forest reserves maintained for timber produ	190	15%
Colonized (up to 1989)	170	13%
Total officially earmarked for development	810	63.5%

Environment and Society

What is Desertification?

Desertification, or the spread of deserts, threatens over a third of the world's land surface. Severe deterioration and loss of soil can turn productive land into desert. Every year, an area the size of the United Kingdom is either lost or severely degraded. In some cases deserts appear to invade good land from the outside, but in fact it is deterioration of soil in the border regions which causes them to expand. By the year 2000, the situation is likely to become critical especially in the Sahel in Africa, the Andes in South America, and parts of South Asia.

At one time lush trees and shrubs surrounded this Nile valley village.

The Causes

Desertification often begins when people decide or are forced to use land in dry areas too intensively. Overcultivation, overgrazing and the clearance of trees for fuel combine to degrade the soil. In other places, badly damaged irrigation schemes can make the land so salty it can no longer grow crops. The diagram below shows two ways in which desertification is triggered. Once desertification is started, natural factors, such as drought accelerate the process.

Where is Desertification Taking Place?

Fertile areas on the edge of existing deserts are most at risk. Here, harsh conditions mean that the land is only just able to grow crops and needs particularly careful management. Some 850 million people live in desert border regions and the population is growing rapidly.

WORLD LAND AT RISK

Existing desert 6%
Other land 66%
Moderate 13%
Severe 12%
Very severe 3%

Land at risk of desertification

In Spain, ten percent of the land is affected by severe desertification.

Europe 2%

Southwest United States

Turkestan
Iranian
Thar
Sahara
Arabian
Somali

North and South America 19%

Atacama

Namib
Kalahari

Cattle ranching and overgrazing have degraded the soil in the western parts of the United States and parts of Mexico. Further south, unsuitable land is being cleared for crops in Brazil and Argentina.

Africa 34%

Overgrazing and the removal of trees threaten the Sahel, Mediterranean coast, and southern Africa.

Two Models of Desertification

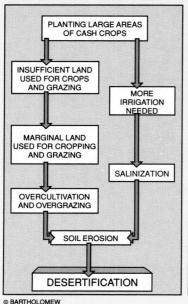

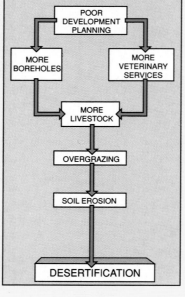

Effects of Desertification

Effects on People
Desertification is slow and insidious. Developing countries suffer most. Here, rural communities become trapped in a cycle of poverty which forces them to exploit the land beyond its capacity. This makes them very vulnerable to natural hazards, such as drought.

As crops fail and water sources dry up, people have no alternative but to leave the land. One sixth of the population of Burkina fled the country in the drought of the early 1970 s. In India and Brazil many victims of desertification have gone to live in the big cities, swelling the urban population.

Effects on Climate
Desertification can have a significant effect on the climate. The increase in dust prevents air from rising freely and forming clouds. In addition, the loss of vegetation reduces the amount of moisture in the air and allows temperatures to rise. Both these factors tend to make droughts worse.

© BARTHOLOMEW

Poor irrigation schemes are causing desertification in several Central Asian Republics. Parts of the Middle East are also at risk.

Gobi

Asia 31%

Great Australian

Australia 75%

Most of Australia is at risk due to poor stock raising.

Moderate desertification (Productivity reduced by up to 25%)

Severe desertification (Productivity reduced by 25-50%)

Very severe desertification (Productivity reduced by over 50%)

Existing desert (Unproductive)

The removal of tree and plant cover exposes the soil. In irrigated areas, salts build up in the ground, killing crops.

Dust storms and floods strip away much of the top soil. Plants struggle to survive.

Bare ground is baked hard in the sun and plants wither. Sand, grit, and dust storms are common.

Combatting Desertification

There is nothing new about desertification. Before people cut them down, there were forests in the Sahara Desert which supported a good variety of wildlife. Desertification has played a role in the downfall of early civilizations, including the Roman Empire. What is new is the scale of the problem.

Human action causes desertification. By the same token it can also control and cure it. Reforestation, improved farming methods, and better land use can halt the advance of the desert. There are many successful projects around the world.

- In Rajasthan, India, trees have been planted as shelter belts along roads.

- In Senegal coastal sand dunes have been stabilised.

- Lines of stones have been placed to follow the contours of the land to trap soil in fields in Burkina.

- Watersheds have been terraced in Ethiopia.

- In northern China a forest 4,350 miles long has been planted to protect the farmland from the Gobi Desert.

Where local people are given responsibility for the schemes and supported by their government the results have been particularly impressive. At the heart of the issue is the control of the land itself. If people feel secure and have a stake in the future they will act accordingly.

Africa - Population Affected by Desertification

Mediterranean Africa 8.5 million

Sahel 28.5 million

👤 1 million people

Africa South of the Sahel 25 million

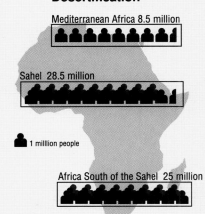

During the 1960s and 1970s the Sahara Desert spread 60 miles further south, forcing millions of people to leave their homes.

Preventative Measures

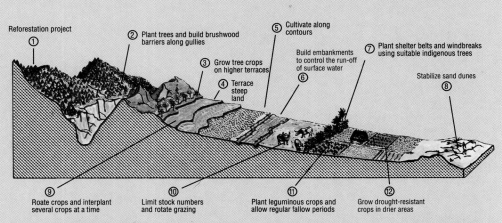

① Reforestation project
② Plant trees and build brushwood barriers along gullies
③ Grow tree crops on higher terraces
④ Terrace steep land
⑤ Cultivate along contours
⑥ Build embankments to control the run-off of surface water
⑦ Plant shelter belts and windbreaks using suitable indigenous trees
⑧ Stabilize sand dunes
⑨ Roate crops and interplant several crops at a time
⑩ Limit stock numbers and rotate grazing
⑪ Plant leguminous crops and allow regular fallow periods
⑫ Grow drought-resistant crops in drier areas

Although we know how to halt desertification, we are not winning the battle against it. Too little money is spent on preventative measures and there is a lack of long-term planning. Many people are at risk and a massive effort will be needed to avoid famine in the years ahead.

Environment and Society

What is Pollution?

All damage to the environment is known as pollution. Some pollution comes from natural sources. Volcanoes, for example, release poisonous gases into the atmosphere. Most pollution, however, is caused by people. As the population of the world increases and the number of industries grows, pollution problems become more severe.

Air Pollution

The earth is covered by a layer of air which extends far into space. Only the lowest few miles can support life. As more and more wastes enter the atmosphere important changes begin to occur. If people continue polluting the atmosphere, the earth will eventually become uninhabitable.

Ozone Destruction

The earth is surrounded by a layer of ozone, O_3, in the stratosphere about 15miles above the surface. The ozone layer filters out harmful ultraviolet rays from the sun which can cause skin cancer. Recently scientists have noticed that the ozone layer is getting thinner. They were alarmed to discover a hole in the ozone over Antarctica each spring.

Ozone destruction is caused by gases known as *chlorofluorocarbons* (CFCs). These are used in foams, refrigerants, and aerosols. In 1987 many countries undertook to reduce their use of CFCs by signing an agreement called the Montreal Protocol.

The expanding hole in the ozone layer

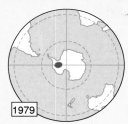

1979

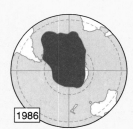

1986

Each year the hole in the ozone layer over Antarctica gets larger. Places as far away as Australia and New Zealand are affected by the reduction in the ozone layer.

Atmospheric Pollution

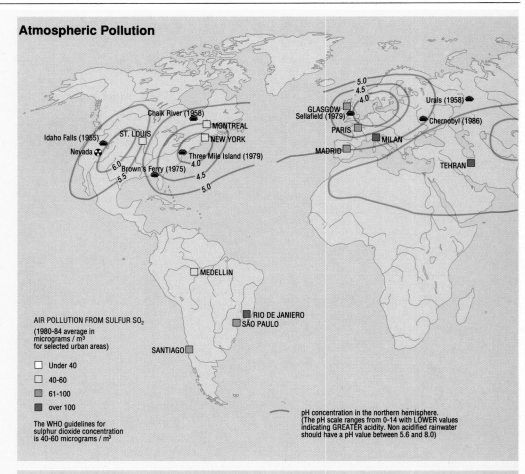

AIR POLLUTION FROM SULFUR SO_2
(1980-84 average in micrograms / m³ for selected urban areas)

☐ Under 40
☐ 40-60
▨ 61-100
■ over 100

The WHO guidelines for sulphur dioxide concentration is 40-60 micrograms / m³

pH concentration in the northern hemisphere. (The pH scale ranges from 0-14 with LOWER values indicating GREATER acidity. Non acidified rainwater should have a pH value between 5.6 and 8.0)

Global Warming

The world is now warmer than at any time since the last Ice Age. Scientists believe that in future temperatures will rise even faster. This is called global warming. Global warming is caused by a blanket of "greenhouse gases" building up around the earth trapping heat from the sun. Carbon dioxide, CO_2, released by burning fossil fuels is one of the main causes.

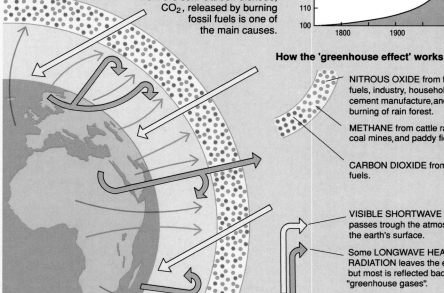

CO₂ LEVELS
1750 level = 100 units

How the 'greenhouse effect' works

NITROUS OXIDE from fossil fuels, industry, households, cement manufacture, and burning of rain forest.

METHANE from cattle ranching, coal mines, and paddy fields.

CARBON DIOXIDE from fossil fuels.

VISIBLE SHORTWAVE LIGHT passes trough the atmosphere to the earth's surface.

Some LONGWAVE HEAT RADIATION leaves the earth - but most is reflected back by "greenhouse gases".

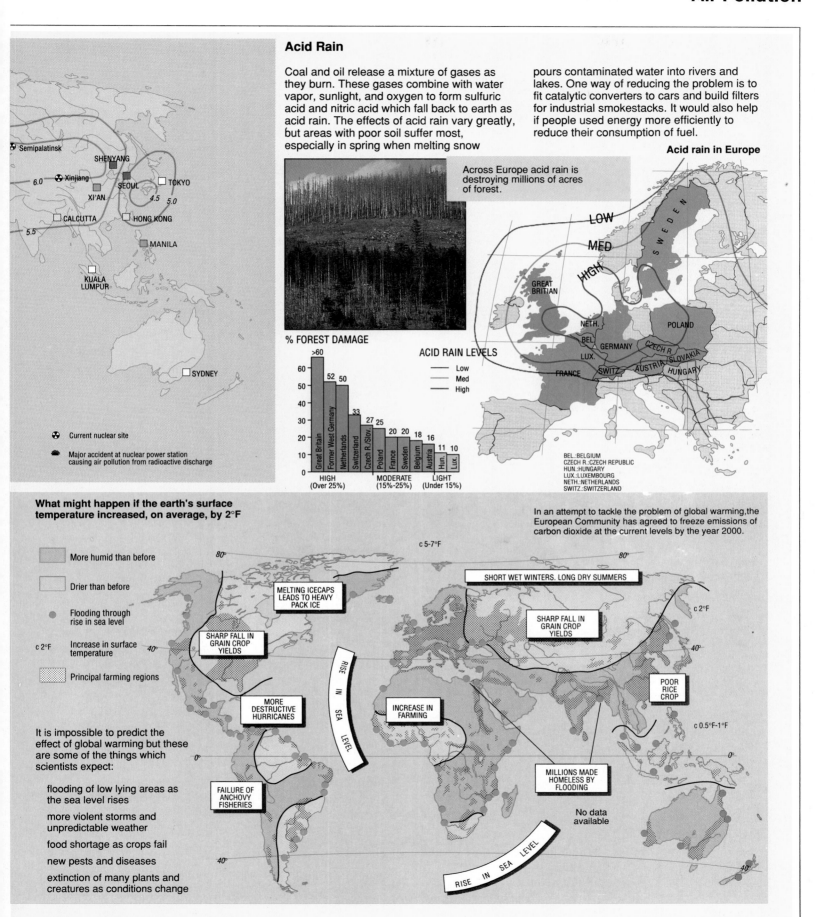

Acid Rain

Coal and oil release a mixture of gases as they burn. These gases combine with water vapor, sunlight, and oxygen to form sulfuric acid and nitric acid which fall back to earth as acid rain. The effects of acid rain vary greatly, but areas with poor soil suffer most, especially in spring when melting snow pours contaminated water into rivers and lakes. One way of reducing the problem is to fit catalytic converters to cars and build filters for industrial smokestacks. It would also help if people used energy more efficiently to reduce their consumption of fuel.

Acid rain in Europe

Across Europe acid rain is destroying millions of acres of forest.

Semipalatinsk

SHENYANG

6.0   Xinjiang
SEOUL   TOKYO
XI'AN   4.5   5.0

CALCUTTA   HONG KONG

5.5

MANILA

KUALA LUMPUR

SYDNEY

☢ Current nuclear site

☣ Major accident at nuclear power station causing air pollution from radioactive discharge

% FOREST DAMAGE

	>60	52	50	33	27	25	20	20	18	16	11	10
	Great Britain	Former West Germany	Netherlands	Switzerland	Czech R./Slov.	Poland	France	Sweden	Belgium	Austria	Hun.	Lux.

HIGH (Over 25%)   MODERATE (15%-25%)   LIGHT (Under 15%)

ACID RAIN LEVELS

— Low
— Med
— High

LOW
MED
HIGH

SWEDEN

GREAT BRITAIN

NETH.
BEL.
LUX.   GERMANY   CZECH R.   POLAND
FRANCE   SWITZ   AUSTRIA   SLOVAKIA
HUNGARY

BEL.:BELGIUM
CZECH R.:CZECH REPUBLIC
HUN.:HUNGARY
LUX.:LUXEMBOURG
NETH.:NETHERLANDS
SWITZ.:SWITZERLAND

What might happen if the earth's surface temperature increased, on average, by 2°F

In an attempt to tackle the problem of global warming, the European Community has agreed to freeze emissions of carbon dioxide at the current levels by the year 2000.

More humid than before

Drier than before

● Flooding through rise in sea level

c 2°F   Increase in surface temperature

Principal farming regions

c 5-7°F
80°   80°
c 2°F

MELTING ICECAPS LEADS TO HEAVY PACK ICE

SHORT WET WINTERS. LONG DRY SUMMERS

SHARP FALL IN GRAIN CROP YIELDS

40°   RISE IN SEA LEVEL   40°

SHARP FALL IN GRAIN CROP YIELDS

POOR RICE CROP
c 0.5°F-1°F

MORE DESTRUCTIVE HURRICANES

INCREASE IN FARMING

0°   0°

MILLIONS MADE HOMELESS BY FLOODING

It is impossible to predict the effect of global warming but these are some of the things which scientists expect:

FAILURE OF ANCHOVY FISHERIES

No data available

flooding of low lying areas as the sea level rises

more violent storms and unpredictable weather

food shortage as crops fail

new pests and diseases

40°   RISE IN SEA LEVEL   40°

extinction of many plants and creatures as conditions change

Environment and Society

Hazardous Waste - Production and Trade

Hazardous and toxic waste damages the environment and poisons people and animals. Most toxic waste comes from the chemical industry. It is produced in increasing quantities each year.

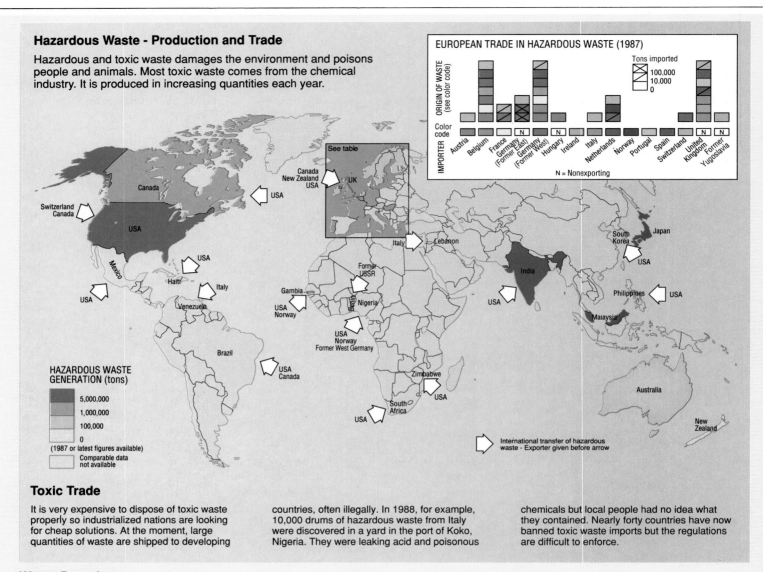

EUROPEAN TRADE IN HAZARDOUS WASTE (1987)

Tons imported
100,000
10,000
0

ORIGIN OF WASTE (see color code)

Color code

IMPORTER: Austria, Belgium, France, Germany (Former East), Germany (Former West), Hungary, Ireland, Italy, Netherlands, Norway, Portugal, Spain, Switzerland, United Kingdom, Former Yugoslavia

N = Nonexporting

HAZARDOUS WASTE GENERATION (tons)

5,000,000
1,000,000
100,000
0
(1987 or latest figures available)
Comparable data not available

International transfer of hazardous waste - Exporter given before arrow

Toxic Trade

It is very expensive to dispose of toxic waste properly so industrialized nations are looking for cheap solutions. At the moment, large quantities of waste are shipped to developing countries, often illegally. In 1988, for example, 10,000 drums of hazardous waste from Italy were discovered in a yard in the port of Koko, Nigeria. They were leaking acid and poisonous chemicals but local people had no idea what they contained. Nearly forty countries have now banned toxic waste imports but the regulations are difficult to enforce.

Waste Dumping

Some 350 million tons of hazardous waste are produced each year and there are over 70,000 different chemicals in regular use. Many of them have never been tested for their effect on the environment and nobody knows what happens when the chemicals are mixed together.

For years toxic waste has been dumped in landfill sites. If these are unlined, dangerous chemicals can seep into the soil and contaminate water supplies. The problem of indiscriminate dumping affects most industrialized countries and there are thousands of sites which need to be cleaned up.

DILUTE AND DISPERSE LANDFILL DISPOSAL

Wastes seep out of landfill

Polluted groundwater

Polluted streams and water supply

% WASTE DISPOSAL BY LANDFILL
(selected countries - 1987 or latest figures available)

100
75
50
25
0

Australia, Canada, W. Germany (former), Ireland, Italy, Japan, Netherlands, Spain, Sweden, Switzerland, United Kingdom

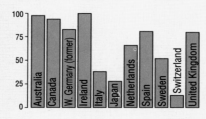

Toxic waste dump, Czech Republic

In Britain toxic waste is mixed with domestic rubbish in the controversial "dilute and disperse" method. Many other countries favor the opposite approach and concentrate their most dangerous waste in specific places. Incineration is also increasingly favored.

The best way of solving the problem of toxic waste is not to produce it in the first place. It is estimated that over the next decade industry could cut its production by a third. More waste could also be recycled or reused.

© BARTHOLOMEW

Agrochemicals

Around the world farmers are putting more and more chemicals on their land. This has led to great increases in crop yields but has also brought environmental problems. Nutrients from fertilizers are polluting rivers and lakes, while residues from pesticides have been detected in crops and drinking water. In addition, pesticides are losing their effectiveness as insects develop immunity to them. In the future, agrochemicals will need to be used much more selectively.

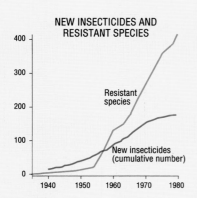

NEW INSECTICIDES AND RESISTANT SPECIES

Resistant species

New insecticides (cumulative number)

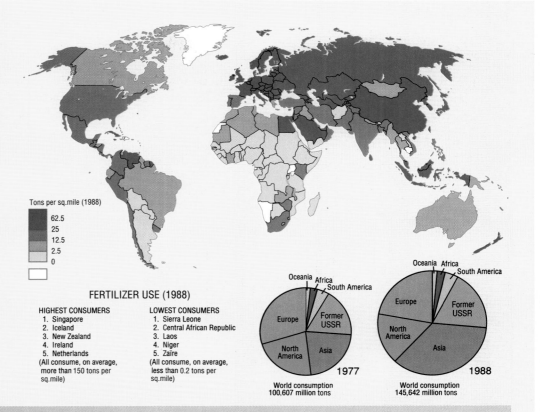

Tons per sq.mile (1988)

62.5
25
12.5
2.5
0

FERTILIZER USE (1988)

HIGHEST CONSUMERS
1. Singapore
2. Iceland
3. New Zealand
4. Ireland
5. Netherlands
(All consume, on average, more than 150 tons per sq.mile)

LOWEST CONSUMERS
1. Sierra Leone
2. Central African Republic
3. Laos
4. Niger
5. Zaïre
(All consume, on average, less than 0.2 tons per sq.mile)

1977
World consumption
100,607 million tons

Oceania Africa
South America
Europe
Former USSR
North America
Asia

1988
World consumption
145,642 million tons

Oceania Africa
South America
Europe
Former USSR
North America
Asia

The Aral Sea Disaster

The Aral Sea in Southwestern Asia used to be the fourth biggest lake in the world. It supported a thriving fishing industry, mixed agriculture, and many species of plants and animals. Now the Aral Sea is drying up as more and more water is diverted to irrigate cotton crops. Unless something is done the sea could disappear completely over the next thirty years.

Environmental Consequences

The dry sea bed has become a desert, poisoned by salt and residues from the chemicals sprayed on the cotton crop. Huge dust storms sweep up the contaminated soil and dump it back on the fields. Deposits have been found up to 2,000 mls. away on the shores of the Arctic Ocean.

The climate of the region has also begun to change. The Aral Sea used to act as a battery, storing heat in the summer and releasing it in the winter. Now temperatures have become more extreme and there is less rainfall.

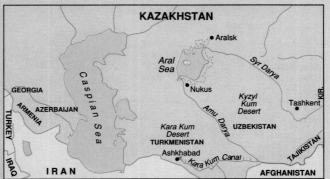

The location of the Aral Sea

The effect on the surrounding communities has been disasterous. Towns which used to depend on fishing are now up to 25 miles from the shore. Diseases and illnesses have increased among adults and one in ten babies die before their first birthday.

ARAL SEA FACTS

▲ Only 4 out of 24 species of fish survive.

▲ The salinity of the water has increased from 10 to 27%.

▲ Surface area has decreased by 40% since 1960.

▲ 173 animal species have been cut to 38.

What could be done?

At present most of the irrigation canals leak. If they were lined with plastic or concrete, it would save large amounts of water. Also, the acreage under cotton could be reduced to cut down the need for irrigation. It will take massive changes to halt the present process and the Aral Sea will probably never be restored properly.

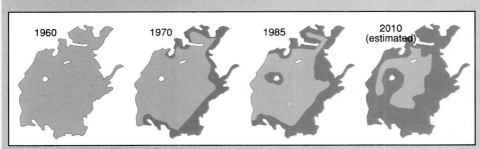

1960 1970 1985 2010 (estimated)

The changing shape of the Aral Sea

Aralsk, Kazakhstan - rusting boats lie in the wasteland that was once part of the Aral Sea.

Environment and Society

The Water Budget

Seventy percent of the earth's surface is covered by water. However, fresh water represents only 2.5% of the total. The rest is found in the oceans where the presence of salt makes it difficult to use.

Most of the fresh water lies deep underground or is frozen in the polar ice caps. Only a small proportion is freely available. Nevertheless there is enough to meet people's needs. The problem is that supplies are unevenly distributed around the world.

Fresh Water 2.5%

97.5% Salt Water

Water Pollution

Water pollution is a worldwide problem. Waste from factories, farms, and cities is poisoning rivers and seeping into groundwater. Lakes are particularly at risk as they allow pollutants to build up. Coastlines and shallow seas are highly vulnerable. The discharge of oil from tanker accidents and ships that wash out their tanks illegally is another problem. It is estimated that several million tons of oil are put into the sea each year.

EXXON VALDEZ (1989)

AMOCO CADIZ (1978)

IRENES SERENADE (1980)

ATLANTIC EXPRESS (1979)

CASTELLO DE BELVER (1983)

Severe oil pollution

Moderate oil pollution

Water Availability

FORMER USSR

FRANCE

USA

MEXICO

INDIA

TANZANIA

WATER AVAILABILITY PER PERSON PER YEAR (CUBIC YARDS)

High (>10)

Medium (5-10)

Low (1-4.9)

Very low (<1)

WATER USE PER PERSON PER YEAR (SELECTED COUNTRIES)

1 square represents 1 cubic yard of water

Agricultural use

Industrial use

Domestic use

Pollution in the North Sea

North Sea Facts

- Average water depth 300 ft.
- Rich variety of flora and fauna, including commercial fish stocks.
- 150 oil and gas platforms.
- 5,000 ships operating at any one time.
- Water replaced every 18 months on average

B - BELGIUM
N - NETHERLANDS
D - DENMARK

NORWAY

North Sea

IRELAND   UK

GERMANY

SOURCES OF POLLUTION

The North Sea receives much of the pollution that is generated in northwestern Europe. Some is dumped directly into the water or absorbed from the atmosphere. Rivers are the single biggest source of pollution and contribute nearly half of the total.

Pollution has begun to have a serious effect on the ecology of the North Sea. Heavy metals from industry, sewage from towns, and oil from ships have all added to the problem. In 1988, large numbers of seals were killed by a mystery virus. Countries bordering the North Sea have now agreed on various measures to control pollution. A lot more still needs to be done and many people would like to see stricter controls.

Pollution via the atmosphere

Oil refineries

Transport

Power stations

Agriculture

Domestic pollution

Industry

Pollution via rivers

Waste disposal

Shipping

Dredging spoil

Offshore industry

Wastes dumped at sea

Sewage outfall

SOURCES OF POLLUTION (1985)

Nitrogen
Total = 1,483,000 tons

Phosphorous
Total = 102 tons

Mercury & Cadmium
Total = 403 tons

Copper, Lead, Zinc, Chromium, Nickel & Arsenic
Total = 39,918 tons

River Inputs
Industrial Waste
Sewage Sludge
Dredging
Atmospheric
Direct Discharge

Source - North Sea Quality Status Report 1987

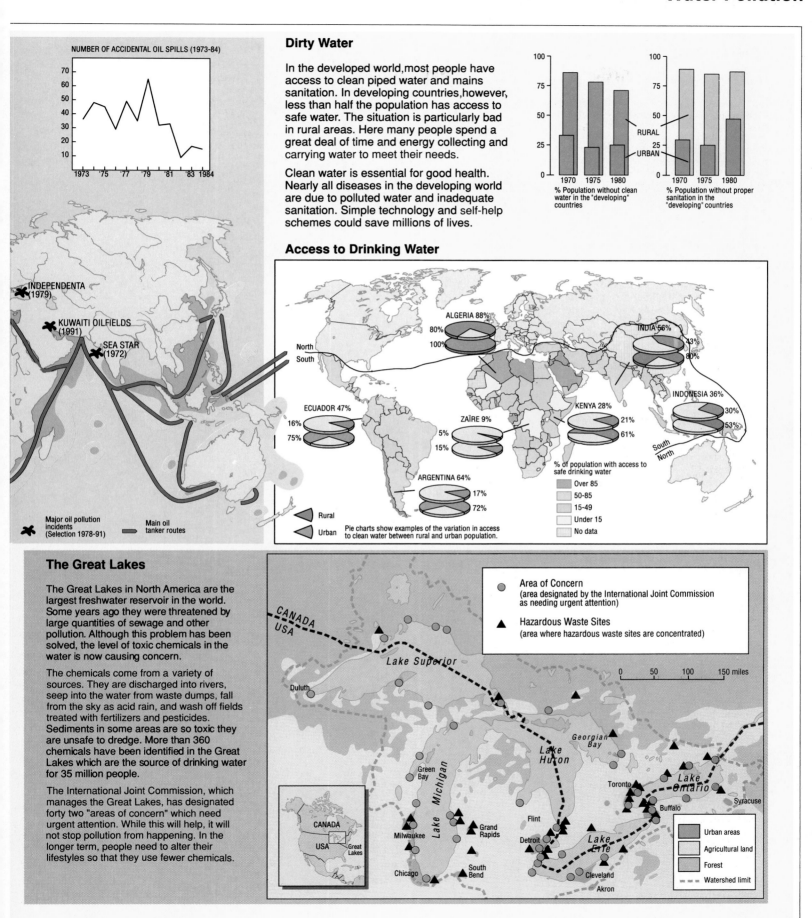

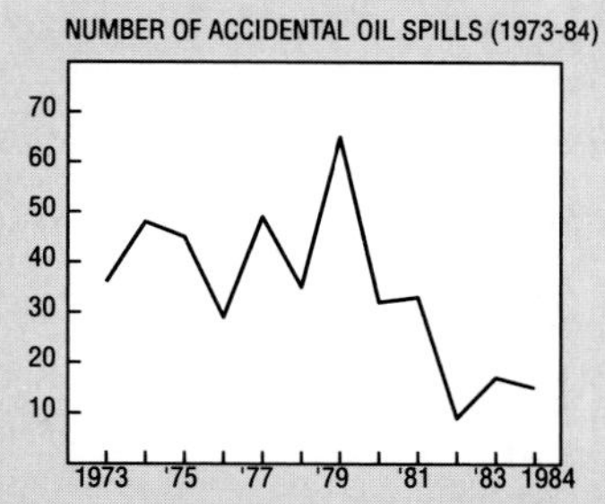
NUMBER OF ACCIDENTAL OIL SPILLS (1973-84)
70
60
50
40
30
20
10
1973
'75
'77
'79
'81
'83
1984

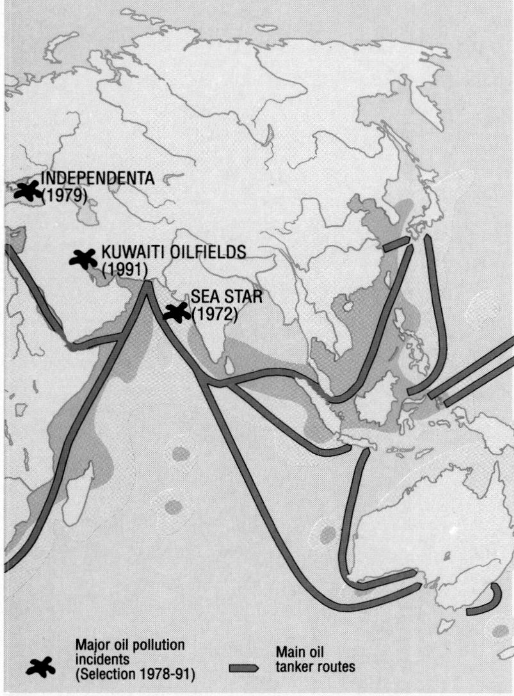
INDEPENDENTA (1979)
KUWAITI OILFIELDS (1991)
SEA STAR (1972)
Major oil pollution incidents (Selection 1978-91)
Main oil tanker routes

Dirty Water

In the developed world,most people have access to clean piped water and mains sanitation. In developing countries,however, less than half the population has access to safe water. The situation is particularly bad in rural areas. Here many people spend a great deal of time and energy collecting and carrying water to meet their needs.

Clean water is essential for good health. Nearly all diseases in the developing world are due to polluted water and inadequate sanitation. Simple technology and self-help schemes could save millions of lives.

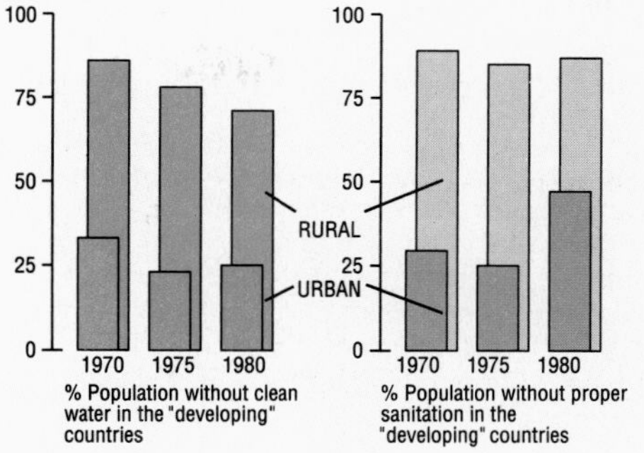
100
75
50
25
0
1970
1975
1980
% Population without clean water in the "developing" countries
RURAL
URBAN
1970
1975
1980
% Population without proper sanitation in the "developing" countries

Access to Drinking Water

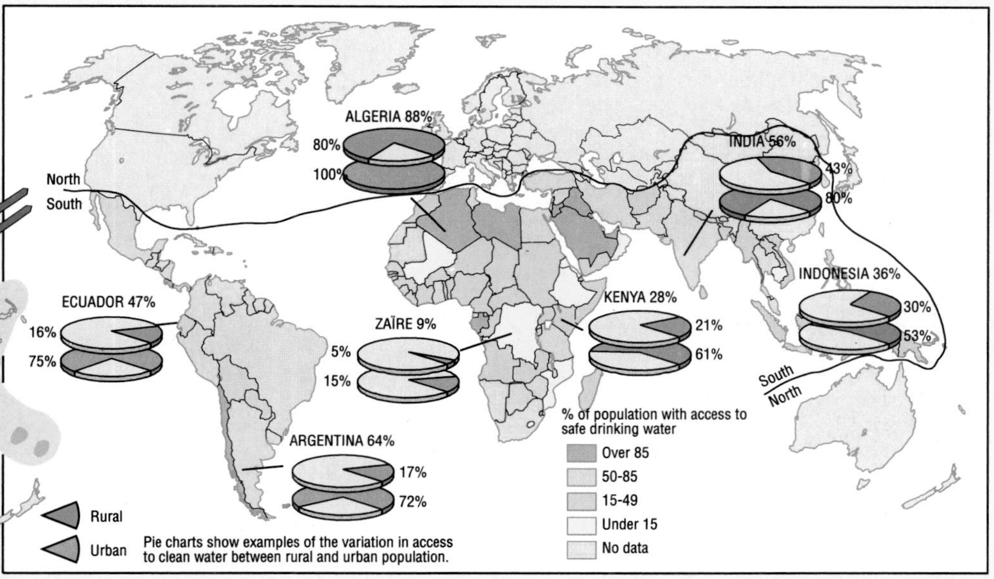
North
South
ALGERIA 88%
80%
100%
INDIA 56%
43%
80%
INDONESIA 36%
30%
53%
ECUADOR 47%
16%
75%
ZAÏRE 9%
5%
15%
KENYA 28%
21%
61%
ARGENTINA 64%
17%
72%
South
North
% of population with access to safe drinking water
Over 85
50-85
15-49
Under 15
No data
Rural
Urban
Pie charts show examples of the variation in access to clean water between rural and urban population.

The Great Lakes

The Great Lakes in North America are the largest freshwater reservoir in the world. Some years ago they were threatened by large quantities of sewage and other pollution. Although this problem has been solved, the level of toxic chemicals in the water is now causing concern.

The chemicals come from a variety of sources. They are discharged into rivers, seep into the water from waste dumps, fall from the sky as acid rain, and wash off fields treated with fertilizers and pesticides. Sediments in some areas are so toxic they are unsafe to dredge. More than 360 chemicals have been identified in the Great Lakes which are the source of drinking water for 35 million people.

The International Joint Commission, which manages the Great Lakes, has designated forty two "areas of concern" which need urgent attention. While this will help, it will not stop pollution from happening. In the longer term, people need to alter their lifestyles so that they use fewer chemicals.

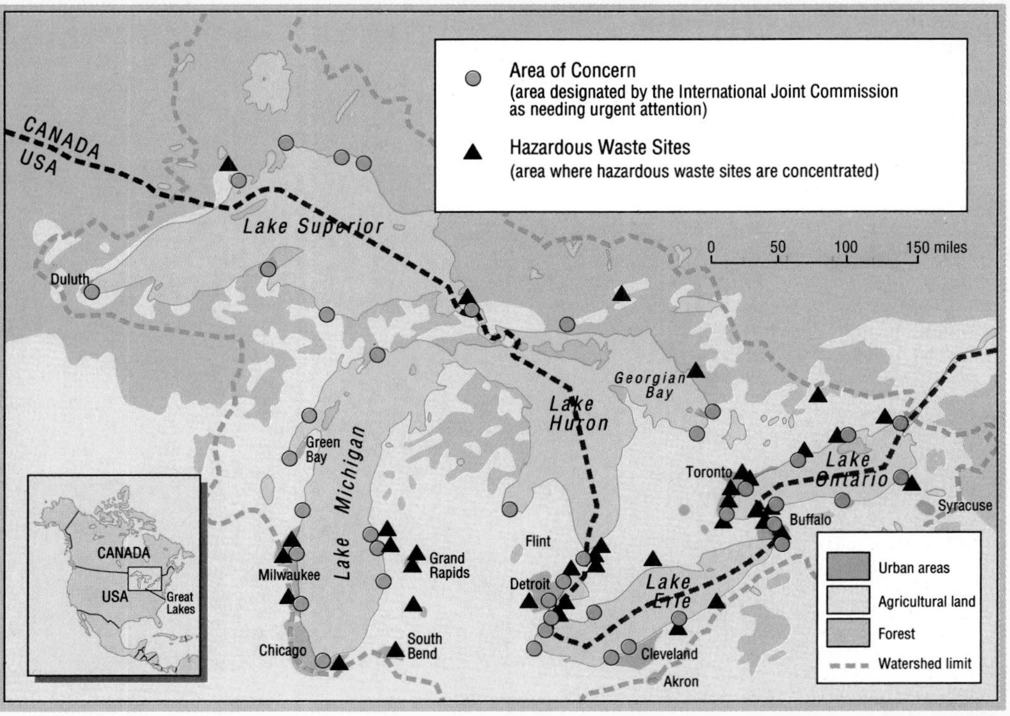
Area of Concern
(area designated by the International Joint Commission as needing urgent attention)
Hazardous Waste Sites
(area where hazardous waste sites are concentrated)
0
50
100
150 miles
CANADA
USA
Lake Superior
Duluth
Georgian Bay
Lake Huron
Lake Michigan
Green Bay
Milwaukee
Chicago
Grand Rapids
South Bend
Flint
Detroit
Toronto
Lake Ontario
Syracuse
Buffalo
Lake Erie
Cleveland
Akron
CANADA
USA
Great Lakes
Urban areas
Agricultural land
Forest
Watershed limit

Environment and Society

What are Natural Resources?

Minerals, water, plants, and animals are all natural resources. Human beings depend on using them for their survival.

For thousands of years people only used natural resources in small quantities. With the growth of industry and population, the demand has escalated. The world now uses three times the amount of minerals that it did in 1950. This is causing people to be concerned about whether there will always be enough.

Renewable Resources

When people use resources they sometimes consume them completely. Many machines, for instance, burn up gasoline in order to generate energy. Resources which are used in this way are said to be nonrenewable. They include oil, chemicals, and a variety of metals.

Other sources can be replaced. Timber, for example, is sometimes grown on plantations which are harvested at regular intervals. It is a renewable resource.

Renewable resources hold the key to the future. Sooner or later all the nonrenewable resources will be used up. By contrast, we can go on using renewable resources for ever.

Exploitation of Natural Resources

Natural resources are unevenly distributed around the world. Large countries such as the United States, former USSR, China, and Australia are rich in resources. Some smaller countries also have big reserves. Jamaica and Guinea, for example, have important bauxite mines which provide the raw material for aluminum.

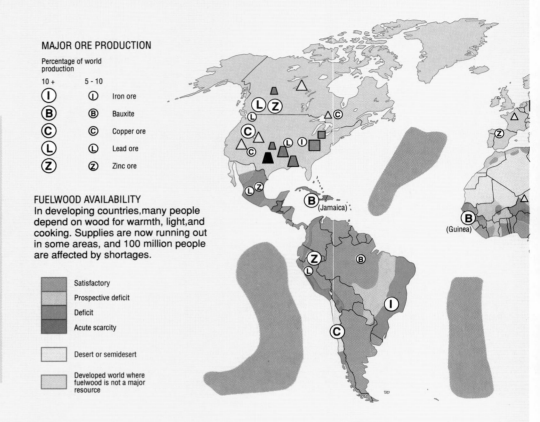

MAJOR ORE PRODUCTION

Percentage of world production

10 +	5 - 10	
Ⓘ	ⓘ	Iron ore
Ⓑ	ⓑ	Bauxite
Ⓒ	ⓒ	Copper ore
Ⓛ	ⓛ	Lead ore
Ⓩ	ⓩ	Zinc ore

FUELWOOD AVAILABILITY
In developing countries, many people depend on wood for warmth, light, and cooking. Supplies are now running out in some areas, and 100 million people are affected by shortages.

- Satisfactory
- Prospective deficit
- Deficit
- Acute scarcity

- Desert or semidesert
- Developed world where fuelwood is not a major resource

Environmental Issues in Mining

Mining is having a greater and greater effect on the environment. Ugly slag heaps and open pits have left scars in areas of scenic beauty. Even more serious is the damage done to rivers as poisonous metals are washed into the water. For example, this is a cause of concern in Brazil where prospectors are panning for gold in the tributaries of the Amazon.

Many countries have laws to control mining. Some old quarries have been restored to farmland or flooded to create attractive lakes.

The environmental damage caused by extensive mining.

Uranium Mining in Australia

Australia possesses about one third of the world's reserves of uranium. This mineral has become imporant in the present century because it is the raw material for nuclear power stations and nuclear weapons. Most of its reserves are concentrated in the Northern Territory. The decision to use the reserves was highly controversial.

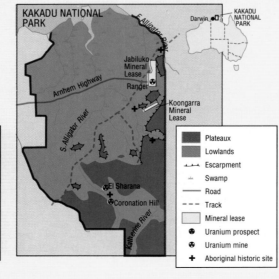

	Plateaux
	Lowlands
⊥⊥⊥	Escarpment
⊥⊥	Swamp
———	Road
- - -	Track
	Mineral lease
⚛	Uranium prospect
⚛	Uranium mine
✛	Aboriginal historic site

Arguments in favor

- The mines earn money and provide employment
- Nuclear power can help solve the world's energy crisis
- Strict safeguards control how the uranium is used

Arguments against

- Nuclear power stations are not safe
- The uranium could fall into the hands of terrorists
- The mines threatened a beautiful area where aborigines live

In 1977 the Australian government decided to go ahead with the mines. At the same time it created a National Park in the surrounding area and agreed to give some of the profits to the aborigines. Despite this compromise many people are still not satisfied.

NATURAL RESOURCES FROM THE OCEANS

There are large quantities of minerals deep beneath the ocean floor. Unfortunately these are difficult to get at and exploit.

Metal-rich sediments beneath ocean floor

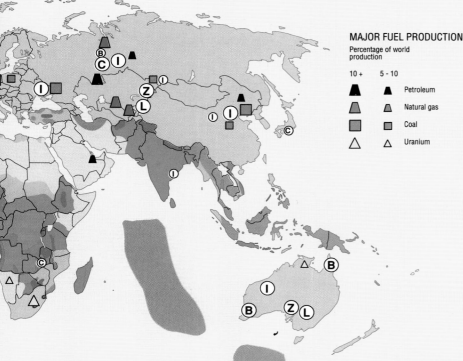

MAJOR FUEL PRODUCTION
Percentage of world production

	10 +	5 - 10	
▲	▲	Petroleum
		Natural gas
		Coal
△	△	Uranium

Depleting Resources

Some minerals are plentiful. Reserves of iron ore, for example, should last for 400 years at present rates of consumption. Other minerals are not so abundant and supplies may run low within our lifetime. These include diamonds, silver, gold, tin and zinc. One solution is to look for and use alternative materials. Another is to recycle waste products so the resources can be used again.

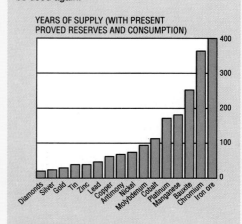

YEARS OF SUPPLY (WITH PRESENT PROVED RESERVES AND CONSUMPTION)

Substitution

In the past, tin was used extensively in the canning and packaging industry. Now that supplies are becoming scarcer alternative materials are being used. Glass, plastics, steel, and aluminum have all proved suitable. However, the answer is not always this simple. Manganese is essential for high-grade steel and there are no substitutes for chromium and platinum.

Recycling

Most waste products can be recycled. On a domestic level, many people now sort out paper and glass from their household rubbish. In industry, scrap metal provides almost half the iron needed for steelmaking.

Recycling not only reduces the demand on natural resources, it saves energy, conserves water, and reduces pollution. It also helps to solve the problem of waste disposal.

Recycling has enormous scope. As individuals we can all play our part, but nations also need to help by putting taxes on pollution and encouraging conservation.

ENVIRONMENTAL BENEFITS OF RECYCLING (Percentage reduction)			
	ALUMINUM	PAPER	GLASS
REDUCTION IN ENERGY USE	90-97	23-24	4-32
REDUCTION IN AIR POLLUTION	95	74	20
REDUCTION IN WATER POLLUTION	97	35	-
REDUCTION IN WATER USE	-	58	50

Recycling Aluminum Cans

Aluminum cans are cheap and easy to recycle. It takes twenty times more energy to make new aluminum from bauxite than to use scrap.

RECYCLING PROCESS

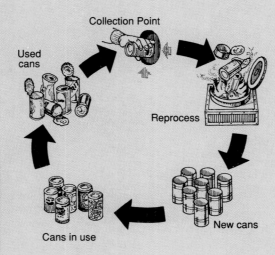

Collection Point

Used cans

Reprocess

New cans

Cans in use

In the United States nearly 80% of aluminum cans are recycled. Other countries, especially in Europe, are beginning to follow suit.

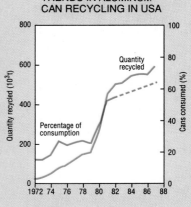

TRENDS IN ALUMINUM CAN RECYCLING IN USA

Quantity recycled

Percentage of consumption

Environment and Society

The Energy Problem

We depend on energy for almost everything that we do. Factories, farms, houses, and vehicles all need power to make them work.

It was the discovery of new sources of power - chiefly wind, water, and coal - which caused the Industrial Revolution. Since 1945 the boom in world economic activity has been based on oil.

Fossil fuels - coal, oil, and gas - provide most of the world's energy. Consumption is very uneven. The United States, Western Europe, and Japan use nearly three quarters of the total. Africa and South Asia use only small quantities.

Fumes from fossil fuels contribute to many pollution problems and are major factors in acid rain and global warming. This is one reason why plans to save energy are receiving so much attention. Wiser use of energy would also help to conserve supplies.

WORLD ENERGY PRODUCTION

Production of pound equivalents of all types of energy (lbs per person), 1988

- 66,000 - 264,000
- 4,500 - 65,999
- 660 - 4,499
- 0 - 659
- No data

WORLD ENERGY PRODUCTION

South America
Africa
Asia
Europe (Inc. Former USSR)
North America
Australasia

Total : 9,203,695 thousand tons equivalent

WORLD ENERGY CONSUMPTION

Consumption of pound equivalents of all types of energy (lbs per person), 1988

- 17,600 - 44,000
- 4,200 - 17,599
- 1,100 - 4,199
- 0 - 1,099
- No data

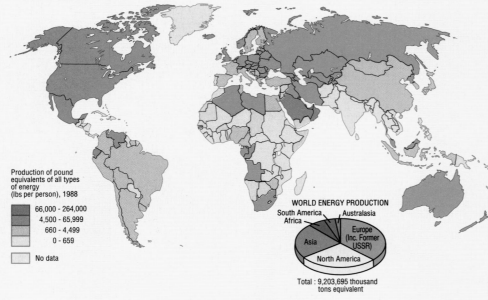

GROWTH IN CONSUMPTION (BY TYPE)

Million tons of oil equivalent

Oil
Coal
Natural gas
Hydro
Nuclear

3 000
2 000
1 000
0
1972 74 76 78 80 82 84 86 88

© BARTHOLOMEW

Fuel Reserves

Fossil fuels will not last forever. It took a million years to create the fuel people now burn every twelve months. At present rates of consumption, the known supplies of oil will be used up in about 45 years. Coal is much more plentiful and will last for several centuries.

WORLD RESERVES (BY TYPE), 1989

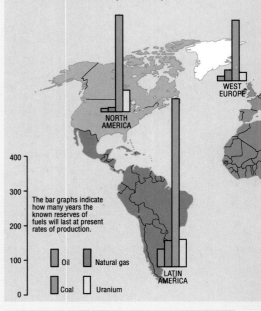

The bar graphs indicate how many years the known reserves of fuels will last at present rates of production.

- Oil
- Coal
- Natural gas
- Uranium

WEST EUROPE
NORTH AMERICA
LATIN AMERICA

400
300
200
100
0

Nuclear Energy

At one time nuclear power appeared to offer almost limitless supplies of cheap and clean electricity. However, there have always been doubts. There is the problem of disposing of nuclear waste and there is the risk of accidents. The catastrophe of Chernobyl in 1986, which spread radiation across the whole of Europe, made such dangers abundantly clear. It is now known that electricity from nuclear power is more expensive than electricity from coal.

In1989 there were 426 commercial nuclear reactors producing one sixth of the world's electricity. The map shows the number of reactors in the European Community. Countries like the United Kingdom have invested heavily in nuclear power.Others, like Denmark, Ireland and Greece have never become involved.

NUCLEAR POWER IN THE EC

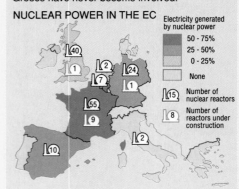

Electricity generated by nuclear power

- 50 - 75%
- 25 - 50%
- 0 - 25%
- None
- Number of nuclear reactors
- Number of reactors under construction

The search for new supplies will almost certainly result in valuable new finds. In addition, developments in technology will make it possible to make use of reserves that are currently uneconomical. The disadvantage is that many of these are likely to be in remote areas and difficult to extract.

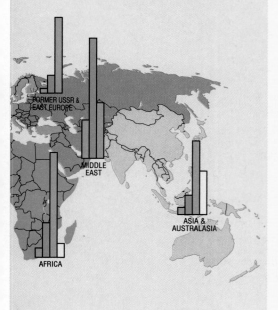

Renewable Energy

Fossil fuels are likely to become more expensive as they get scarcer, and nuclear power is surrounded by questions. The alternative is to harness renewable energy from natural sources. This has the added advantage of avoiding the problem of air pollution.

Hydroelectric Power

Hydroelectric power works by storing water in dams to drive turbines. It now provides more than a fifth of the world's electricity. One of the drawbacks of hydroelectric power is that the dams flood good farmland and in hot countries encourage the spread of waterborne diseases.

Solar Power

The simplest way of using the sun's rays is to use flat-plate collectors to heat water and buildings. Solar power can be converted into electricity using reflectors. The most promising areas are in the tropics where solar radiation is highest.

Solar panels for powering a borehole pump, Somali Republic.

Geothermal Power

Hot rocks beneath the earth's surface are a valuable source of energy. Most houses in Iceland are heated with steam from underground reservoirs. In the United Kingdom experiments are being undertaken in Cornwall and Southampton.

Wind Power *see below*

Wave Power

The motion of the waves can be used to generate electricity. It is estimated that half the United Kingdom's supplies could come from an area off northwest Scotland. Much more research is needed but the world's first wave power scheme is operating off the coast of Norway.

A tidal barrage on the River Rance, Brittany, France.

Tidal Power

Dams can trap sea water as it rises and falls with the tide. Estuaries make the best sites as they have a large tidal range. A dam on the Severn estuary could generate 5% of the United Kingdom's electricity but would cause ecological problems.

Biomass Power

Rotting waste matter from plants and animals produces methanol which can be collected in tanks and used as fuel. In some places special power stations run on crop waste. India, Malaysia, the Philippines and the United States, for example, have power stations which burn rice husks.

Wind Power in the United Kingdom

LOCATION OF UNITED KINGDOM WIND DEVELOPMENTS

Modern wind turbines can harness the power of the wind, much as windmills did in the past. Coasts and mountains are the best sites as the turbines need winds of over 15miles per hour to make them work. Unfortunately, as shown on the map, these coincide with many of the United Kingdom's most scenic areas. Offshore locations might provide a better solution.

A wind turbine in operation at Burgar Hill, Orkney.

Ovenden Moor Wind Farm

At Ovenden Moor in West Yorkshire, a local company plans to build a wind farm with 35 turbines. The turbines will be about 100 feet high and painted so they blend in with the landscape. The site is on windy moorland remote from towns and villages.

Some people are worried about how the scheme will affect the landscape. They are also concerned about the disruption to a peaceful part of the country. A proposed wind farm in mid Wales has met with similar objections.

LOCATION MAP OF PROPOSED SITE

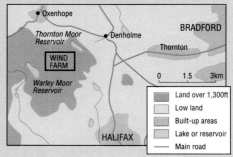

Environment and Society

The Growth of Cities

Cities were first built in the Middle East about 8,000 years ago. Here, the development of settled agriculture provided enough surplus food to support an urban population.

Today cities play a crucial role in human affairs. Athens, Rome, and Venice, for example, are famous for their contributions to European civilization and culture. Administration and government is also organized from cities which explains their political importance.

The largest cities have vast populations. About 18 million people live in New York and Mexico City has over 20 million inhabitants. By the year 2000, over half the world's population will be living in urban areas. This rapid expansion of cities in the developing world is causing a crisis.

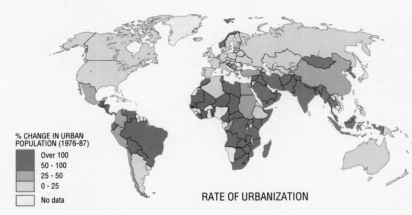

% CHANGE IN URBAN POPULATION (1976-87)
- Over 100
- 50 - 100
- 25 - 50
- 0 - 25
- No data

RATE OF URBANIZATION

The World's Largest Cities

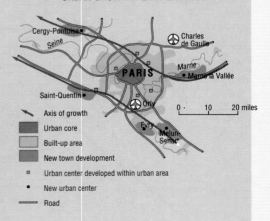

NORTH AMERICA
RURAL | URBAN 55%

Toronto
Detroit | Montreal
Chicago
San Francisco | Boston
NEW YORK
Philadelphia
LOS ANGELES | Washington
Dallas
Houston
Monterrey
Havana
Guadalajara
MEXICO CITY
Santo Domingo
Caracas
Casablanca
Bogotá
Lima
Rio de Janeiro
São Paulo
Santiago
Buenos Aires
SOUTH AMERICA
RURAL | URBAN 67%

% URBAN POPULATION, (1987)
- 75 - 100
- 50 - 75
- 25 - 50
- 0 - 25
- No data available

Cities
- ■ Over 10,000,000
- ● 5,000,000 - 10,000,000
- • 2,000,000 - 5,000,000

Pies show the percentage of the population living in cities

Planned Growth?

Developing World : Jakarta

Jakarta is one of the largest cities in the world. Almost half the people have no real jobs but survive by providing services for others. This has created an underclass of people living in miserable shanties that sprawl along the surrounding roads. The population increases by approximately a million every three years. Coping with such huge numbers is an immense challenge for the city authorities.

URBAN SPRAWL OF JAKARTA

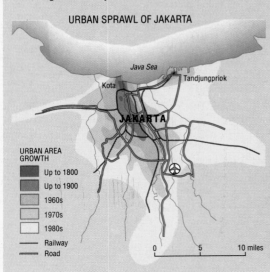

Java Sea
Kota
Tandjungpriok
JAKARTA

URBAN AREA GROWTH
- Up to 1800
- Up to 1900
- 1960s
- 1970s
- 1980s
- Railway
- Road

0   5   10 miles

POPULATION GROWTH

20 millions

15

10

Paris
Jakarta

5

0
1950   1980   2000

Sprawling slums of suburban Jakarta

Developed World : Paris

Paris is another large city. It suffers from overcrowding, traffic congestion, and poor housing. To tackle these problems, new buildings have been put up in the historic center, satellite towns established round the edge, and public transportation systems improved. These measures have helped to protect the city and maintain the quality of life of the people who live there.

URBAN GROWTH PLAN FOR PARIS

Cergy-Pontoise
Seine
Charles de Gaulle
Marne
Marne la Vallée
Saint-Quentin
PARIS
Orly
Evry
Melun Sénart

- Axis of growth
- Urban core
- Built-up area
- New town development
- ▫ Urban center developed within urban area
- • New urban center
- Road

0   10   20 miles

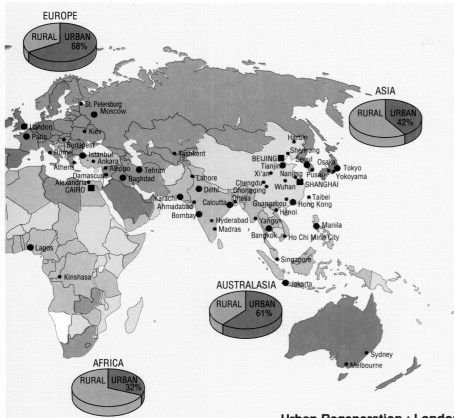

EUROPE
RURAL | URBAN 68%

ASIA
RURAL | URBAN 42%

AUSTRALASIA
RURAL | URBAN 61%

AFRICA
RURAL | URBAN 32%

Why do People come to Cities?

People come to cities for a variety of reasons. Some are attracted by the bright lights, greater freedom, better living conditions, and the prospect of work. Others are driven off the land by wars, famines, and development schemes.

This mixture of forces, which both encourages people to move and drives them forward, is known as the "push-pull" process. It affects almost every country in the developing world.

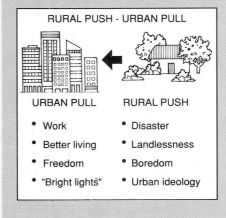

RURAL PUSH - URBAN PULL

URBAN PULL	RURAL PUSH
• Work	• Disaster
• Better living	• Landlessness
• Freedom	• Boredom
• "Bright lights"	• Urban ideology

Urban Problems

Since 1950 the number of people living in cities has almost tripled.

Housing
All big cities have homeless people. In the developing world, over half the city dwellers live in shanties where dirty water and poor sanitation cause disease. A quarter of all slum children die before the age of five.

Transport
Cities are busy, congested places and it is difficult to get about. In Athens, traffic fumes are eroding the historic buildings.

Waste
New York produces so much garbage it has run out of places to dispose of it. Human sewage has helped make the Mediterranean one of the dirtiest seas in the world.

Resources
As they grow, cities cover valuable farmland, and make huge demands on the surrounding countryside for food, water, and energy. Due to the shortage of firewood, Delhi is supplied from forests 450 miles away.

Welfare
Overcrowding, noise, and stress can have an adverse effect on the health of city dwellers. The number of violent crimes tends to be high.

Careful planning can help to provide better housing and services for city dwellers. Governments around the world could take a lead in tackling these issues.

Urban Regeneration : London Docklands

The London Docklands stretch down the Thames River from Tower Bridge. A large community depended on the docks, but during the 1960s trade began to decline. This was due, to some extent to changing patterns of trade, larger ships, labor disputes, and poor management. By 1981, all the docks had closed.

People had different ideas about what to do. One suggestion was to try and halt the job losses. The alternative, adopted by the government, was to attract new companies to the area. An airport and public railway to the center of London were built to encourage new businesses.

The population of the area has now begun to increase. Fifteen thousand new homes have been built and a major office center opened at Canary Wharf. This may benefit newcomers but local people question if it has helped the old community.

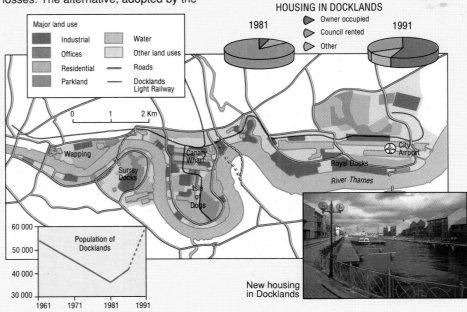

HOUSING IN DOCKLANDS
1981   1991

◗ Owner occupied
◗ Council rented
◗ Other

Major land use

Industrial
Offices
Residential
Parkland
Water
Other land uses
— Roads
--- Docklands Light Railway

0   1   2 Km

Wapping
Surrey Docks
Canary Wharf
Isle of Dogs
City Airport
Royal Docks
River Thames

Population of Docklands

60 000
50 000
40 000
30 000
1961   1971   1981   1991

New housing in Docklands

Spatial Dynamics and Connections

Ways of Travelling

For centuries the speed of travel depended on human effort or horse power. The Industrial Revolution changed all this. In the nineteenth century, railways revolutionized land travel, linking in hours places which had previously been days apart. Now modern jet aircraft fly around the world at 600 miles per hour. At this speed, it takes less than 24 hours to reach the other side of the earth.

Some people have better access to travel than others. In industrialized countries, extensive communications networks ensure that most of the people can move quickly from one place to another. In poorer countries, many people do not have access to these facilities. There are also big variations between sections of the population. Men, for example, are more likely to drive cars than women. Children and the elderly also tend to be disadvantaged.

In general people are making more journeys than ever before. Some travel voluntarily for vacations. Others are forced to travel in search of work or to escape war and famine. This increase in mobility is having a profound effect on social customs and values.

Major International Migrations

Much of world history is the story of the migration of people from one place to another. Many of these movements have been marked by battles and conflicts. They have also tended to occur in waves over a period of time, rather than as single events.

The map shows how Europe's expansion in the past has affected many parts of the world. In the present century, poverty, war, and famine have led to an unprecedented movement of people. As a result, many countries now have significant immigrant populations.

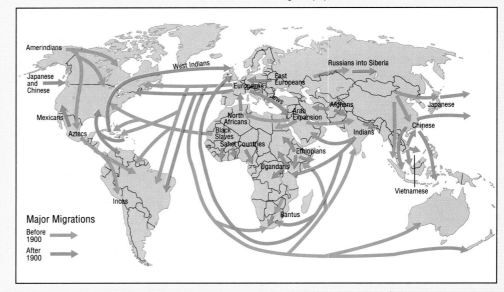

Major Migrations

Before 1900	→
After 1900	→

Car Culture

There are about 400 million cars in the world. Most of them are in industrialized countries. The United States, with 140 million, is still the home of the car culture.

The number of cars in the world has doubled in the last twenty years. Car making is the largest industry in the world economy. It is dominated by a handful of powerful international companies.

TOTAL NUMBER OF CARS PER COUNTRY

- 10,000,000
- 1,000,000
- 100,000
- 25,000
- 0
- No data

1988 or latest figures available

Cars may be convenient, but they cause widespread environmental damage. They are expensive to build, consume scarce resources, and are difficult to dispose of when they wear out. In addition, car fumes make a major contribution to acid rain and greenhouse gases. About a third of the land in towns and cities is devoted to roads and car parking. Around the world, a quarter of a million people die each year in car accidents.

Many people believe that the car culture needs to be better controlled. In the United Kingdom, for example, traffic is expected to double over the next thirty years. The government is planning a massive road-building program. Yet new roads gobble up valuable land and quickly attract more vehicles. One solution is to have more efficient public transport. The use of catalytic converters and lead free petroleum is a positive trend because it reduces air pollution.

CAR TRAVEL IN THE USA

Population	246,330,000
Area	3,619,000 sq.miles
Total number of cars	140,655,000
Car ownership (per 1,000 people)	571
Total length of road network	3,873,303 miles
Total length of motorways	51,087 miles
Road density	0.26 sq.miles
Annual fuel consumption	353,094,000 tons of petroleum
Average distance travelled per person per year	7,770 miles

CAR TRAVEL IN ITALY

Population	57,440,000
Area	113,500 sq.miles
Total number of cars	25,490,000
Car ownership (per 1,000 people)	444
Total length of road network	187,564 miles
Total length of motorways	3,726 miles
Road density	0.4 sq.miles
Annual fuel consumption	12,249,000 tons of petroleum
Average distance travelled per person per year	3,015 miles

The Impact of Tourism

The Alps form a chain of mountains 600 miles long. The snowy peaks, glaciers, and beautiful alpine scenery are major tourist attractions. Every year 50 million people visit the Alps for their vacations, two thirds of them for winter skiing.

The tourism boom has led to tree clearance to make room for ski resorts, and encouraged development on steep and unsuitable slopes. As a result, the risk of floods and avalanches has substantially increased. Areas above 6,500 feet are particularly at risk as their environment is delicately balanced.

Tourism and industry have caused an enormous increase in motor traffic and road building. Seven million vehicles cross the Alps each year contributing significantly to noise and air pollution. Acid rain affects 60% of the trees. Attempts are now being made to control vehicle fumes, replant trees, and restore damaged landscapes. If there is enough public pressure, much can be done to protect the Alps.

Around the world, tourism is on the increase. It creates jobs for local people, brings new community facilities, and helps to preserve cultural and natural heritage. But it also puts pressure on the environment, undermines traditional values, and tends to spoil the landscape. Careful planning can help to maximize the benefits and minimize the disturbance.

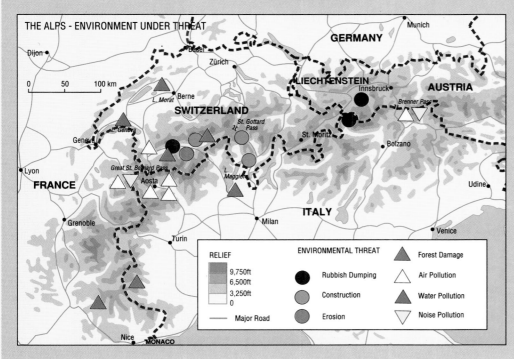

THE ALPS - ENVIRONMENT UNDER THREAT

RELIEF
9,750ft
6,500ft
3,250ft
0

Major Road

ENVIRONMENTAL THREAT
- Rubbish Dumping
- Construction
- Erosion
- Forest Damage
- Air Pollution
- Water Pollution
- Noise Pollution

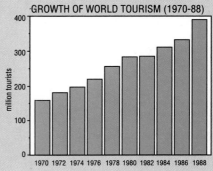

GROWTH OF WORLD TOURISM (1970-88)

million tourists

1970 1972 1974 1976 1978 1980 1982 1984 1986 1988

Refugees

There are about fifteen million refugees in the world. They are the victims of a variety of different forces. These include:

    war and conflict
    violence between different ethnic and
      religious groups
    government repression
    natural disasters such as floods, drought,
      and earthquakes

Poor people tend to be affected the most as they do not have the means to protect themselves. The majority of refugees are women and children.

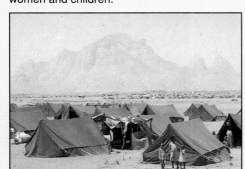

Refugee camp in Ethiopia

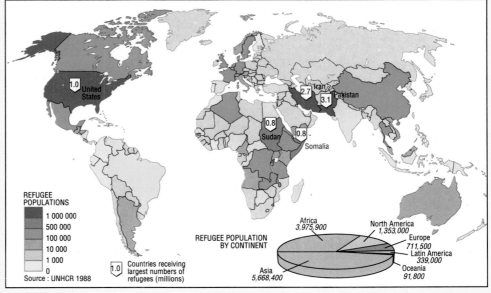

REFUGEE POPULATIONS
1 000 000
500 000
100 000
10 000
1 000
0
Source : UNHCR 1988

1.0 Countries receiving largest numbers of refugees (millions)

REFUGEE POPULATION BY CONTINENT

Africa 3,975,900
North America 1,353,000
Europe 711,500
Latin America 339,000
Oceania 91,800
Asia 5,668,400

Pakistan has the largest refugee population in the world. It accommodates over three million refugees who fled from the Afghan War during the 1980s. In 1990 and 1991, the Gulf Crisis caused the displacement of thousands of migrant workers, Kurds, and other minorities from Iraq.

Although some refugees go to live permanently in Western Europe and North America, governments are often unwilling to accept large numbers of displaced people. The United Nations High Commission for Refugees (UNHCR) provides valuable international assistance. In the long term the best solution is for refugees to return to their homelands.

Spatial Dynamics and Connections

What is Development?

Countries with a high standard of living such as the United States, Japan, and those in Western Europe are generally said to be "developed". They belong to the industrialized parts of the world where many people work in service industries and material possessions are plentiful. Countries which have not been industrialized are said to be economically "developing". Here the majority of the people are poor in material terms and earn their living by working on the land.

There are many different ways of measuring development. The first map below shows the percentage of income generated by service industries in each country. The second shows the quality of life based on life expectancy, infant mortality, and literacy. The maps need to be interpreted with care. People's need's are not the same in all environments for example, and there may well be big differences in wealth within a country whatever the average may be.

One World or Two?

In 1980 a group of political and economic experts published a report on the differences in wealth around the world. Known as the Brandt Report, it drew attention to the contrast between the rich, developed countries of the "North" and the poor, developing countries of the "South". The report argued that the countries of the North had a moral duty to help the South, and close the gap between them.

SERVICE INDUSTRY

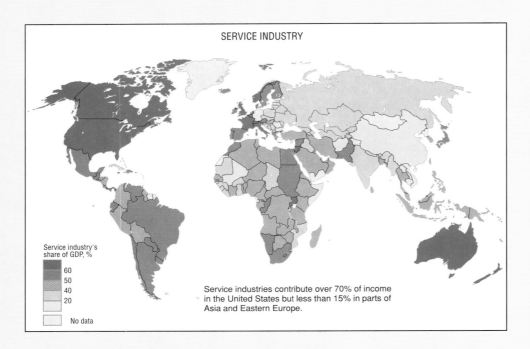

Service industries contribute over 70% of income in the United States but less than 15% in parts of Asia and Eastern Europe.

Service industry's share of GDP, %
- 60
- 50
- 40
- 20
- No data

Contrasts within the European Community

There are wide variations in living standards within the European Community. In the central area, Germany, France, Luxembourg, and Denmark form a group of countries where people have the highest incomes. Many international companies and government departments have their headquarters here.

QUALITY OF LIFE

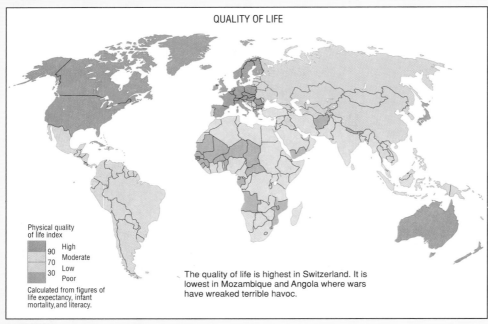

The quality of life is highest in Switzerland. It is lowest in Mozambique and Angola where wars have wreaked terrible havoc.

Physical quality of life index
- 90 High
- 70 Moderate
- 30 Low
- Poor

Calculated from figures of life expectancy, infant mortality, and literacy.

GDP PER CAPITA IN THE EC

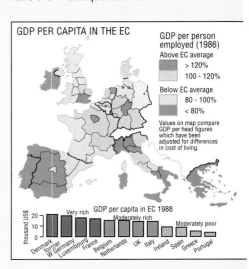

GDP per person employed (1986)

Above EC average
- > 120%
- 100 - 120%

Below EC average
- 80 - 100%
- < 80%

Values on map compare GDP per head figures which have been adjusted for differences in cost of living.

Unequal Development in South Africa

Nowadays the terms "North" and "South" are used as a kind of shorthand. Like all generalizations they conceal big differences. The countries of the South are not all equally poor, nor is the North universally rich. In addition, conditions are always changing. Recent events in Eastern Europe and the Soviet Union, for example, have shown that these countries are much less "developed" than previously thought.

For many years South Africa has had a policy of segregating black and white people, known as apartheid. Homelands have been created as national states for the black population. These cover less than a fifth of the country although blacks form the majority of the population. Apartheid is the main cause of poverty in the black population of South Africa.

Blacks earn much lower wages than whites for doing exactly the same job. Most people think it is wrong to discriminate against people because of the color of their skin. Recently the laws have begun to change. However, it seems likely that white South Africans will continue to earn more and receive better services for many years to come.

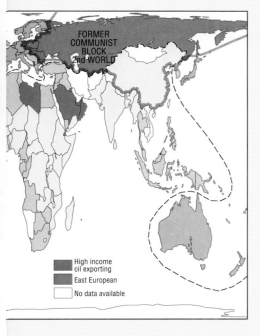

High income
oil exporting

East European

No data available

APARTHEID IN SOUTH AFRICA

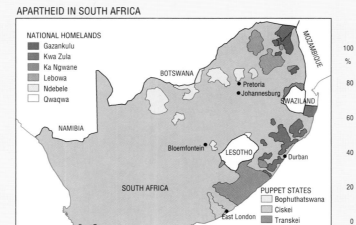

NATIONAL HOMELANDS
- Gazankulu
- Kwa Zula
- Ka Ngwane
- Lebowa
- Ndebele
- Qwaqwa

PUPPET STATES
- Bophuthatswana
- Ciskei
- Transkei
- Venda

PERCENTAGE OF POPULATION & INCOME
- Population
- Income

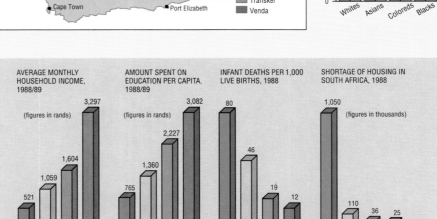

AVERAGE MONTHLY HOUSEHOLD INCOME, 1988/89
(figures in rands)
- Blacks 521
- Coloreds 1,059
- Asians 1,604
- Whites 3,297

AMOUNT SPENT ON EDUCATION PER CAPITA, 1988/89
(figures in rands)
- Blacks 765
- Coloreds 1,360
- Asians 2,227
- Whites 3,082

INFANT DEATHS PER 1,000 LIVE BIRTHS, 1988
- Blacks 80
- Coloreds 46
- Asians 19
- Whites 12

SHORTAGE OF HOUSING IN SOUTH AFRICA, 1988
(figures in thousands)
- Blacks 1,050
- Coloreds 110
- Asians 36
- Whites 25

Around this core there are a number of moderately rich countries such as the United Kingdom, Belgium, the Netherlands, and Italy. They have good communications with the center but are not so prosperous. Further afield, Spain, Portugal, Ireland, and Greece form a third group of poorer countries.

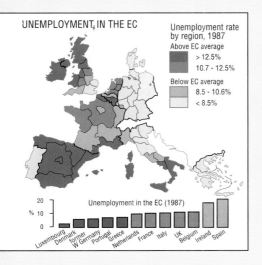

UNEMPLOYMENT IN THE EC

Unemployment rate by region, 1987

Above EC average
- > 12.5%
- 10.7 - 12.5%

Below EC average
- 8.5 - 10.6%
- < 8.5%

Unemployment in the EC (1987)
Luxembourg, Denmark, former W Germany, Portugal, Greece, Netherlands, France, Italy, UK, Belgium, Ireland, Spain

Modern flats and offices in Nairobi, Kenya

Rural housing near Kakamega, Kenya.

There are often striking differences of wealth even within the same country.

Spatial Dynamics and Connections

The Roots of Modern Trade

Modern trade dates back to the sixteenth century when European explorers began to make journeys to India and the Americas. It developed dramatically in the eighteenth and nineteenth centuries. By then Europe had extensive overseas colonies and the Industrial Revolution was gathering pace. These two factors created a world economic system with European needs and interests at its core. Present patterns of trade continue to reflect this. The income of many developing countries still depends on exporting products such as copper, coffee, and tea. Manufacturing industries, by contrast, are concentrated in the developed countries of the "North". Machines, chemicals, and consumer goods are produced here in large volumes. This accounts for the huge disparity in the value of trade between countries.

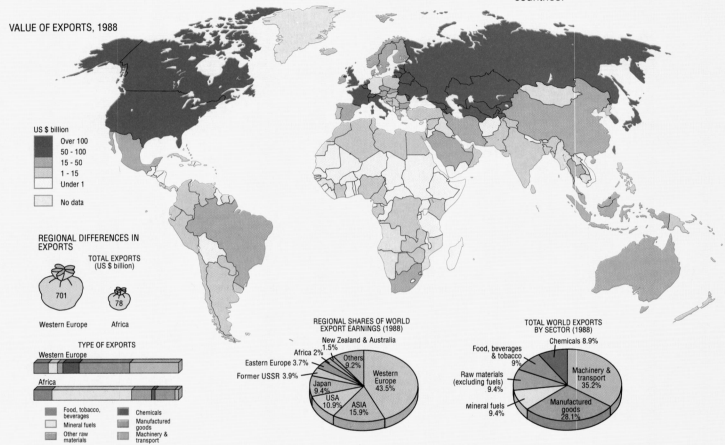

VALUE OF EXPORTS, 1988

US $ billion
- Over 100
- 50 - 100
- 15 - 50
- 1 - 15
- Under 1
- No data

REGIONAL DIFFERENCES IN EXPORTS

TOTAL EXPORTS (US $ billion)

701 — Western Europe
78 — Africa

TYPE OF EXPORTS

Western Europe

Africa

- Food, tobacco, beverages
- Mineral fuels
- Other raw materials
- Chemicals
- Manufactured goods
- Machinery & transport

REGIONAL SHARES OF WORLD EXPORT EARNINGS (1988)

- New Zealand & Australia 1.5%
- Africa 2%
- Eastern Europe 3.7%
- Former USSR 3.9%
- Japan 9.4%
- USA 10.9%
- ASIA 15.9%
- Western Europe 43.5%
- Others 9.2%

TOTAL WORLD EXPORTS BY SECTOR (1988)

- Chemicals 8.9%
- Food, beverages & tobacco 9%
- Raw materials (excluding fuels) 9.4%
- Mineral fuels 9.4%
- Machinery & transport 35.2%
- Manufactured goods 28.1%

The Terms of Trade

One of the problems facing countries which export raw materials is that commodity prices fluctuate considerably. This is partly due to changing weather conditions. A bumper crop, for example, causes a glut and forces prices down.

The graph below shows how the terms of trade have changed. Between 1975 and 1983 most commodities halved their value in comparison with oil. Since then prices have to some extent recovered, but many producers are still struggling to recover from heavy losses in the early 1980s.

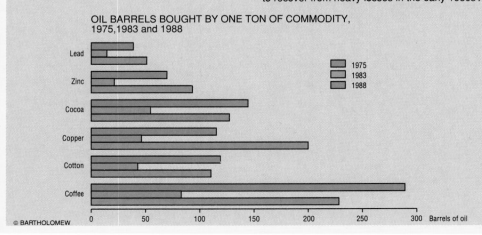

OIL BARRELS BOUGHT BY ONE TON OF COMMODITY, 1975, 1983 and 1988

- 1975
- 1983
- 1988

Lead, Zinc, Cocoa, Copper, Cotton, Coffee

0   50   100   150   200   250   300   Barrels of oil

© BARTHOLOMEW

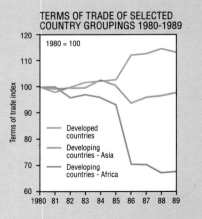

TERMS OF TRADE OF SELECTED COUNTRY GROUPINGS 1980-1989

1980 = 100

Terms of trade index

- Developed countries
- Developing countries - Asia
- Developing countries - Africa

120 110 100 90 80 70 60

1980 81 82 83 84 85 86 87 88 89

Africa has been particularly hard hit by changes in the terms of trade. During the 1980s, the value of its goods fell by a third. This has forced governments to borrow money, reducing economic and political independence.

Trade Dependency

Many developing countries depend on exporting one or two products which puts them in a very vulnerable position. Uganda, for example, earns 92% of its income from coffee. If the crops fails the results are disasterous. Also, the countries of the "North" are often able to push prices down by playing one producer off against another.

To stop this from happening, producers have formed themselves into associations called cartels. These have been largely unsuccessful, apart from OPEC (Organization of Petroleum Exporting Countries) which managed to quadruple oil prices during the 1973 Middle East War.

Diversifying Production

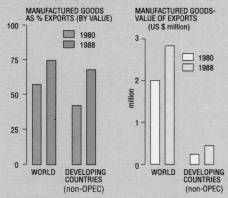

Developing countries are trying to diversify their economies to reduce trade dependency. More than half now have important manufacturing industries. As the graphs show, over the last decade the percentage of income from manufacturing has increased faster in the developing countries than in the rest of the world. In financial terms, however, these industries continue to be dwarfed by the developed countries of the "North".

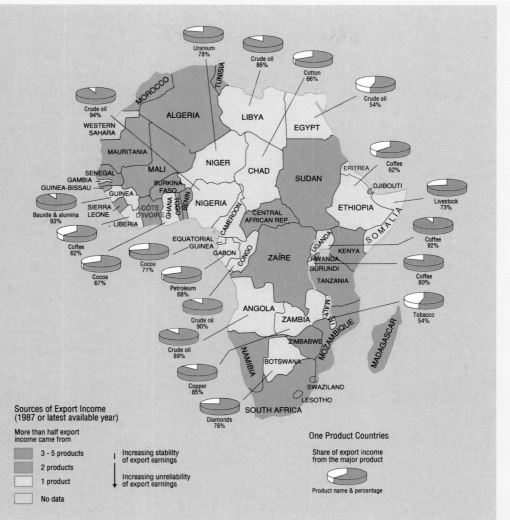

Sources of Export Income
(1987 or latest available year)

More than half export income came from

- 3 - 5 products
- 2 products
- 1 product
- No data

↑ Increasing stability of export earnings

↓ Increasing unreliability of export earnings

One Product Countries

Share of export income from the major product

Product name & percentage

The Debt Crisis

Unequal patterns of trade have driven many developing countries into debt. Repayments on loans often consume all their income.

As they struggle for survival, developing countries have to exploit their environment. Forests are cut down and the soil impoverished for short-term gains.

One solution is to cancel all debts. Another is to exchange them for environmentally sound policies. It is clear that in many developing countries economic well-being and protection of the environment are inseparable.

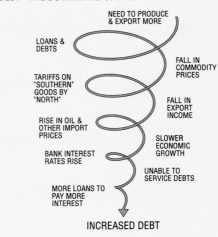

DEBT - THE DOWNWARD SPIRAL

Repayment as a percentage of exports (1988)

- Over 40
- 30 - 40
- 20 - 30
- 10 - 20
- Under 10
- No data

INTERNATIONAL DEBT:
REPAYMENTS AS A PERCENTAGE OF EXPORTS

Regions

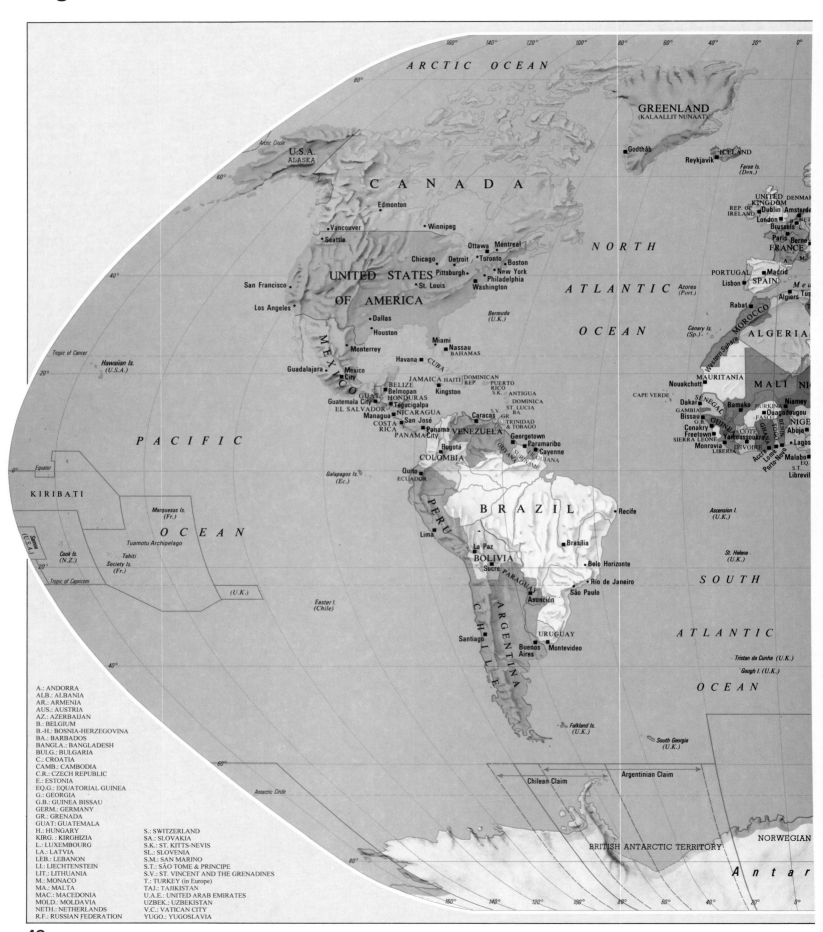

ARCTIC OCEAN

80°

GREENLAND
(KALAALLIT NUNAAT)

• Godthåb

60°

Arctic Circle

U.S.A.
ALASKA

Reykjavík • ICELAND

Faroe Is.
(Den.)

C A N A D A

UNITED DENMARK
KINGDOM
REP. OF Dublin Amsterdam
IRELAND London NET
Brussels L.
Paris Berne
FRANCE

• Edmonton

NORTH

• Vancouver   • Winnipeg

60°

• Seattle

Ottawa Montreal
Chicago • Toronto
• Detroit • Boston

ATLANTIC

40°

UNITED STATES   Pittsburgh • New York
• St. Louis Philadelphia
OF AMERICA   Washington

PORTUGAL Madrid
Lisbon SPAIN Me
Azores   Tur
(Port.)   Algiers

San Francisco •

OCEAN

Rabat MOROCCO ALGERIA

Los Angeles •

• Dallas

Bermuda
(U.K.)

Canary Is.
(Sp.)

Tropic of Cancer

Hawaiian Is.
(U.S.A.)

20°

• Houston

• Monterrey

MEXICO

• Miami
• Nassau
BAHAMAS

Western Sahara

MAURITANIA   MALI   NI

Guadalajara •

Mexico
City

Havana • CUBA

Nouakchott •

CAPE VERDE   SENEGAL
Dakar •   BURKINA
Bamako • FASO
JAMAICA HAITI DOMINICAN   GAMBIA   Ouagadougou •
BELIZE   REP.   Bissau   Niamey •
Belmopan   PUERTO   G.B. GUINEA NIGE
GUAT. Kingston RICO   Conakry •   Abuja •
HONDURAS   S.K. ANTIGUA   Freetown • CÔTE
Guatemala City • Tegucigalpa   DOMINICA   SIERRA LEONE Yamoussoukro
EL SALVADOR NICARAGUA   ST. LUCIA   Monrovia D'IVOIRE Lagos
Managua   S.V. BA.   LIBERIA   Accra Lomé
COSTA San José   GR. TRINIDAD   Porto-Novo
RICA   Caracas & TOBAGO   Malabo
Panama VENEZUELA   S.T.
PANAMA City   Libreville EQ.

BELIZE
Belmopan

PACIFIC

Georgetown
Paramaribo
Cayenne
FR. GUIANA

Bogotá GUYANA
SURINAME

KIRIBATI

COLOMBIA

Quito
ECUADOR

Galapagos Is.
(Ec.)

0° Equator

OCEAN

PERU

B R A Z I L

• Recife

Ascension I.
(U.K.)

Marquesas Is.
(Fr.)

Lima •

Samoa
(U.S.A.)

Cook Is.
(N.Z.)

Tuamotu Archipelago

Tahiti
Society Is.
(Fr.)

20°

La Paz •
BOLIVIA
Sucre •

PARAGUAY

• Brasília

• Belo Horizonte

St. Helena
(U.K.)

SOUTH

Tropic of Capricorn

(U.K.)

Easter I.
(Chile)

• Rio de Janeiro
Asunción • São Paulo •

CHILE ARGENTINA

ATLANTIC

URUGUAY

Tristan da Cunha (U.K.)

Gough I. (U.K.)

40°

Santiago •

Buenos
Aires

Montevideo

OCEAN

Falkland Is.
(U.K.)

South Georgia
(U.K.)

60°

Chilean Claim Argentinian Claim

Antarctic Circle

NORWEGIAN

BRITISH ANTARCTIC TERRITORY

80°

Antar

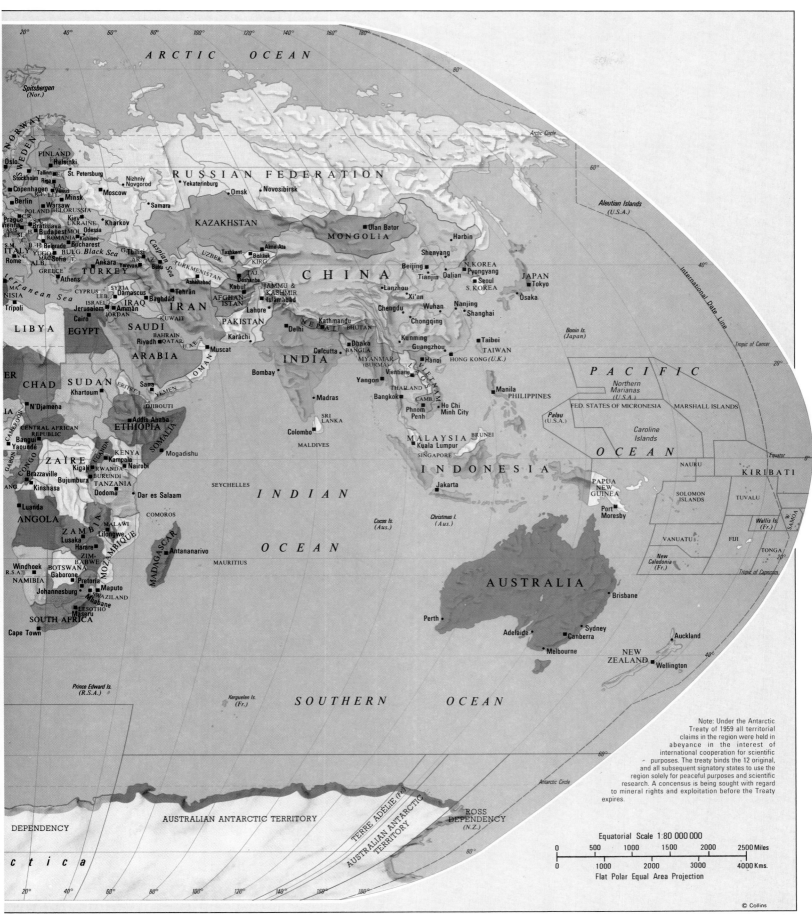

ARCTIC OCEAN

Spitsbergen (Nor.)

NORWAY

SWEDEN

FINLAND

Oslo

Helsinki

Stockholm

Tallinn

St. Petersburg

Copenhagen

Riga

Berlin

Vilnius

Minsk

Moscow

Warsaw

POLAND BELORUSSIA

Prague

Vienna

Bratislava

UKRAINE

Kharkov

Budapest

Odessa

ITALY

Belgrade

Bucharest

Rome

ROMANIA

BULG.

Black Sea

Sofia

Athens

GREECE

TURKEY

Ankara

Tbilisi

Baku

Caspian Sea

CYPRUS

SYRIA

Damascus

Yerevan

Mediterranean Sea

ISRAEL

LEB.

Baghdad

Jerusalem

Amman

IRAQ

IRAN

JORDAN

Cairo

KUWAIT

LIBYA

EGYPT

SAUDI

Riyadh

QATAR

BAHRAIN

ARABIA

U.A.E.

Muscat

OMAN

CHAD

SUDAN

ERITREA

YEMEN

N'Djamena

Khartoum

DJIBOUTI

CENTRAL AFRICAN REPUBLIC

Addis Ababa

CAMEROON

Bangui

ETHIOPIA

SOMALIA

Yaoundé

UGANDA

KENYA

ZAIRE

Kigali

Kampala

Nairobi

CONGO

RWANDA

Brazzaville

BURUNDI

Bujumbura

TANZANIA

Kinshasa

Dodoma

Dar es Salaam

Luanda

ANGOLA

ZAMBIA

MALAWI

Lilongwe

Lusaka

Harare

ZIMBABWE

MOZAMBIQUE

Windhoek

BOTSWANA

NAMIBIA

Gaborone

MADAGASCAR

Antananarivo

Johannesburg

Pretoria

Maputo

SWAZILAND

LESOTHO

Maseru

SOUTH AFRICA

Cape Town

RUSSIAN FEDERATION

Nizhniy Novgorod

Yekaterinburg

Omsk

Novosibirsk

KAZAKHSTAN

Samara

Tashkent

UZBEK.

Alma-Ata

Bishkek

KIRG.

TURKMENISTAN

Ashkhabad

Dushanbe

TAJ.

MONGOLIA

Ulan Bator

Harbin

Shenyang

Beijing

N. KOREA

Pyongyang

CHINA

Lanzhou

Tianjin

Dalian

Seoul

S. KOREA

Kabul

AFGHAN-ISTAN

JAMMU & KASHMIR

Islamabad

Xi'an

PAKISTAN

Lahore

Chengdu

Wuhan

Nanjing

Shanghai

Karachi

NEPAL

Delhi

Kathmandu

BHUTAN

Chongqing

Kunming

Guangzhou

Calcutta

Dhaka

BANGLA.

Taibei

TAIWAN

INDIA

MYANMAR (BURMA)

Hanoi

HONG KONG (U.K.)

Bombay

Vientiane

Madras

Yangon

THAILAND

Bangkok

CAMB.

Ho Chi Minh City

Phnom Penh

SRI LANKA

Colombo

MALDIVES

MALAYSIA

Kuala Lumpur

BRUNEI

SINGAPORE

INDONESIA

Jakarta

JAPAN

Tokyo

Osaka

Bonin Is. (Japan)

PACIFIC

Northern Marianas (U.S.A.)

Aleutian Islands (U.S.A.)

International Date Line

Manila

PHILIPPINES

FED. STATES OF MICRONESIA

MARSHALL ISLANDS

Palau (U.S.A.)

Caroline Islands

OCEAN

NAURU

KIRIBATI

PAPUA NEW GUINEA

Port Moresby

SOLOMON ISLANDS

TUVALU

W. SAMOA

Wallis Is. (Fr.)

VANUATU

FIJI

TONGA

New Caledonia (Fr.)

Tropic of Cancer

Tropic of Capricorn

Equator

INDIAN

OCEAN

SEYCHELLES

COMOROS

MAURITIUS

Cocos Is. (Aus.)

Christmas I. (Aus.)

AUSTRALIA

Brisbane

Perth

Sydney

Adelaide

Canberra

Auckland

Melbourne

NEW ZEALAND

Wellington

Prince Edward Is. (R.S.A.)

Kerguelen Is. (Fr.)

SOUTHERN

OCEAN

DEPENDENCY

AUSTRALIAN ANTARCTIC TERRITORY

TERRE ADÉLIE (Fr.)

AUSTRALIAN ANTARCTIC TERRITORY

ROSS DEPENDENCY (N.Z.)

ctica

Arctic Circle

Antarctic Circle

Note: Under the Antarctic Treaty of 1959 all territorial claims in the region were held in abeyance in the interest of international cooperation for scientific purposes. The treaty binds the 12 original, and all subsequent signatory states to use the region solely for peaceful purposes and scientific research. A concensus is being sought with regard to mineral rights and exploitation before the Treaty expires.

Equatorial Scale 1:80 000 000

| 0 | 500 | 1000 | 1500 | 2000 | 2500 Miles |

| 0 | 1000 | 2000 | 3000 | 4000 Kms. |

Flat Polar Equal Area Projection

© Collins

Relief

Meters		Feet
5000		16 404
3000		9843
2000		6562
1000		3281
500		1640
200		656
Sea Level		0
200		Land Dep. 656
4000		13 123
7000		22 966

ARCTIC OCEAN

Asia

Kamchatka Pen.
Koryak Range
Chukot Range
St. Lawrence I.
Bering Str.
Point Hope
Pt. Barrow
Wrangel I.

BERING SEA
Aleutian Is.
Bristol Bay
Alaska Pen.
Kodiak I.
Gulf of Alaska

Beaufort Sea
Banks I.
Victoria Island
Parry Islands
Queen Elizabeth Islands
Ellesmere I.

Greenland
Mt. Forel 3360
Denmark Strait
Iceland
Arctic Circle
C. Brewster

Baffin Bay
Davis Strait
C. Farewell

Yukon
6194 Mt. Mckinley
Alaska Range
Brooks Range
Mt. Logan 6050
Coast Mountains
Yukon
Mackenzie Mts.
Mackenzie

Great Bear Lake
Great Slave Lake
Baffin Island
Foxe Basin
Southampton I.
Hudson Strait
C. Chidley
Labrador

PACIFIC OCEAN
Vancouver Island
Alexander Archipelago
Cascade Range
Fraser
Columbia
Peace
Athabasca
Mt. Robson 3954
L. Athabasca
Churchill
Saskatchewan
Nelson
L. Winnipeg
Severn
Albany
Canadian Shield
Hudson Bay
Belcher Is.
Newfoundland
Gulf of St. Lawrence
Cape Breton I.

ROCKY MOUNTAINS
Great Plains
Missouri
Yellowstone
Snake
Great Salt Lake
Gannett Pk. 4202
Platte
Missouri
Mississippi
L. Superior
L. Michigan
L. Huron
St. Lawrence
L. Ontario
L. Erie
C. Sable
C. Cod
Long I.

Sierra Nevada
Great Basin
Colorado
Colorado Plateau
Mt. Elbert 4399
Gila
Arkansas
Red
Canadian
Ozark Plateau
Ohio
Tennessee
Mt. Mitchell 2037
Appalachian Mts.
C. Hatteras
ATLANTIC OCEAN
Bermuda

Pt. Arena

Lower California
Gulf of California
C. San Lucas
Rio Grande
Pecos
Edwards Plateau
Brazos
Mississippi
C. Canaveral
C. Sable
Strs. of Florida
Bahamas
Tropic of Cancer

Sierra Madre Occidental
Altiplano
Sierra Madre Oriental
Mexicano
Popocatépetl 5452
Campeche Bay
Yucatan Pen.
Gulf of Mexico
Cuba
Greater Antilles
Hispaniola
Puerto Rico
Caribbean Sea
C. Gallinas

Sierra Madre del Sur
Sierra Madre
Coco
Gulf of Honduras
L. Nicaragua
Isthmus of Panama
Gulf of Panama
C. San Francisco
L. Maracaibo
Cordillera Occidental
Cordillera Central
Cordillera Oriental
Cotopaxi 5897
Chimborazo 6272
Llanos
Guaviare
Amazon
C. San Francisco
Equator
Galapagos Is.

© Collins ◇ Longman Atlases

Inset map

GREENLAND
U.S.A.
CANADA
UNITED STATES OF AMERICA
MEXICO
BAHAMAS
CUBA
HAITI D.R. P.R.
GUATEMALA JAMAICA
BELIZE
HONDURAS
EL SALVADOR NICARAGUA
COSTA RICA PANAMA

D.R.:DOMINICAN REP.
P.R.:PUERTO RICO

Scale 1:80 000 000
0 500 1000 1500 Miles
0 800 1600 2400 km
Bonne Projection

Scale 1:40 000 000
0 200 400 600 800 1000 Miles
0 400 800 1200 1600 km
Bonne Projection

Climate : Natural Vegetation : Land Use : Population

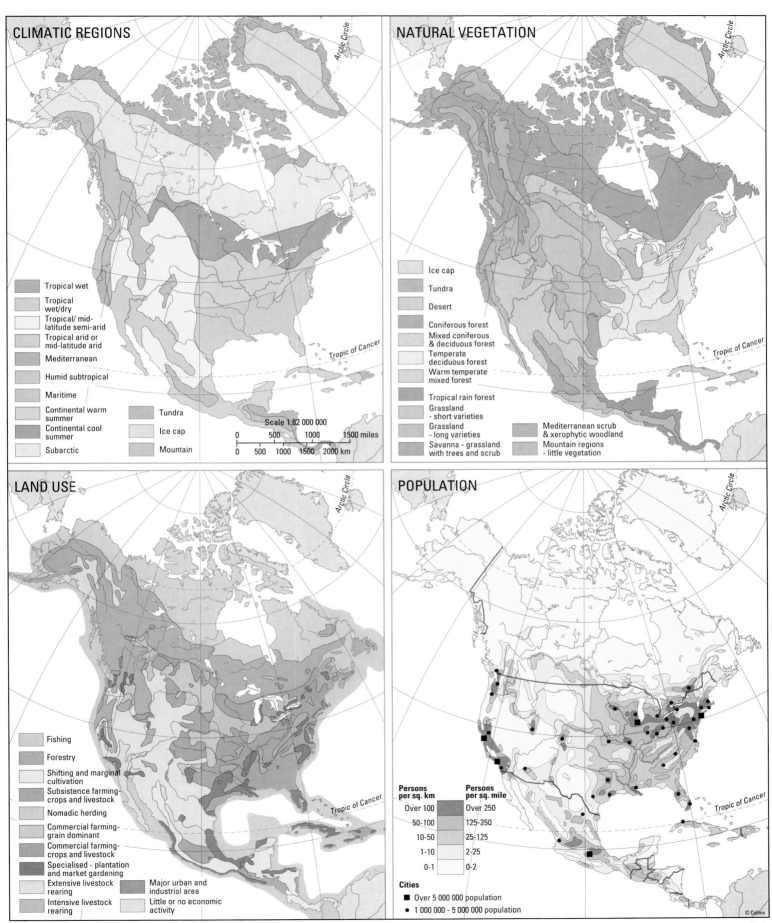

CLIMATIC REGIONS

- Tropical wet
- Tropical wet/dry
- Tropical/ mid-latitude semi-arid
- Tropical arid or mid-latitude arid
- Mediterranean
- Humid subtropical
- Maritime
- Continental warm summer
- Continental cool summer
- Subarctic
- Tundra
- Ice cap
- Mountain

Scale 1:82 000 000

0   500   1000   1500 miles
0   500   1000   1500   2000 km

NATURAL VEGETATION

- Ice cap
- Tundra
- Desert
- Coniferous forest
- Mixed coniferous & deciduous forest
- Temperate deciduous forest
- Warm temperate mixed forest
- Tropical rain forest
- Grassland - short varieties
- Grassland - long varieties
- Savanna - grassland with trees and scrub
- Mediterranean scrub & xerophytic woodland
- Mountain regions - little vegetation

LAND USE

- Fishing
- Forestry
- Shifting and marginal cultivation
- Subsistence farming- crops and livestock
- Nomadic herding
- Commercial farming- grain dominant
- Commercial farming- crops and livestock
- Specialised - plantation and market gardening
- Extensive livestock rearing
- Intensive livestock rearing
- Major urban and industrial area
- Little or no economic activity

POPULATION

Persons per sq. km	Persons per sq. mile
Over 100	Over 250
50-100	125-250
10-50	25-125
1-10	2-25
0-1	0-2

Cities
- ■ Over 5 000 000 population
- ● 1 000 000 - 5 000 000 population

© Collins

51

Regions (North America)

Relief

Feet		Meters
16404		5000
9843		3000
6562		2000
3281		1000
1640		500
656		200
0		Sea Level
Land Dep.		
656		200
13123		4000
22966		7000

Scale 1 : 17 000 000

0   100   200   300   400   500 Miles

0 100 200 300 400 500 600 700 800 Kms.

Bonne Projection

Canada

53

Regions (North America)

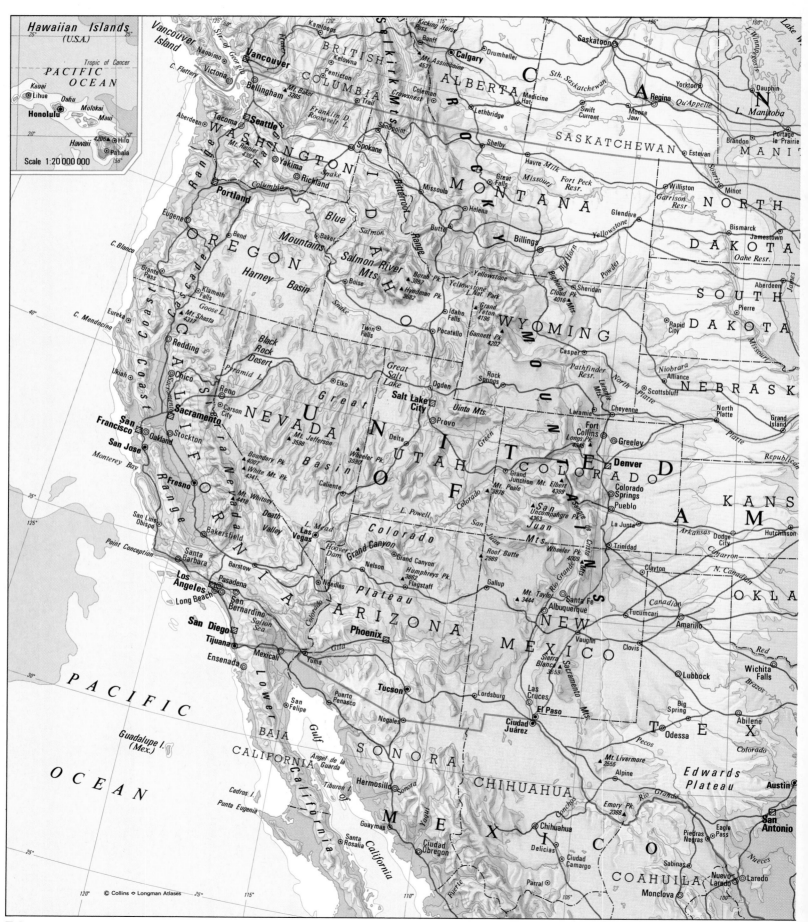

Hawaiian Islands (U.S.A.)

PACIFIC OCEAN

Tropic of Cancer

Kauai
Lihue
Oahu
Molokai
Maui
Honolulu
Hawaii 4206 Hilo
Pahala

Scale 1:20 000 000

PACIFIC OCEAN

BRITISH COLUMBIA
Vancouver Island
Vancouver
Victoria
C. Flattery
Bellingham
Kamloops
Kelowna
Penticton
Trail
Kicking Horse Pass
Banff
Mt. Assiniboine 4533
Crowsnest
Coleman
Calgary
Drumheller
ALBERTA
Lethbridge
Medicine Hat
Sth. Saskatchewan
Saskatoon
Regina
Qu'Appelle
Yorkton
Dauphin
L. Manitoba
Brandon
Portage la Prairie
MANIT

WASHINGTON
Aberdeen
Tacoma
Seattle
Mt. Baker 3285
Mt. Rainier 4392
Yakima
Richland
Spokane
Sandpoint
Franklin D. Roosevelt L.
ROCKY MTS
Shelby
MONTANA
Great Falls
Helena
Butte
Missoula
Bitterroot Range
Salmon
Havre
Milk
Missouri
Fort Peck Resr.
Williston
Glendive
Yellowstone
Bismarck
Jamestown
NORTH DAKOTA
Garrison Resr.

OREGON
Portland
Eugene
Bend
Grants Pass
Klamath Falls
Goose L.
Mt. Shasta 4317
Coastal
Cascade Range
Blue Mountains
Harney Basin
Baker
Salmon
Salmon River Mts.
IDAHO
Boise
Borah Pk. 3859
Hyndman Pk. 3682
Snake
Twin Falls
Idaho Falls
Pocatello
Yellowstone L. Nat. Park
Grand Teton 4196
Gannett Pk. 4202
WYOMING
Billings
Big Horn
Cloud Pk. 4016 Mts.
Sheridan
Powder
SOUTH DAKOTA
Pierre
Rapid City
Aberdeen
James

C. Blanco
C. Mendocino
Eureka
Redding
Ukiah
Chico
CALIFORNIA
Sacramento
San Francisco
Oakland
San Jose
Monterey Bay
Stockton
Reno
Carson City
Pyramid L.
Black Rock Desert
NEVADA
Great Basin
Mt. Jefferson 3598
Boundary Pk. 4007
White Mt. Pk. 4341
Elko
Salmon
Great Salt Lake
Salt Lake City
Ogden
Provo
Uinta Mts.
UTAH
Delta
Green
Rock Springs
Pathfinder Resr.
Laramie Mts.
North Platte
Casper
Laramie
Cheyenne
Fort Collins
Longs Pk. 4345
Greeley
Niobrara
Alliance
Scottsbluff
NEBRASK
North Platte
Grand Island
Platte

40°
35°
125°

Fresno
San Luis Obispo
Santa Barbara
Point Conception
Bakersfield
Mt. Whitney 4418
Death Valley
Sierra Nevada
L. Mead
Las Vegas
Needles
Hoover Dam
Wheeler Pk. 3980
Caliente
L. Powell
Colorado
COLORADO
Grand Junction
Mt. Peale 3878
Mt. Elbert 4399
San Juan
Uncompahgre 4363
Mts.
Wheeler Pk. 4009
Roof Butte 2989
Sangre de Cristo Mts.
Mt. Elbert
Colorado Springs
Pueblo
La Junta
Trinidad
Clayton
Arkansas
Dodge City
Hutchinson
KANSAS
Cimarron
M

Los Angeles
Pasadena
Long Beach
San Bernardino
San Diego
Tijuana
Salton Sea
Barstow
Gila
Grand Canyon
Grand Canyon
Nelson
Humphreys Pk. 3862
Flagstaff
Plateau
ARIZONA
Phoenix
Mexicali
Yuma
Gallup
Mt. Taylor 3444
Albuquerque
Santa Fe
NEW MEXICO
Tucumcari
Amarillo
Clovis
OKLA
N. Canadian
Canadian
Red

PACIFIC OCEAN
Guadalupe I. (Mex.)
Cedros I.
Punta Eugenia
Ensenada
San Felipe
Puerto Peñasco
Nogales
Lower California
BAJA CALIFORNIA
Angel de la Guarda
Tiburon I.
Gulf of California
SONORA
Hermosillo
Sonora
Guaymas
Santa Rosalia
Tucson
Lordsburg
Las Cruces
El Paso
Ciudad Juárez
Nogales
Sierra Blanca 3659
Sacramento Mts.
Vaughn
Roswell
Mt. Livermore 2555
Alpine
Pecos
Big Spring
Odessa
Edwards Plateau
Lubbock
Wichita Falls
Brazos
Abilene
TEXAS
Colorado
Austin
San Antonio

MEXICO
CHIHUAHUA
Chihuahua
Delicias
Ciudad Camargo
Parral
COAHUILA
Emory Pk. 2388
Rio Grande
Conchos
Fuerte
Yaqui
Ciudad Obregon
Eagle Pass
Piedras Negras
Sabinas
Monclova
Nuevo Laredo
Laredo
Nueces

PACIFIC OCEAN
UNITED STATES OF AMERICA

© Collins ○ Longman Atlases

Conterminous United States

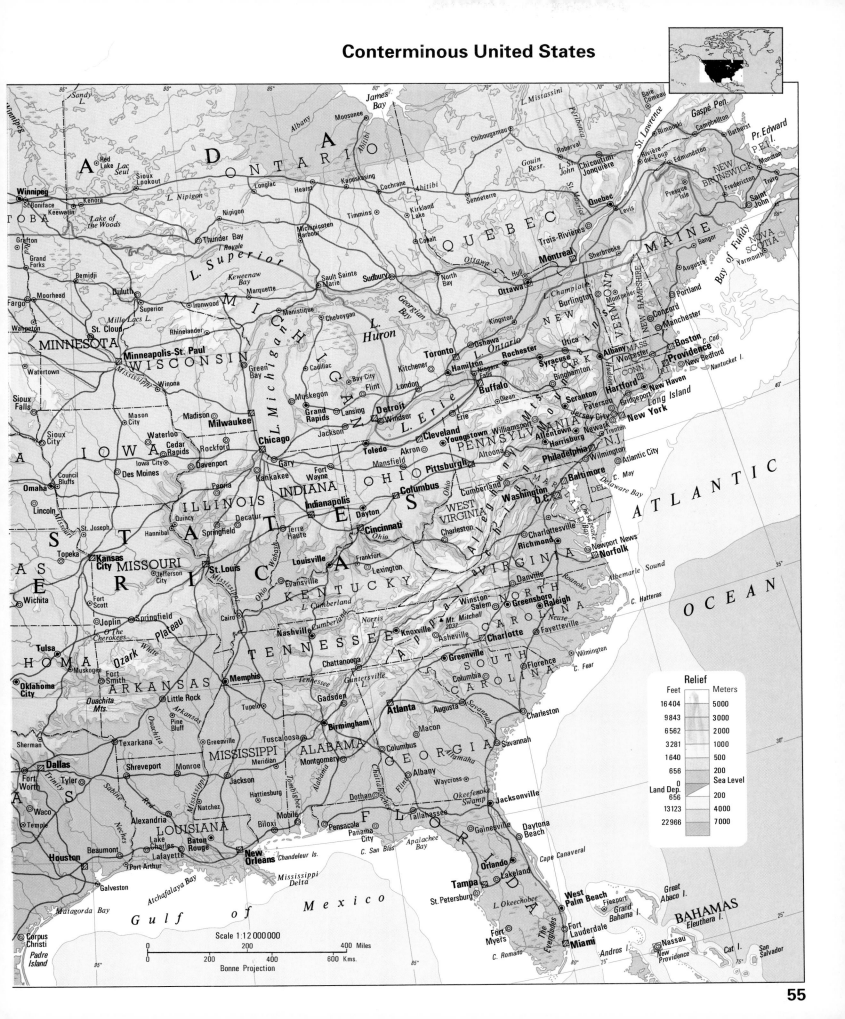

Regions (North America)

Guam, American Samoa, Micronesia

US OUTLYING AREAS

RUSSIAN FEDERATION

Arctic Circle

ALASKA
⊙Anchorage

CANADA

Hudson Bay

⊙Edmonton

Sea of Okhotsk

Bering Sea

Gulf of Alaska

☑Vancouver Winnipeg⊙

☑Seattle

PACIFIC

Toronto

Detroit☑ Boston☑

CHINA ⊙Vladivostok

Kuril Is.

UNITED STATES New York☑

☑Beijing N.KOREA

JAPAN

OCEAN

San Francisco Washington Philadelphia

S. KOREA ☑Tokyo

☑Los Angeles

ATLANTIC

☑Shanghai

Midway Is. (U.S.A.)

Houston☑

OCEAN

Tropic of Cancer

Monterrey☑ Miami☑

☑Taibei

Wake (U.S.A.)

HAWAII Johnston (U.S.A.)

Guadalajara☑ Gulf of Mexico ☑Havana

TAIWAN

MEXICO Mexico City

●Manila NORTHERN

BELIZE DOM. REP.

PHILIPPINES GUAM☑ MARIANAS

MARSHALL IS.

GUATEMALA HONDURAS PUERTO RICO

EL SALVADOR NICARAGUA

FEDERATED STATES

OF MICRONESIA

Palmyra Is. (U.S.A.)

PALAU

Equator

Howland (U.S.A.)

PAPUA Baker (U.S.A.) Jarvis

NEW NAURU (U.S.A.)

INDONESIA GUINEA SOLOMON KIRIBATI

IS. TUVALU Cook Is.

AUSTRALIA WEST. AMERICAN

SAMOA SAMOA

Legend:
- U.S. States
- U.S. Commonwealths
- U.S. Territories
- Countries in a Compact of Free Association with U.S.
- U.S. Trust Territory of the Pacific Island

PALAU
1:1 000 000

0 5 miles
0 5 10 kms

Konrei Arekalong Pen.

Ngardmau Bay

Ngardmau Gulitel ▲200 ●Keklau

Pkulagalid Pt ▲218 Makelulu

Namai Bay

▲Melekeiok

Babelthuap

Mukeru

Koror ▲34 30'

Malakal ⊙Garusuun

GUAM
1:1 000 000

Ritidian Pt.

Pati Pt.

Tumon Bay ▲262

Tamuning ●Dededo

13 30'

Piti ▲330

Agana

Orote Pen.

Apra Heights Pago Bay

Agat Santa Rita

Facpi Pt. ▲405 Talofofo

Lamlam

Merizo ▲378 Inarajan

144 45'

SAIPAN & TINIAN
(NORTHERN MARIANAS)
1:1 000 000

Sabaneta Pt.

Tanapag

Garapan Kalabera

▲465

Mt. Tagpochau

Chalan Kanoa

Saipan

Tahgong Pt. Saipan Channel

Naftan Pt.

Tinian

Diablo Pt.

Tachungnya

▲178

15°

Carolinas Pt. 145 40'

TUTUILA
(AMERICAN SAMOA)
1:1 000 000

170 40'

Vatia C. Matatula

Pago Pago Aua Tula

Fagasa ▲652 Pago Pago Harbor

Amanave Nu'uuli 14 20'

Leone Tafuna

Steps Pt.

MANUA
(AMERICAN SAMOA)
1:1 000 000

169 30'

▲484 ▲639

14 10'

Ofu Olosega

Luma ▲931

Ta'u

170 40' 169 30'

MICRONESIA

Scale 1:20 000 000

0 200 400 miles
0 200 400 600 miles

140°E 145°E 150°E 155°E 160°E 165°E 170°E 175°E

20°N Wake I. (U.S.A) 20°N

Farallon de Pajaros

Maug Is.

Asuncion

Agrihan

Pagan NORTHERN

Alamagan

Guguan

Sarigan

Anatahan MARIANAS PACIFIC OCEAN

Farallon de Medinilla

Garapan Saipan

15°N Tinian 15°N

Rota

Agana

GUAM Taongi⊙

Mariana Trench

MARSHALL ISLANDS

Bikar

Enewetak Bikini Rongerik

10°N Ulithi Ailuk 10°N

Yap Is. Fais Rongelap Likiep

Ngulu FEDERATED STATES Ujelang Kwajalein Wotje

Sorol Faraulen Erikub

Babelthuap Namonuito Fayu Ujae Namu Dalap-

Palau Is. Woleai Olimarao West Fayu Hall Is. Alinglapalap Uliga-

Angaur Ifalik Pulap Truk Is. Pakin Pohnpei Darrit

Eauripik Lamotrek Pulusuk Losap Palikir Majuro Mili

OF MICRONESIA Mokil

5°N Sonsorol Is. Satawan Kosrae Jaluit 5°N

Pulo Anna Ebon

Merir Caroline Islands Nukuoro

Tobi PALAU Butaritari

Abaiang K I R I B A T I

Kapingamarangi Tarawa

Equator Maiana Gilbert Islands

INDONESIA 140°E PAPUA NEW GUINEA 160°E NAURU ⊙Yaren 170°E Abemama

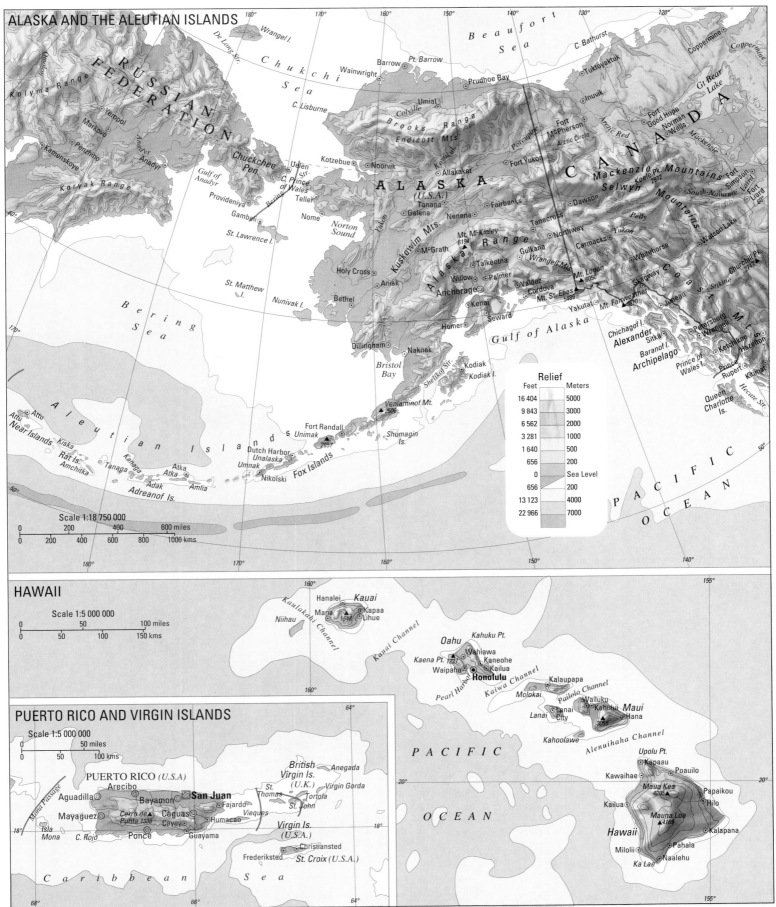

Alaska, Hawaii, Puerto Rico, Virgin Islands

ALASKA AND THE ALEUTIAN ISLANDS

RUSSIAN FEDERATION

Kolyma Range
Omolon
Yeropol
Markovo
Penzhino
Anadyr
Kamenskoye
Koryak Range
Andyr
Anadyr
Gulf of Anadyr
Chuckchee Pen.
Providenya
Gambell
Uelen
Str.
C. Prince of Wales
Teller
Bering Str.

Wrangel I.
De Long Str.
Chukchi Sea
Wainwright
Barrow
Pt. Barrow

Beaufort Sea
C. Bathurst
Coppermine
Tuktoyaktuk
Inuvik
Gt. Bear Lake
Coppermine

C. Lisburne
Kotzebue
Noorvik
Umiat
Colville
Brooks Range
Endicott Mts.
Allakaket
Fort Yukon
Porcupine
Arctic Red
Fort McPherson
Arctic Circle
Fort Good Hope
Norman Wells
Fort Norman
Mackenzie

CANADA
ALASKA (U.S.A.)
Mackenzie Mountains
Selwyn
Keele Pk. 2972
South Nahanni
Fort Simpson
Fort Liard

Nome
Norton Sound
St. Lawrence I.
St. Matthew I.
Nunivak I.

Holy Cross
Aniak
Bethel
Dillingham
Naknek
Bristol Bay

Yukon
Tanana
Galena
Nenana
Fairbanks
Tanacross
Dawson
Pelly
Yukon
Carmacks
Whitehorse
Watson Lake

Kuskokwim Mts.
McGrath
Mt. McKinley 6194
Alaska Range
Willow
Talkeetna
Anchorage
Palmer
Gulkana
Wrangell Mts.
Mt. Logan 6050
Skagway
Churchill Pk. 2743

Kenai
Valdez
Cordova
Mt. St. Elias 5489
Yakutat
Mt. Fairweather 4670
Juneau
Coast Mts.
Srikine
Hazelton

Homer
Seward
Gulf of Alaska
Chichagof I.
Alexander
Sitka
Baranof I.
Archipelago
Prince of Wales I.
Petersburg
Wrangell
Ketchikan
Prince Rupert
Kitimat

Bering Sea

Kodiak
Kodiak I.
Shelikof Str.

Queen Charlotte Is.
Hecate Str.

Veniaminof Mt. 2506
Fort Randall
Unimak 2857
Dutch Harbor
Unalaska
Umnak
Nikolski
Fox Islands
Shumagin Is.

Attu
Attu
Near Islands
Kiska
Rat Is.
Amchitka
Tanaga
Kanaga
Adak
Adreanof Is.
Atka
Atka
Amlia

Aleutian Islands

PACIFIC OCEAN

Relief

Feet		Meters
16 404		5000
9 843		3000
6 562		2000
3 281		1000
1 640		500
656		200
0		Sea Level
656		200
13 123		4000
22 966		7000

Scale 1:18 750 000

0   200   400   600 miles
0   200   400   600   800   1000 kms

HAWAII

Scale 1:5 000 000

0   50   100 miles
0   50   100   150 kms

Kaulakahi Channel
Hanalei
Mana
Kauai
Kapaa
1598
Lihue
Niihau

Kauai Channel

Kahuku Pt.
Oahu
Wahiawa
Kaena Pt. 1227
Kaneohe
Kailua
Waipahu
Honolulu
Pearl Harbor
Kaiwa Channel

Kalaupapa
Molokai
Pailolo Channel
Wailuku
Kahului
Maui
Lanai City
Hana
3055
Lanai
Kahoolawe
Alenuihaha Channel

PACIFIC OCEAN

Upolu Pt.
Kapaau
Poauilo
Kawaihae
Mauna Kea 4205
Papaikou
Kailua
Hilo
Mauna Loa 4169
Hawaii
Milolii
Pahala
Naalehu
Ka Lae
Kalapana

PUERTO RICO AND VIRGIN ISLANDS

Scale 1:5 000 000

0   50 miles
0   50   100 kms

Mona Passage
PUERTO RICO (U.S.A)
Aguadilla
Arecibo
Bayamon
San Juan
Mayaguez
Cerro de Punta 1338
Caguas
Fajardo
Cayey
Humacao
Ponce
Guayama
Isla Mona
C. Rojo

British Virgin Is. (U.K.)
Anegada
Virgin Gorda
St. Thomas
Tortola
St. John
Vieques
Virgin Is. (U.S.A.)
Christiansted
Frederiksted
St. Croix (U.S.A.)

Caribbean Sea

Regions (North America)

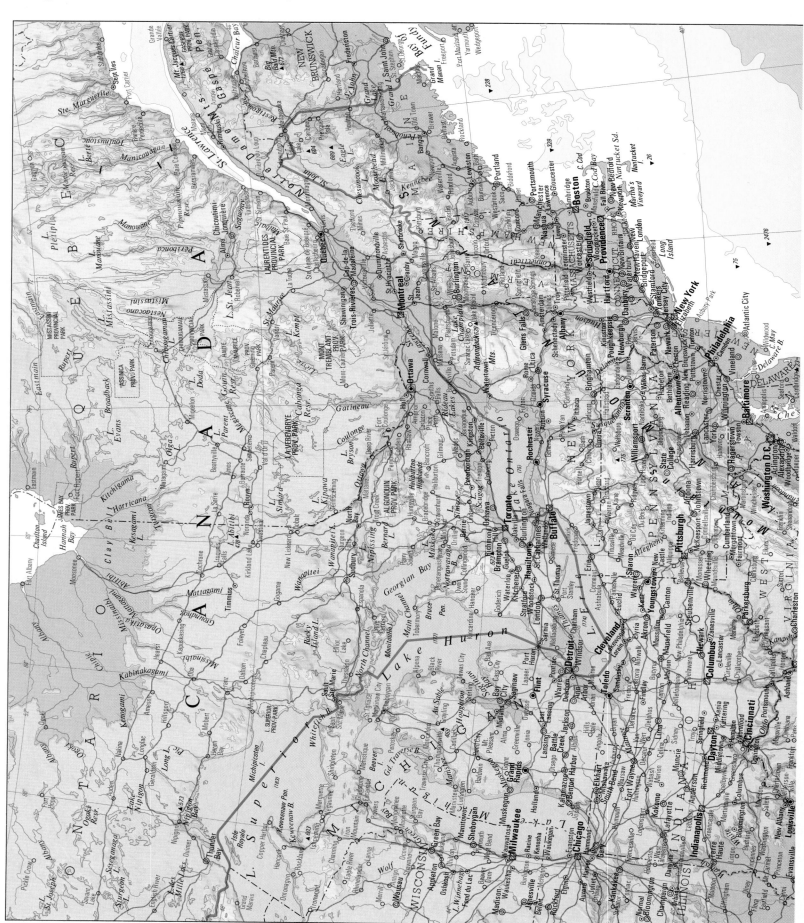

Eastern United States

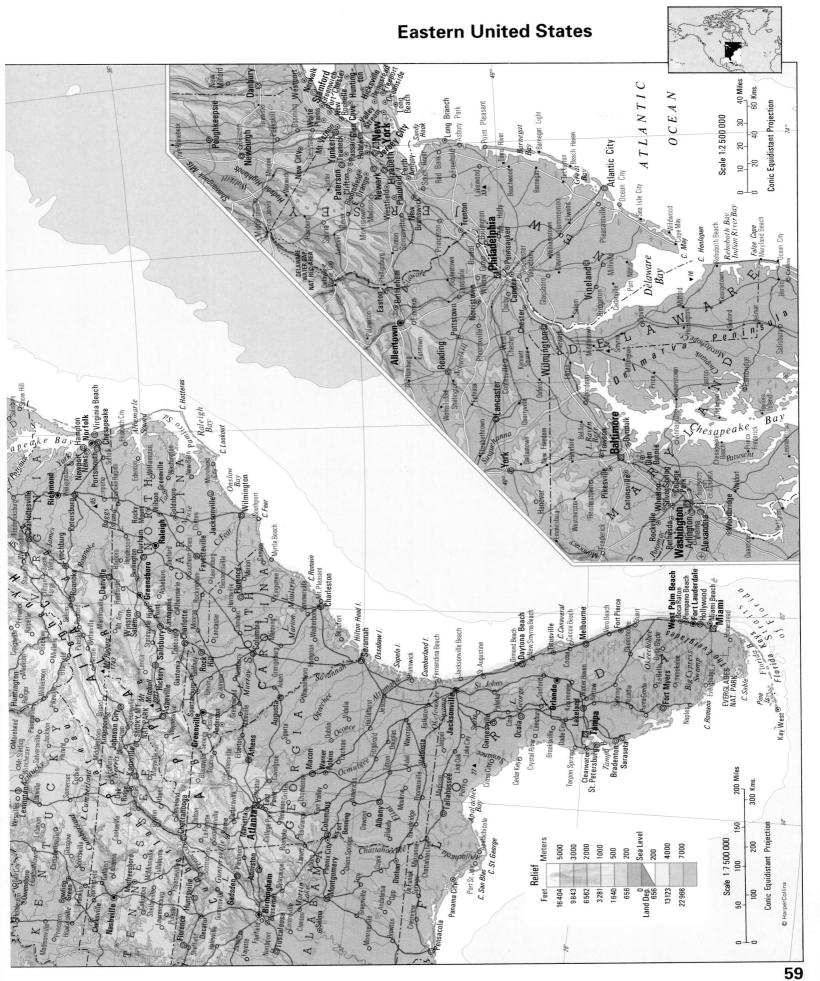

Regions (North America)

Middle United States

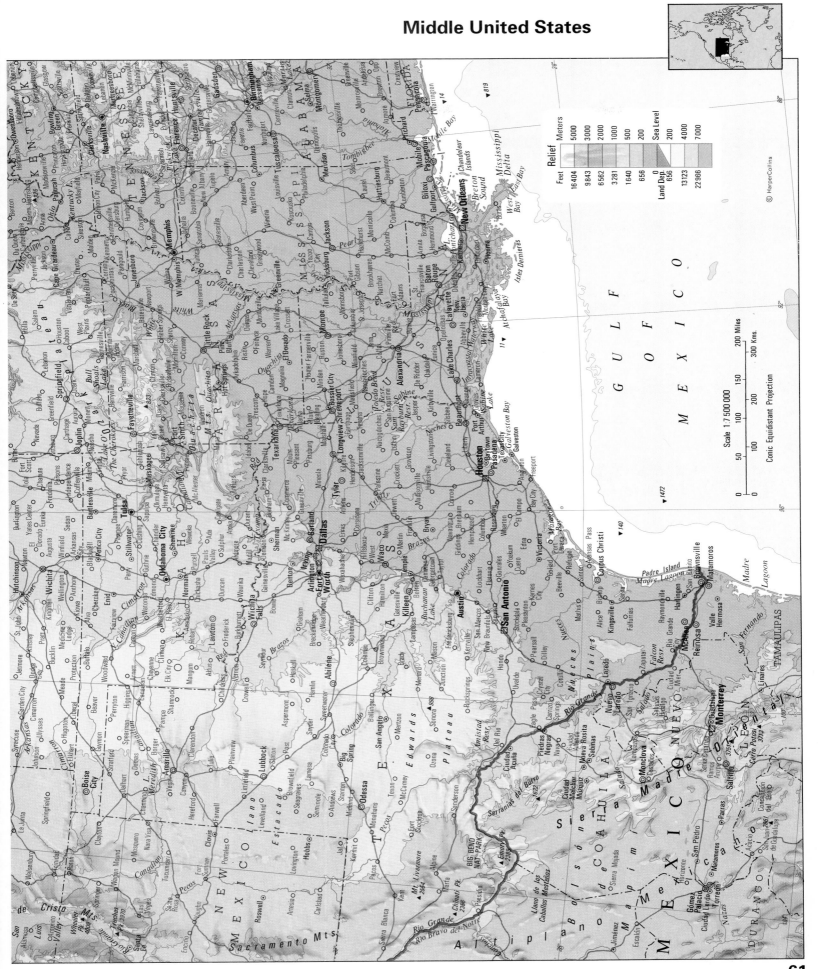

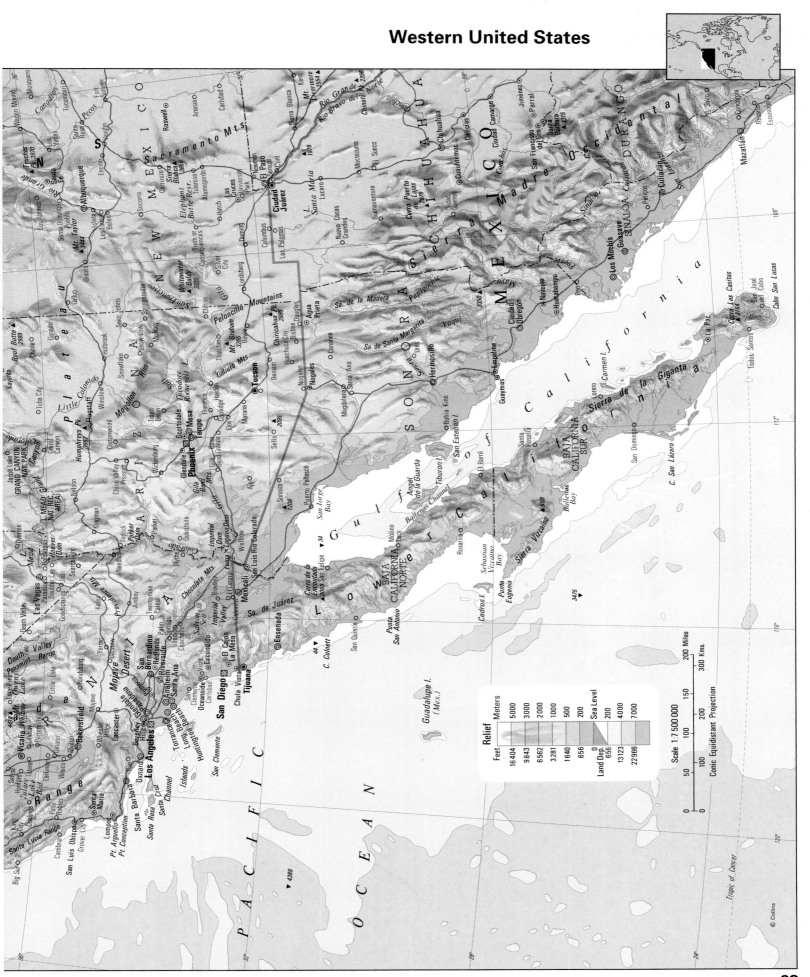

63

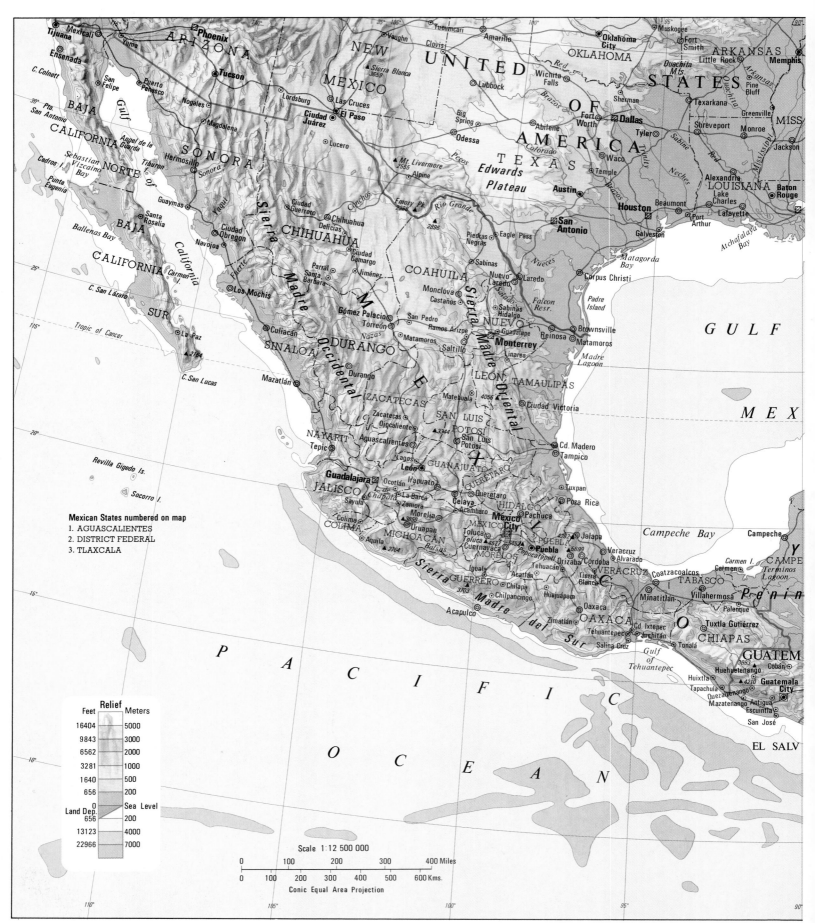

Mexican States numbered on map
1. AGUASCALIENTES
2. DISTRICT FEDERAL
3. TLAXCALA

Relief	
Feet	Meters
16404	5000
9843	3000
6562	2000
3281	1000
1640	500
656	200
0	Sea Level
Land Dep.	
656	200
13123	4000
22966	7000

Scale 1:12 500 000

0   100   200   300   400 Miles
0 100 200 300 400 500 600 Kms.
Conic Equal Area Projection

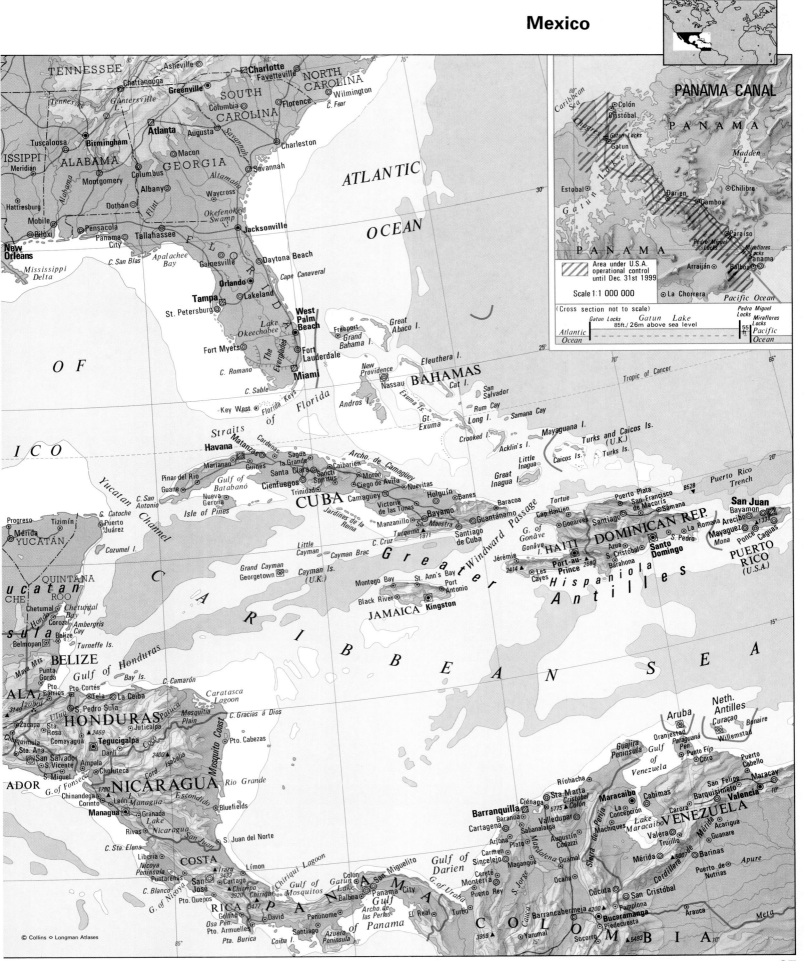

PANAMA CANAL

Area under U.S.A. operational control until Dec. 31st 1999

Scale 1:1 000 000

(Cross section not to scale)

| Gatun Locks | Gatun Lake 85ft./26m above sea level | Pedro Miguel Locks | Miraflores Locks |

Atlantic Ocean — 55 ft — Pacific Ocean

TENNESSEE
Asheville
Chattanooga
Greenville
Charlotte
Fayetteville
NORTH CAROLINA
SOUTH CAROLINA
Columbia
Florence
Wilmington
C. Fear
Guntersville
Tennessee
Atlanta
Augusta
Birmingham
Tuscaloosa
ALABAMA
GEORGIA
Macon
Charleston
Savannah
Meridian
Montgomery
Columbus
Albany
Waycross
Altamaha
ISSISSIPPI
Hattiesburg
Dothan
Flint
Mobile
Biloxi
Pensacola
Panama City
Tallahassee
Jacksonville
New Orleans
Mississippi Delta
C. San Blas
Apalachee Bay
Okefenokee Swamp
Gainesville
Daytona Beach
FLORIDA
Orlando
Cape Canaveral
Tampa
Lakeland
St. Petersburg
West Palm Beach
Lake Okeechobee
Fort Myers
The Everglades
Fort Lauderdale
C. Romano
Miami
C. Sable
Key West
Florida Keys
Straits of Florida

ATLANTIC OCEAN

Freeport
Grand Bahama I.
Great Abaco I.
New Providence
Nassau
BAHAMAS
Eleuthera I.
Cat I.
Andros I.
Exuma Is.
San Salvador
Tropic of Cancer
Rum Cay
Long I.
Samana Cay
Gt. Exuma
Crooked I.
Mayaguana I.
Acklin's I.
Little Inagua
Turks and Caicos Is. (U.K.)
Caicos Is.
Turks Is.

OF
ICO
Yucatan Channel
Progreso
Tizimín
Mérida
G. Catoche
Puerto Juárez
YUCATÁN
Cozumel I.
QUINTANA ROO
CHE
Ucatan
Chetumal
Chetumal Bay
Ambergris Cay
Corozal
Belize
BELIZE
Turneffe Is.
Belmopan
sula
Maya Mts.
Punta Gorda
ALA
Izabal
Zacapa
Chiquimula
Sta. Ana
San Salvador
S. Vicente
S. Miguel
Ampala
ADOR
G. of Fonseca
Chinandega
Corinto
León
Managua
Managua
Granada
Rivas
Lake Nicaragua
C. Sta. Elena
Liberia
Nicoya Peninsula
Puntarenas
COSTA
San José
G. of Nicoya
Pto. Quepos
RICA
Golfito
Osa Pen.
Pto. Armuelles
Pta. Burica
Coiba I.

C. San Antonio
Nueva Gerona
Isle of Pines
Pinar del Rio
Guane
Havana
Marianao
Guines
Matanzas
Cárdenas
Sagua
la Grande
Santa Clara
Cienfuegos
Gulf of Batabanó
Trinidad
Jardines de la Reina
Little Cayman
Cayman Brac
Grand Cayman
Georgetown
Cayman Is. (U.K.)
Archo. de Camagüey
Caibarién
Sancti Spíritus
Morón
Ciego de Avila
CUBA
Camagüey
Nuevitas
Victoria de las Tunas
Bayamo
Holguín
Banes
Manzanillo
Sa. Maestra
Turquino 1971
Santiago de Cuba
Baracoa
Guantánamo
C. Cruz
Greater
Windward Passage

Montego Bay
St. Ann's Bay
Port Antonio
Black River
JAMAICA
Kingston

CARIBBEAN
Gulf of Honduras
Bay Is.
C. Camarón
Caratasca Lagoon
Pto. Cortés
Tela
La Ceiba
S. Pedro Sula
HONDURAS
Sta. Rosa
Comayagua
Juticalpa
Mosquitia Plain
C. Gracias á Dios
Patuca
Tegucigalpa
Danlí
Choluteca
Coco
Pto. Cabezas
NICARAGUA
Rio Grande
Escondido
Bluefields
Mosquito Coast
San Juan
S. Juan del Norte
Chiriquí Lagoon
Colón
Gatun Lake
San Miguelito
PANAMA City
Balboa
Gulf of Panama
Archo. de las Perlas
Azuero Peninsula
Santiago
Penonome
David
Chiriquí
El Real
Gulf of Mosquitos

SEA

Cap Haïtien
Gonaïves
Tortue
G. of Gonâve
Gonâve I.
HAITI
Port-au-Prince
Jérémie
Les Cayes
Hispaniola
Santiago
Puerto Plata
San Francisco de Macorís
Sámana
DOMINICAN REP.
Azua
S. Cristóbal
Santo Domingo
Barahona
La Romana
S. Pedro
Antilles
Mona
Mayagüez
Ponce
PUERTO RICO (U.S.A.)
San Juan
Bayamón
Arecibo
Caguas
Puerto Rico Trench

Aruba
Neth. Antilles
Curaçao
Bonaire
Oranjestad
Willemstad
Guajira Peninsula
Paraguaná Pen.
Gulf of Venezuela
Punto Fijo
Coro
Puerto Cabello
Ríohacha
Sta. Marta
Ciénaga
Barranquilla
Baranoa
Cartagena
Sabanalarga
Arjona
Plato
Magangue
Sincelejo
Cereté
Montería
Puerto Rey
Turbo
Gulf of Darien
G. of Uraba
S. Jorge
El Banco
Carmen
Sincelejo
Valledupar
Maicao
La Concepción
Machiques
Lake Maracaibo
Maracaibo
Cabimas
San Felipe
Barquisimeto
Carora
Valera
Trujillo
Mérida
VENEZUELA
Valencia
Maracay
Acarigua
Guanare
Barinas
Apure
Cordillera
Puerto de Nutrias
Ocaña
Barrancabermeja
Bucaramanga
Piedecuesta
Socorro
Yarumal
Cúcuta
San Cristóbal
Pamplona
Arauca
Meta
Cauca
Magdalena
COLOMBIA

© Collins ◇ Longman Atlases

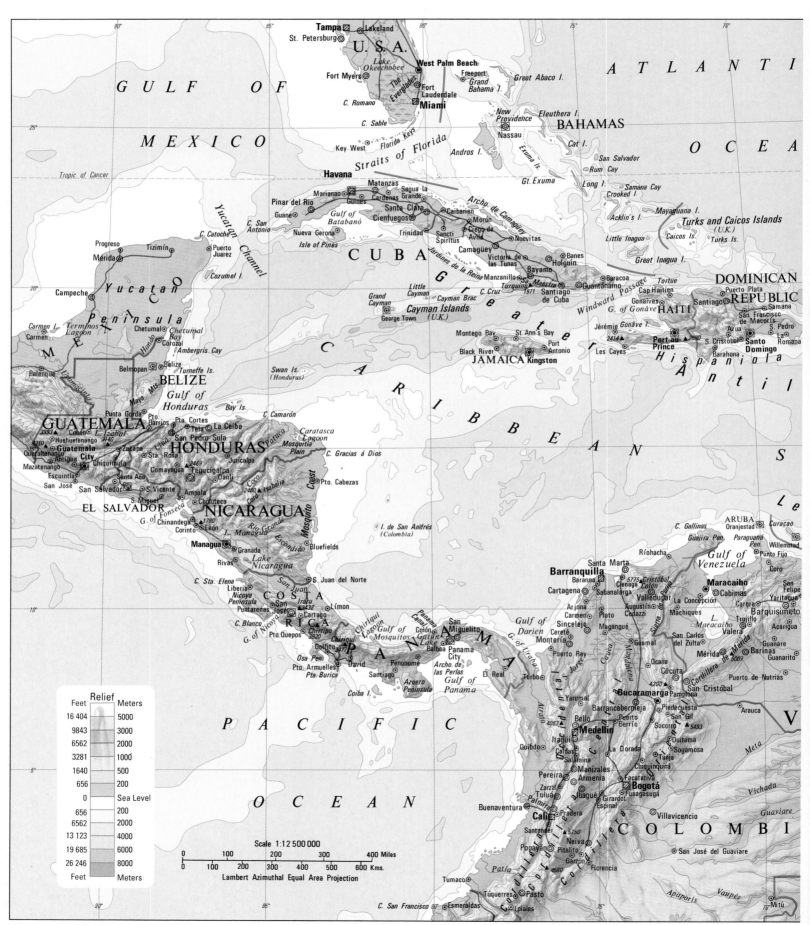

Central America and The West Indies

PUERTO RICO

Isabela · Camuy · Hatillo · Vega Baja · Dorado · Levittown · **San Juan** · Cataño
Quebradillas · Arecibo · Vega Alta · Bayamón · Río Piedras · Carolina · Río Grande · Luquillo · Cabezas de San Juan
Aguadilla · Cord. Jaicoa · Manatí · Ciales · Corozal · Naranjito · Comerío · Aguas Buenas · Caguas · Juncos · Naguabo · Pta. Puerca · Culebra
Moca · San Sebastian · Lares · Utuado · Jayuya · Sa. de El Yunque 1065 · Luquillo · Pto. Medio Mundo · I. Piñeros
Rincón · Añasco · Río Gde. de Añasco · Mtns. de Uroyan · Adjuntas · Cerro de Punta 1338 · Cordillera Central · Barranquitas · San Lorenzo · Humacao · Pta. Lima · Isabel · Vieques
Mayagüez · Maricao · Aibonito · Cayey · Pta. Arenas · Segunda · Pta. Este
Hormigueros · Peñuelas · Coamo · Guayama · Yabucao · Pto. Yabucoa · Esperanza
Cabo Rojo · San Germán · Yauco · Juana Diaz · Pastillo · Central Aguirre · Guayama · Patillas · Pta. Guayanes · Pto. Yeguas
Boquerón · La de Guánica · Guayanilla · Ponce · Salinas · Arroyo · Pta. Ola Grande
Ensenada · Guánica · Santa Isabel · B. de Jobos · Pto. Patillas
Frontón de la Brea · B. de Guayanilla · Pta. Carenero · Bahía de Rincón
Bahía Sucia

Scale 1:1 250 000
0 10 20 30 miles
0 10 20 30 40 50 kms

C A R I B B E A N   S E A

Puerto Rico Trench
8528
San Juan · Bayamón · St. Thomas · Tortola · **British Virgin Is.** (U.K.)
Arecibo · 1338 · Anguilla (U.K.)
Mayagüez · Sint Maarten · St. Martin (Fr.)
Mona · Ponce · Caguas · St. Croix · NETH. ANTILLES · Saba
PUERTO RICO (U.S.A.) · Vieques · **Virgin Is.** (U.S.A.) · Sint Eustatius
St. KITTS-NEVIS · Montserrat (U.K.)
Guadeloupe (Fr.)
Basse Terre · Marie Galante (Fr.)
Roseau · **DOMINICA**
Fort-de-France · **Martinique** (Fr.)
Castries · **ST. LUCIA**
Kingstown · **BARBADOS**
ST. VINCENT AND THE GRENADINES · Bridgetown
Carriacou · **GRENADA** · St. George's
Orchila · La Blanquilla
Los Roques · Tortuga · Margarita I. · Porlamar · **Tobago** · Scarborough
Bonaire · NETH. ANTILLES
Caracas · Cumaná · Carúpano · Güiria · Port of Spain · Arima · **TRINIDAD AND TOBAGO**
Pto. Cabello · Guatire · Barcelona · Pto. La Cruz · Paria Pen. · Gulf of Paria · **Trinidad**
Valencia · Los Teques · Altagracia de Orituco · Maturín · San Fernando
San Carlos · San Juan de los Morros · Anaco · Cantaura · El Tigre
El Baúl · Zaraza · Tucupita · Orinoco Delta
Calabozo
Apure · San Fernando de Apure · Cabruta · Mapire · Upata · Ciudad Guayana
Ciudad Bolívar
La Paragua · El Callao · Matthews Ridge
ENEZUELA · El Dorado · Cuyuni · Parika · Georgetown · New Amsterdam
Puerto Carreño · Angel Falls · **GUYANA** · Bartica · Nieuw Nickerie · Totness · Paramaribo · Albina
Cerro Yavi 2285 · **Guiana** · Mt. Roraima 2772 · Pakaraima · Mahdia · Afobaka · **SURINAME** · Cayenne
Puerto Ayacucho · Venturari · Orinduik · **Highlands** · **FRENCH GUIANA** · St. Georges · C. Orange
San Fernando de Atabapo · Cerro Marahuaca 2579 · Lethem · Boa Vista · **SURINAME**
Almirida · Orinoco · Uraricuera · Branco · Tumuc Humac Mts. · Amapá · C. Norte
Icana · San Felipe · **B R A Z I L** · Serra do Navio · Porto Grande

ISLA MONA
Scale 1:1 250 000
Isla Monito · Cabo Norte
Pta. Arenas · Cabo Este

VIRGIN IS.
Scale 1:1 250 000

British Virgin Is. (U.K.)
Great Camanoe
Jost Van Dyke I. · Guana I. · Virgin Gorda
Virgin Passage · Savana I. · Road Town · Spanish Town
Culebra · Dewey · **Tortola** · Ginger I. · Cooper I.
St. Thomas I. · Charlotte Amalie · Cruz Bay · Coral · Peter I.
Virgin Is. (U.S.A.) · St. John Bay · Norman I.
Vieques · Pillsbury Sd.

C A R I B B E A N   S E A

Hams Bluff · Cane Bay · Baron Bluff · Buck I. · East Pt.
Frederiksted · Christiansted · Grove Place
Southwest Pt. · Long Pt. · **St. Croix** (U.S.A.)

© Collins ◇ Longman Atlases

67

Yucatan Channel

Cuba

Bahama Is.

Greater Antilles

Hispaniola

Puerto Rico

Leeward Is.

ATLANTIC

Yucatan Pen.

Gulf of Honduras

Jamaica

Lesser Antilles

Windward Is.

OCEAN

Sierra Madre

L. Nicaragua

Caribbean Sea

C. Gallinas

Curaçao

Trinidad

Isthmus of Panama

L. Maracaibo

Orinoco Delta

Gulf of Panama

Llanos

Orinoco

Cordillera Occidental

Cordillera Central

Cordillera Oriental

Meta

Orinoco

Roraima 2772

Guiana Highlands

Essequibo

Cotopaxi 5897

Negro

Equator

Chimborazo 6272

Japura

Amazon

Tapajos

Xingu

C. São Roque

Marañon

Javari

Jurua

Selvas

Purus

Madeira

Araguaia

Tocantins

Parnaíba

C. Negra

Ucayali

PACIFIC

Huascaran 6768

ANDES

Guaporé

Planalto do Mato Grosso

Brazilian

OCEAN

L. Titicaca

Paraguay

Highlands

São Francisco

Atacama Desert

L. Poopó

Pilcomayo

Gran Chaco

Paraná

Agulhas Negras 2787

C. Frio

Tropic of Capricorn

Salado

Paraná

Uruguay

SOUTH

Aconcagua 6960

Pampas

Rio de la Plata

ATLANTIC

Patagonia

G. of S. Matias

OCEAN

Chiloé I.

Bahía Grande

Falkland Is.

Magellan's Str.

Tierra del Fuego

S. Georgia

POLITICAL

TRINIDAD & TOBAGO

VENEZUELA

GUYANA FR. GUIANA

COLOMBIA

SURINAME

ECUADOR

PERU

BRAZIL

BOLIVIA

PARAGUAY

CHILE

ARGENTINA

URUGUAY

Falkland Islands

Scale 1 : 80 000 000

0 500 1000 1500 Miles

0 1000 2000 Kms.

Scale 1:35 000 000

0 200 400 600 800 1000 Miles

0 500 1000 1500 Kms.

Lambert Azimuthal Equal Area Projection

© Collins ◇ Longman Atlases

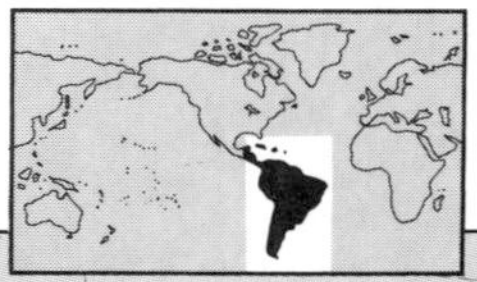

Climate : Natural Vegetation : Land Use : Population

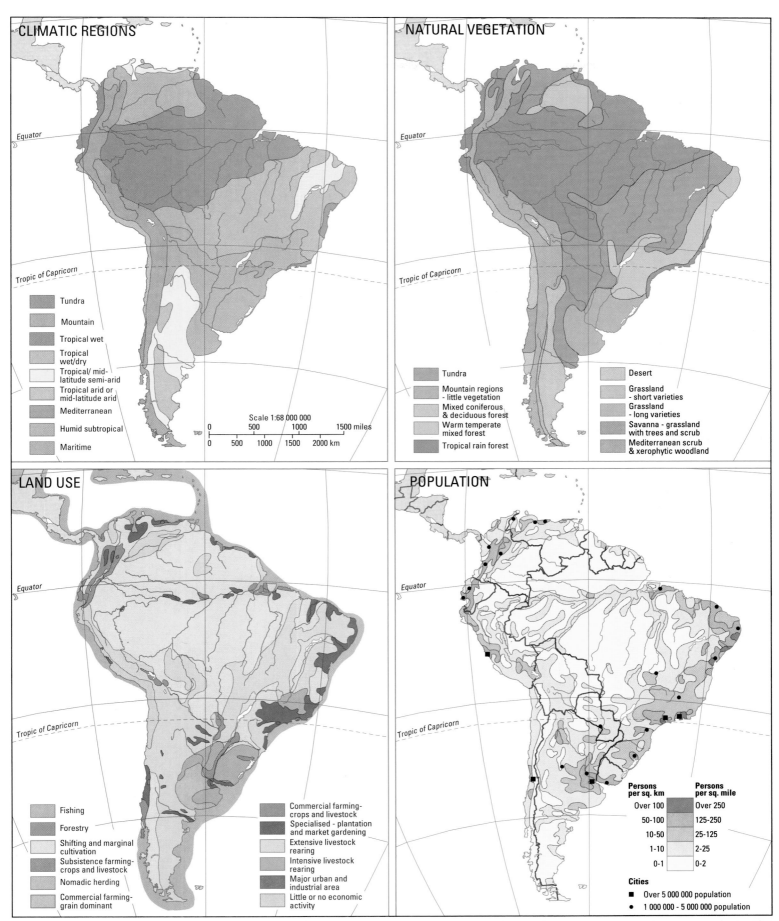

CLIMATIC REGIONS

Equator

Tropic of Capricorn

Scale 1:68 000 000

| 0 | 500 | 1000 | 1500 miles |

| 0 | 500 | 1000 | 1500 | 2000 km |

- Tundra
- Mountain
- Tropical wet
- Tropical wet/dry
- Tropical/ mid-latitude semi-arid
- Tropical arid or mid-latitude arid
- Mediterranean
- Humid subtropical
- Maritime

NATURAL VEGETATION

Equator

Tropic of Capricorn

- Tundra
- Mountain regions - little vegetation
- Mixed coniferous & deciduous forest
- Warm temperate mixed forest
- Tropical rain forest
- Desert
- Grassland - short varieties
- Grassland - long varieties
- Savanna - grassland with trees and scrub
- Mediterranean scrub & xerophytic woodland

LAND USE

Equator

Tropic of Capricorn

- Fishing
- Forestry
- Shifting and marginal cultivation
- Subsistence farming-crops and livestock
- Nomadic herding
- Commercial farming-grain dominant
- Commercial farming-crops and livestock
- Specialised - plantation and market gardening
- Extensive livestock rearing
- Intensive livestock rearing
- Major urban and industrial area
- Little or no economic activity

POPULATION

Equator

Tropic of Capricorn

Persons per sq. km	Persons per sq. mile
Over 100	Over 250
50-100	125-250
10-50	25-125
1-10	2-25
0-1	0-2

Cities

- ■ Over 5 000 000 population
- ● 1 000 000 - 5 000 000 population

69

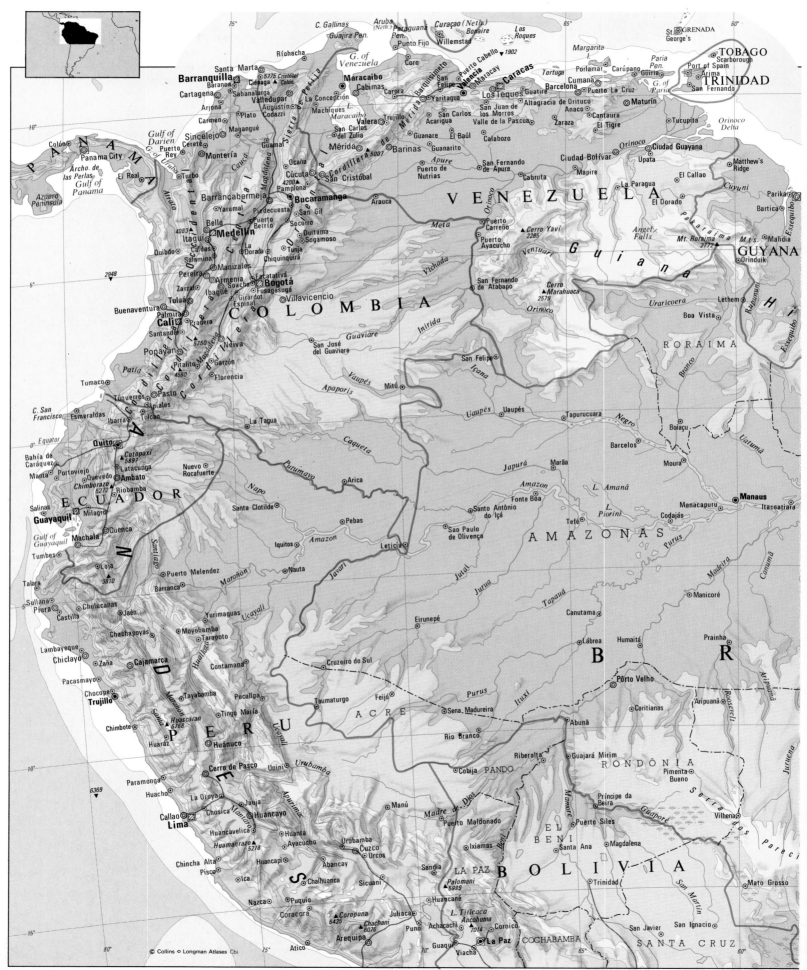

70

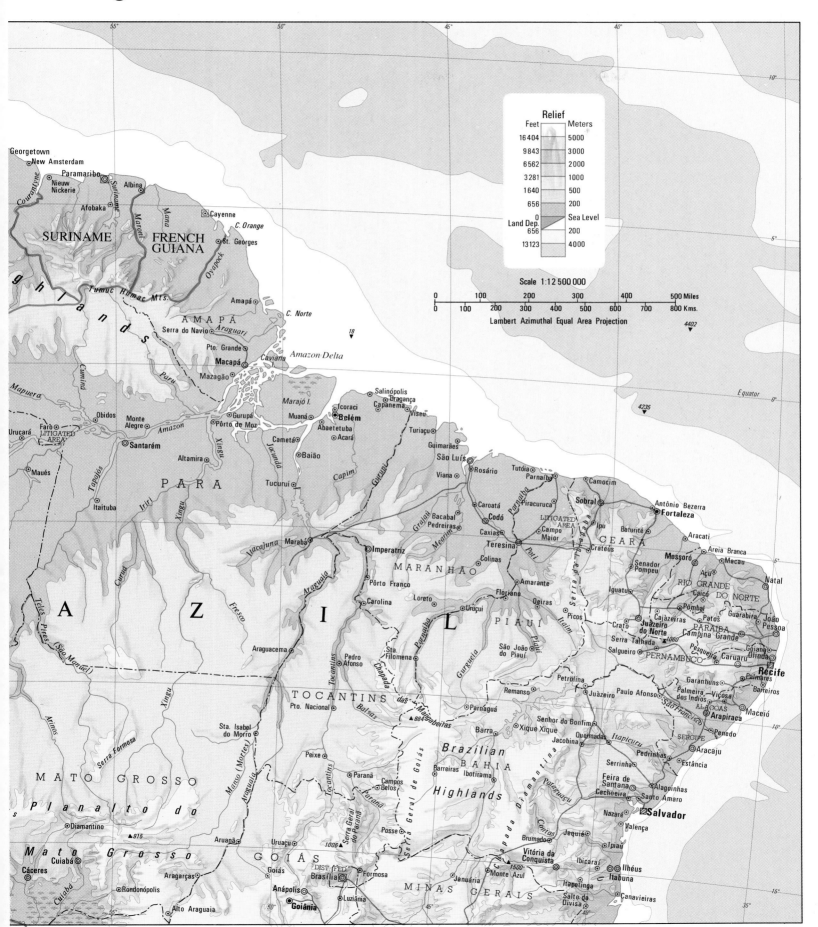

Relief

Feet		Meters
16 404		5000
9843		3000
6562		2000
3281		1000
1640		500
656		200
0 Land Dep.		Sea Level
656		200
13123		4000

Scale 1:12 500 000

Lambert Azimuthal Equal Area Projection

Regions (South America)

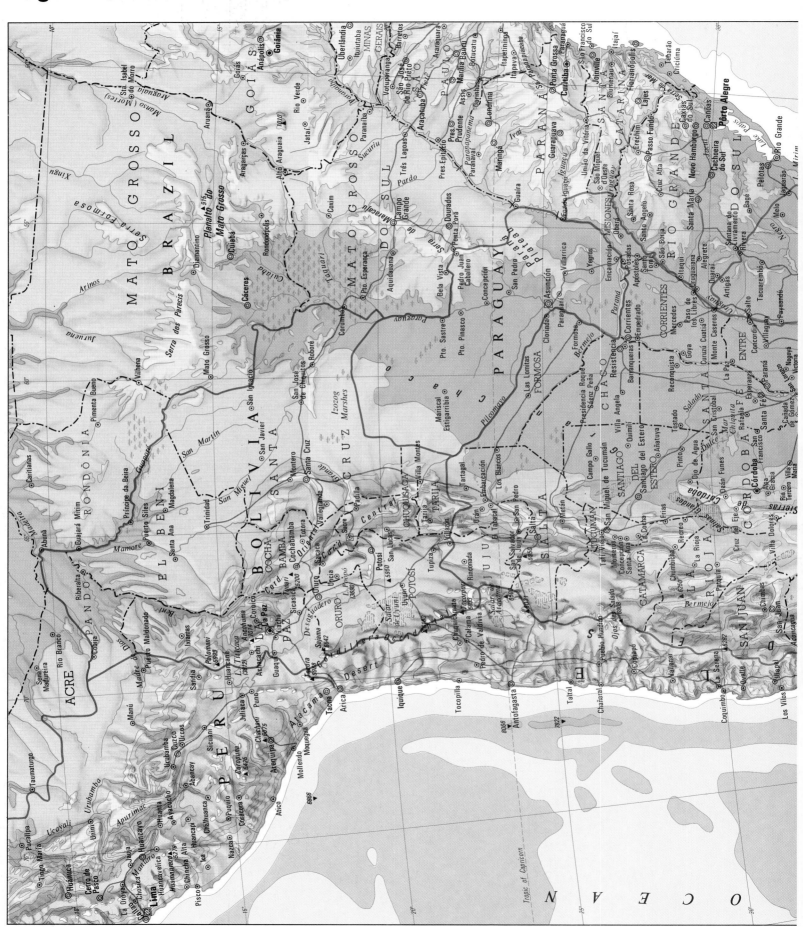

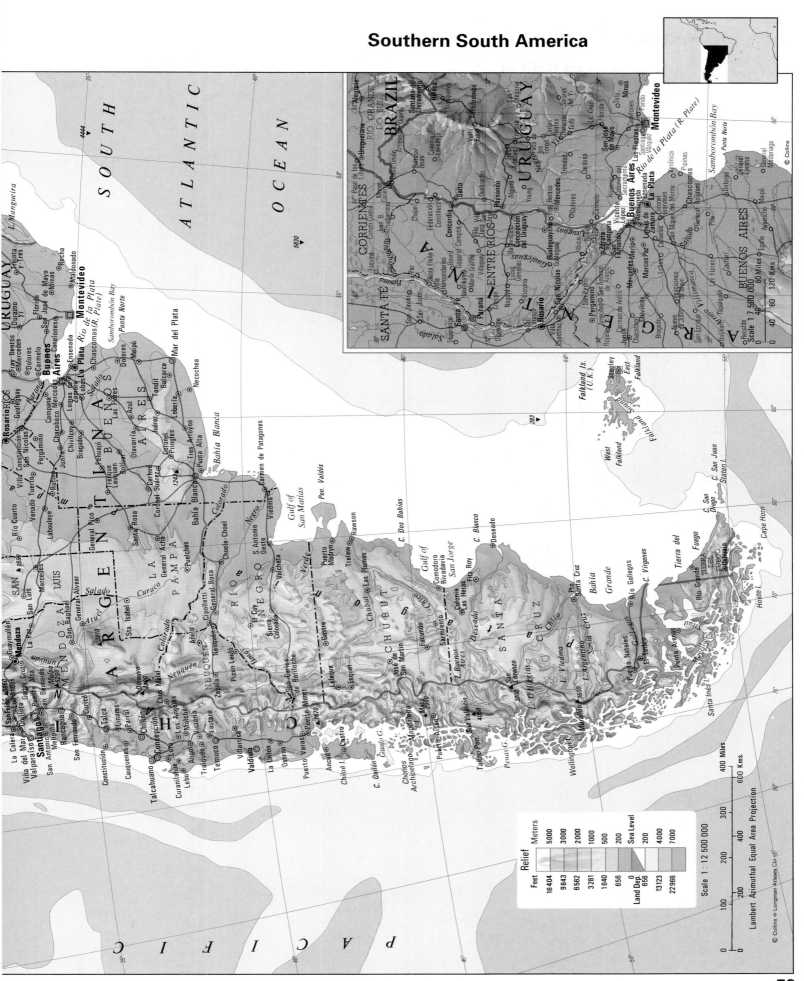

Southern South America

Planalto do Mato Grosso

Serra dos Parecis

TOCANTINS

Brazilian BAHIA *Highlands*

MATO GROSSO

SANTA CRUZ

BOLIVIA

Izozog Marshes

GOIÁS

DISTRITO FEDERAL

Brasília

Goiânia

B R A Z I L

MINAS GERAIS

Belo Horizonte

MATO GROSSO DO SUL

ESPIRITO SANTO

SÃO PAULO

São Paulo
Sto. André
Santos

PARAGUAY

PARANÁ

Curitiba

RIO DE JANEIRO
Rio de Janeiro

FORMOSA

SANTIAGO DEL ESTERO

CHACO

MISIONES

SANTA CATARINA

Florianópolis

Asunción

CORRIENTES

A R G E N T I N A

RIO GRANDE DO SUL

Pôrto Alegre

SANTA FÉ

ENTRE RIOS

URUGUAY

CÓRDOBA

Rosario

BUENOS AIRES

Buenos Aires
La Plata

Montevideo

Rio de la Plata (R. Plate)

Samborombón Bay

LA PAMPA

Bahía Blanca

Relief

Feet		Meters
16 404		5000
9843		3000
6562		2000
3281		1000
1640		500
656		200
0	Sea Level	
Land Dep.		
656		200
13 123		4000

Scale 1:12 500 000

| 0 | 100 | 200 | 300 | 400 Miles |
| 0 | 100 | 200 | 300 | 400 | 500 | 600 Kms. |

Lambert Azimuthal Equal Area Projection

Belo Horizonte

Divinópolis

MINAS GERAIS

SÃO PAULO

RIO DE JANEIRO

Rio de Janeiro

Scale 1:7 500 000

| 0 | 40 | 80 Miles |
| 0 | 40 | 80 | 120 Kms. |

© Collins

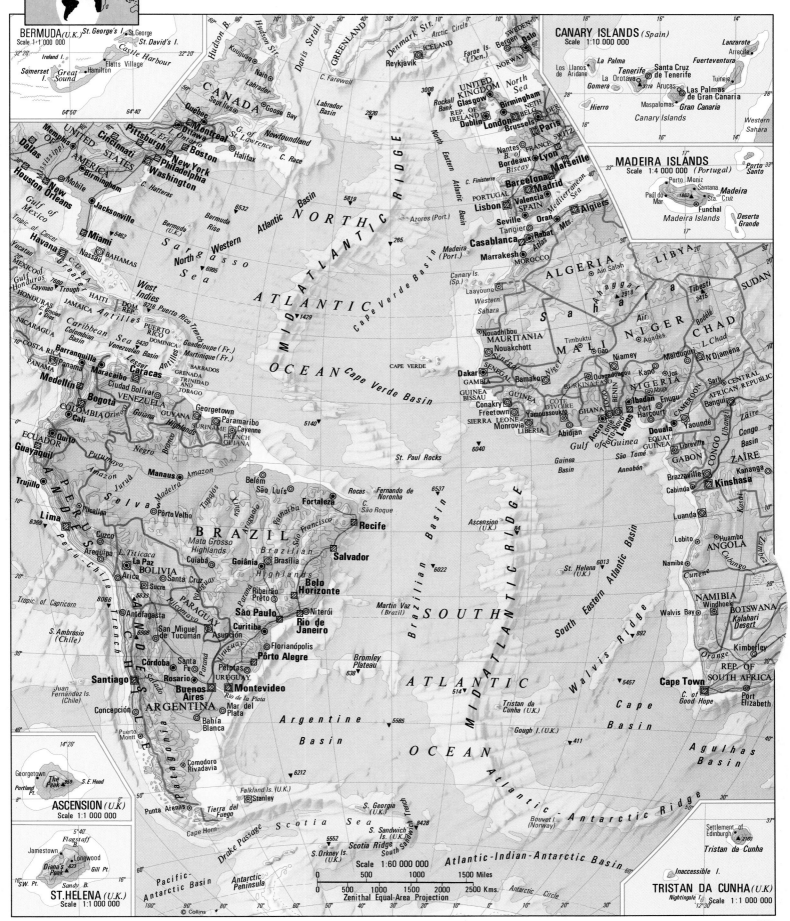

Regions (Europe)

Relief

Feet		Meters
16 404		5000
9 843		3000
6 562		2000
3 281		1000
1 640		500
656		200
0	Land Dep.	Sea Level
656		200
13 123		4000
22 966		7000

Scale 1:16 000 000

0 100 200 300 400 500 Miles

0 100 200 300 400 500 600 700 800 Kms.

Conic Projection

© Collins • Longman Atlases

76

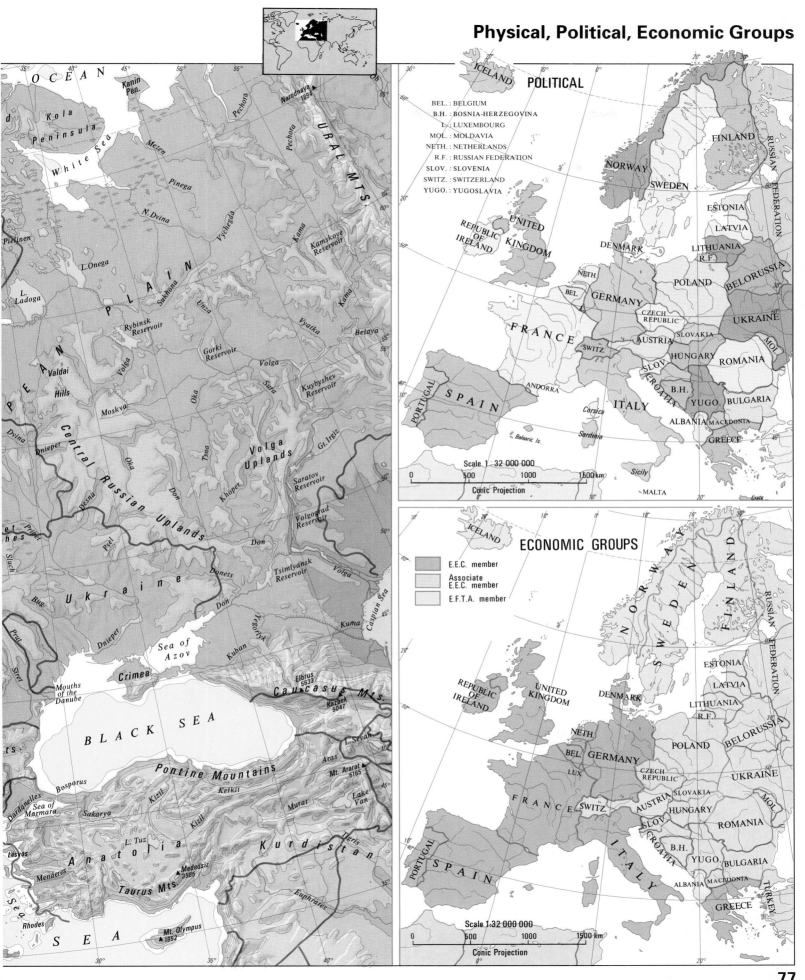

Regions (Europe)

Climate : Natural Vegetation : Land Use : Population

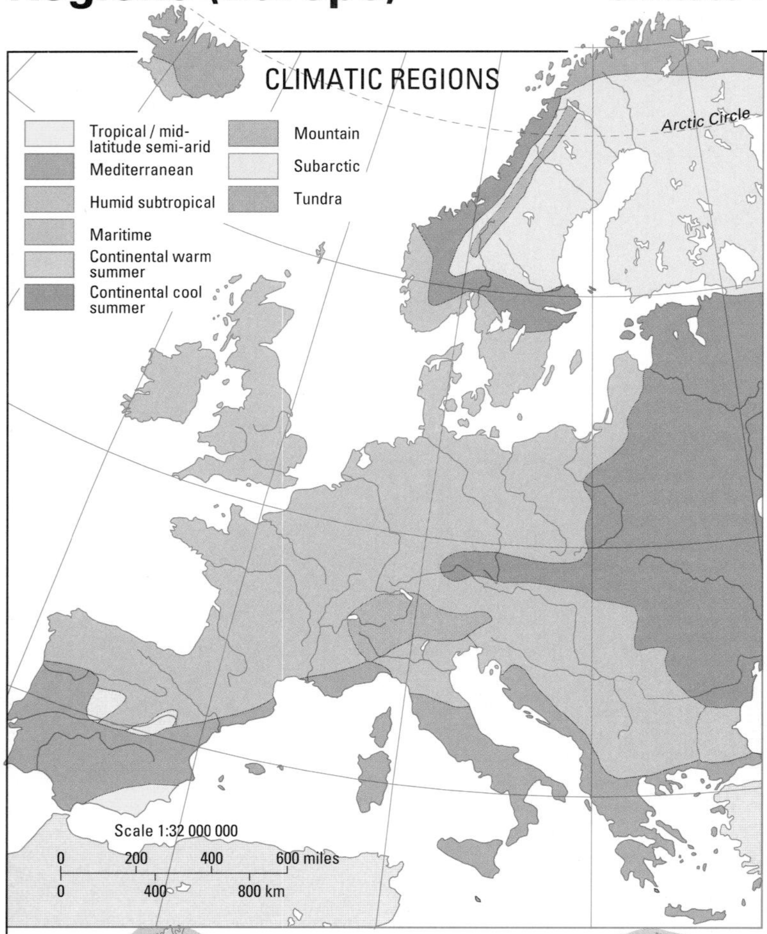

CLIMATIC REGIONS

- Tropical / mid-latitude semi-arid
- Mediterranean
- Humid subtropical
- Maritime
- Continental warm summer
- Continental cool summer
- Mountain
- Subarctic
- Tundra

Arctic Circle

Scale 1:32 000 000

| 0 | 200 | 400 | 600 miles |
| 0 | 400 | | 800 km |

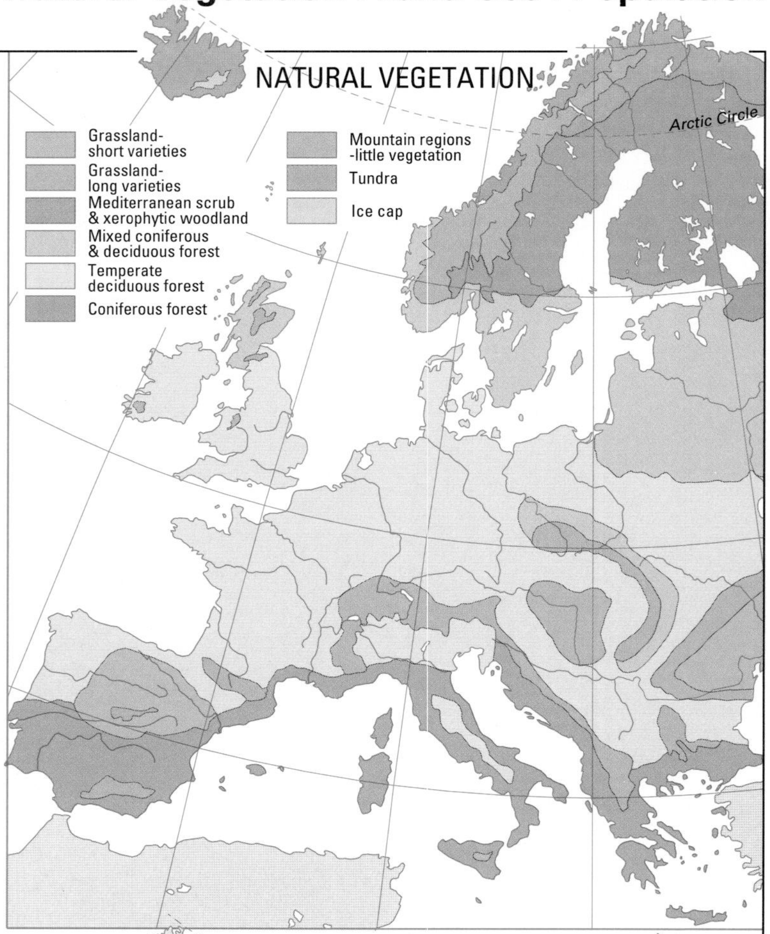

NATURAL VEGETATION

- Grassland-short varieties
- Grassland-long varieties
- Mediterranean scrub & xerophytic woodland
- Mixed coniferous & deciduous forest
- Temperate deciduous forest
- Coniferous forest
- Mountain regions -little vegetation
- Tundra
- Ice cap

Arctic Circle

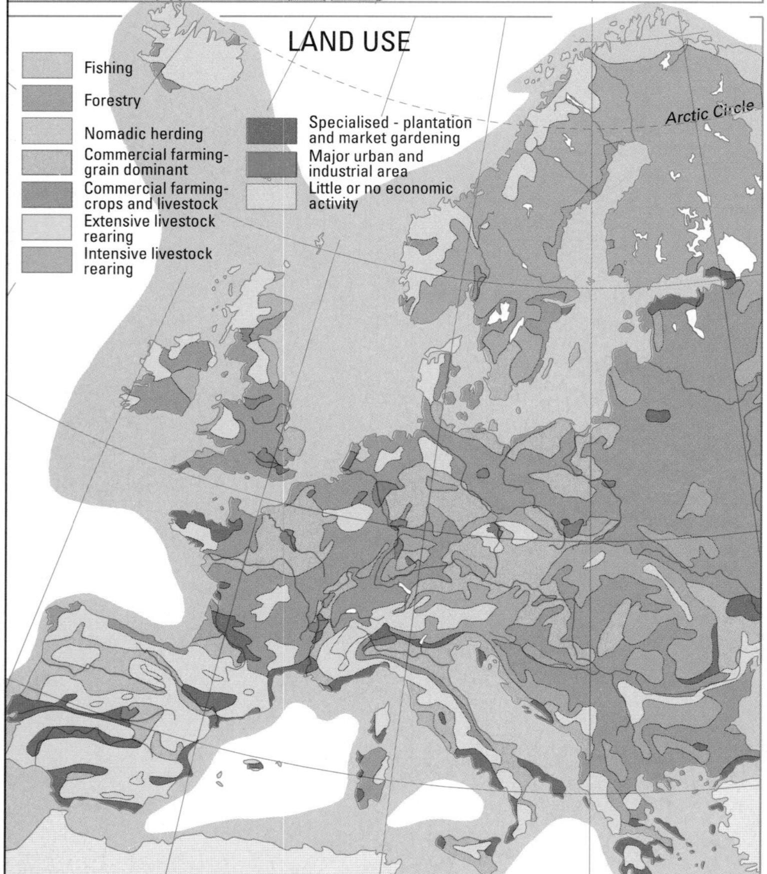

LAND USE

- Fishing
- Forestry
- Nomadic herding
- Commercial farming-grain dominant
- Commercial farming-crops and livestock
- Extensive livestock rearing
- Intensive livestock rearing
- Specialised - plantation and market gardening
- Major urban and industrial area
- Little or no economic activity

Arctic Circle

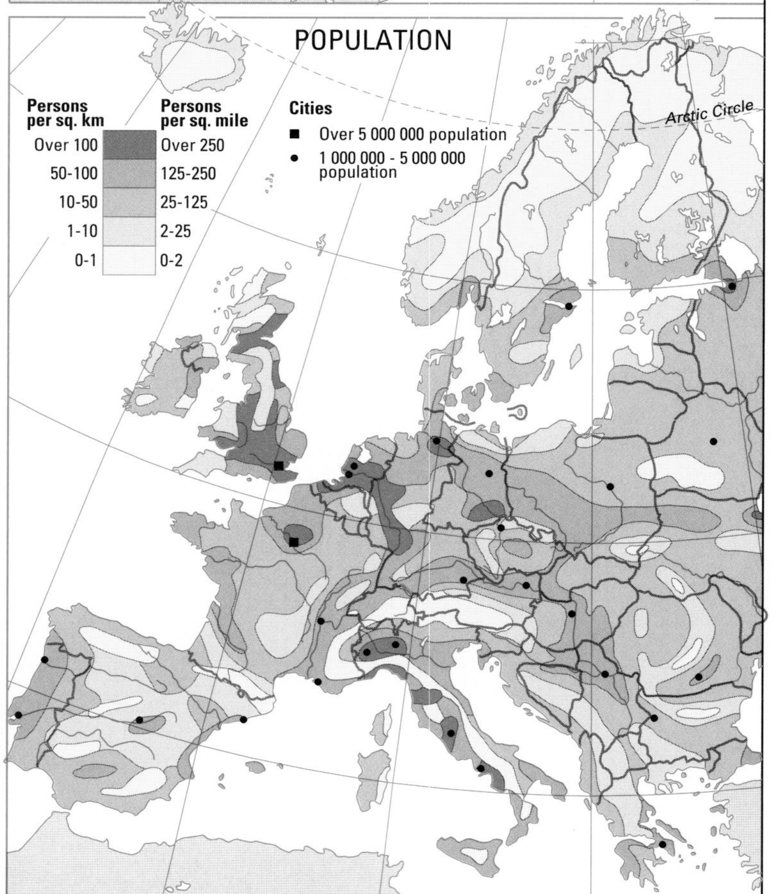

POPULATION

Persons per sq. km	Persons per sq. mile
Over 100	Over 250
50-100	125-250
10-50	25-125
1-10	2-25
0-1	0-2

Cities

- ■ Over 5 000 000 population
- ● 1 000 000 - 5 000 000 population

Arctic Circle

© Collins

78

ORKNEY ISLANDS

SHETLAND ISLANDS

Netherlands, Belgium and Luxembourg

Scale 1:2 000 000

0	10	20	30	40	50	60 Miles

0	20	40	60	80	Kms.

Conic Projection

Relief

Feet		Meters
16 404		5000
9843		3000
6562		2000
3281		1000
1640		500
656		200
0	Sea Level	

Land Dep.
656		200
13123		4000
22 966		7000

NORTH SEA

West Frisian Islands
East Frisian Islands

Texel
Vlieland
Terschelling
Ameland
Schiermonnikoog
Borkum
Norderney
Langeoog
Spiekeroog
Juist

Wadden Sea

Den Helder
Den Burg
Den Oever
Harlingen
Leeuwarden
Dokkum
Zoutkamp
Delfzijl
Emden
Norden
Aurich
Wilhelmshaven
Varel
Emden
Leer
Westerstede
Oldenburg

GRÖNINGEN
Gröningen
Hoogezand
Marum
Winschoten
Bunde
Papenburg
Friesoythe

FRIESLAND
Sneek
Heerenveen
Drachten
Assen
Stadskanaal
Gieten
Cloppenburg

IJsselmeer
Staveren
Lemmer
Steenwijk
DRENTHE
Hoogeveen
Emmen
Rütenbrock
Löningen

N.E. Polder
Emmeloord
Meppel
Coevorden
Meppen
Kusten Canal

NORTH HOLLAND
Enkhuizen
Hoorn
Kampen
Zwolle
OVERIJSSEL
Raalte
Almelo
Nordhorn
Lingen
Fürstenau
Haase

Alkmaar
Markerwaard (U.C.)
Lelystad
E. Flevoland
Beverwijk
Edam
Haarlem
Heemstede
Zaandam
IJmuiden
Amsterdam
S. Flevoland
Harderwijk
Deventer
Hengelo
Enschede
Oldenzaal
Rheine
Ibbenbüren
Osnabrück

Katwijk aan Zee
Bussum
Hilversum
Veluwe
Apeldoorn
Burgsteinfurt
Ahaus
Lengerich

Scheveningen
Leiden
Alphen
NETHERLANDS
Amersfoort
Zutphen
Lochem
Münster
Warendorf

The Hague
Voorburg
SOUTH
Old Rhine
Zeist
Utrecht
Ede
Arnhem
GELDERLAND
Dieren
Berkel
Coesfeld

Rijswijk
Gouda
UTRECHT
Renkum
Wageningen
Winterswijk
Doetinchem

Hook of Holland
Delft
Lek
IJssel
Culemborg
Tiel
Waal
Nijmegen
Emmerich
Kleve
Bocholt
Borken
Dülmen
Lüdinghausen
Haltern

Europoort
Rotterdam
Schiedam
Vlaardingen
Gorinchem
Oss
s'Hertogenbosch
Wesel
Dorsten
Lippe
Recklinghausen
Werne
Hamm
Soest

Hellevoetsluis
HOLLAND
Dordrecht
Sliedrecht
Waalwijk
Boxtel
Niers
Geldern
Gelsenkirchen
Bottrop
Herne
Dortmund

Schouwen
Duiveland
Overflakkee
Zevenbergen
Oosterhout
Maas
NOORD BRABANT
Helmond
Venray
Duisburg
Oberhausen
Mülheim
Essen
Bochum
Witten
Iserlohn
Hagen

Walcheren
East Schelde
Tholen
Bergen op Zoom
Roosendaal
Breda
Tilburg
Eindhoven
Venlo
Krefeld
Mönchen-Gladbach
Düsseldorf
Wuppertal
Remscheid
Solingen
Lüdenscheid

Middelburg
ZEELAND
South Beveland
N. Beveland
Flushing
West Schelde
Terneuzen
Valkenswaard
Weert
LIMBURG
Roermond
Maaseik
Neuss
Rheydt
Leverkusen
Bergisch Gladbach
Olpe

Zeebrugge
Ostend
Sluis
Bruges
Eeklo
St. Nicolas
Antwerp
Turnhout
Geel
Albert Canal
Sittard
Geleen
Jülich
Cologne (Köln)
Siegen

Nieuwpoort
FLANDERS
Gent
Deurne
Wilrijk
Lier
Campine
LIMBOURG
Sittard
Erkelenz
Brühl
Siegburg
Siegen

Dixmude
WEST FLANDERS
EAST FLANDERS
Lokeren
Malines
Gt. Nete
Dijle
Demer
Hasselt
Maastricht
Tongres
Heerlen
Aachen
Eupen
Bonn
Altenkirchen

Poperinge
Roulers
Deinze
Aalst
Dendermonde
Aarschot
Louvain
St Trond
Geleen
Euskirchen
GERMANY

Ypres
Menin
Courtrai
Oudenaarde
Ninove
BRABANT
Tirlemont
Namur
Meuse
Liège
Herstal
Verviers
Eschweiler
Düren
Westerwald

Armentières
Tourcoing
Renaix
Geraardsbergen
Halle
Waterloo
Wavre
Ramillies
HESBAYE
LIÈGE
Seraing
Spa
Botrange 692
Schleiden
Neuwied

Lille
Roubaix
Ath
Tournai
Soignies
Nivelles
Gembloux
Huy
Malmédy
Stadtkyll
Andernach
Koblenz

Béthune
Villeneuve d'Ascq
BELGIUM
La Louvière
Mons
Binche
Charleroi
Namur
Ciney
Marche
St.Vith
696
Prüm
746
Mayen
Lahnstein

Bruay-en-Artois
Lens
Orchies
St. Amand
HAINAUT
Beaumont
NAMUR
Dinant
Rochefort
La Roche
Bastogne
Bitburg
Daun
Boppard
Bernkastel

ARTOIS
Douai
Valenciennes
Bavay
Maubeuge
Thuin
Sambre
Philippeville
Givet
Ciney
ARDENNES
St Hubert
Wittlich
Bad Kreuznach

PICARDY
Arras
Cambrai
Le Cateau
Avesnes
Chimay
Fumay
LUXEMBOURG
Neufchâteau
Süre
Ettelbrück
Idar 816
Simmern
Bingen

Somme
Péronne
Bohain
Oise
Hirson
Charleville-Mézières
Sedan
Bouillon
Arlon
LUXEMBOURG
Trier
Hunsrück
Nahe

St. Quentin
Guise
Marle
Vervins
Rethel
Aisne
Montmédy
Longwy
Esch
Saarburg
Remich
Idar

Roye
Noyon
Oise
La Fère
Laon
Le Chesne
Longuyon
Thionville
Merzig
St. Wendel
Kaiserslautern

FRANCE

© Collins • Longman Atlases

Scandinavia and The Baltic Lands

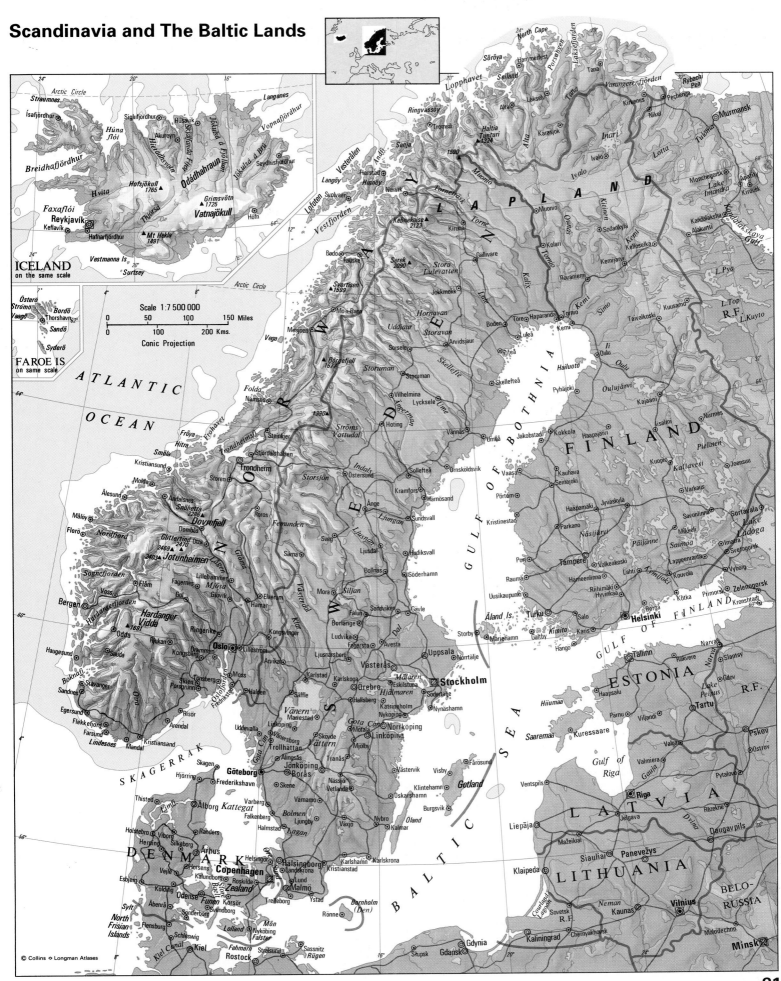

ICELAND
on the same scale

FAROE IS
on same scale

Scale 1:7 500 000

50   100   150 Miles

100   200 Kms.

Conic Projection

ATLANTIC
OCEAN

N O R W A Y

S W E D E N

L A P L A N D

FINLAND

GULF OF BOTHNIA

GULF OF FINLAND

BALTIC SEA

ESTONIA

LATVIA

LITHUANIA

DENMARK

Skagerrak

Kattegat

BELO-RUSSIA

© Collins ◇ Longman Atlases

Regions (Europe)

Central Europe

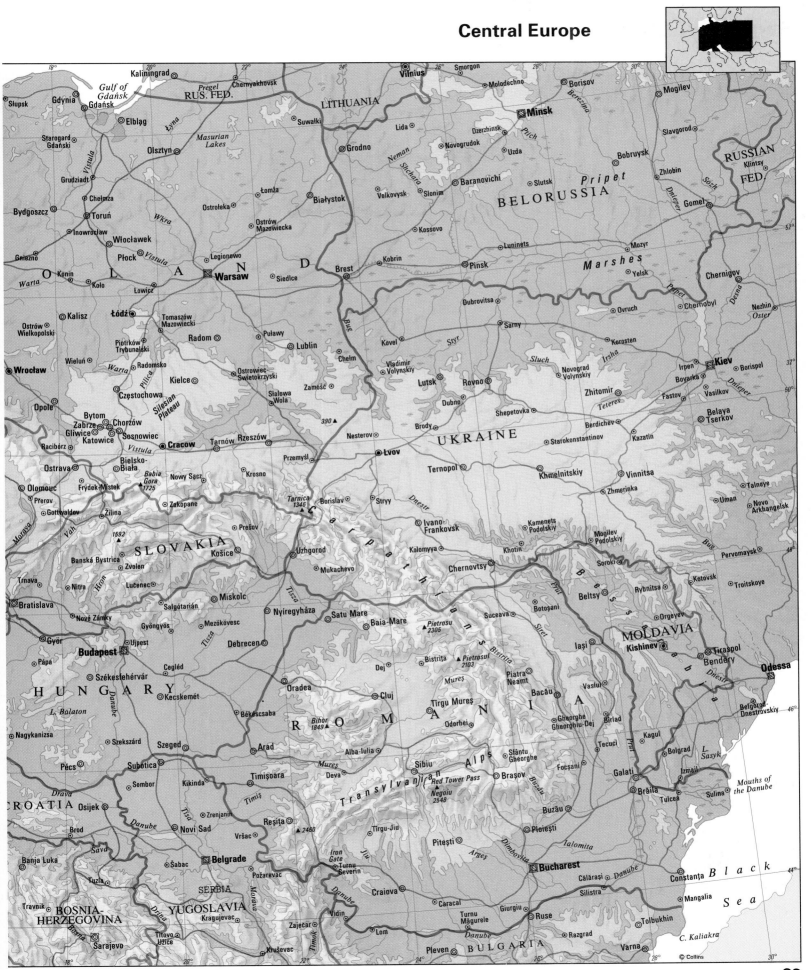

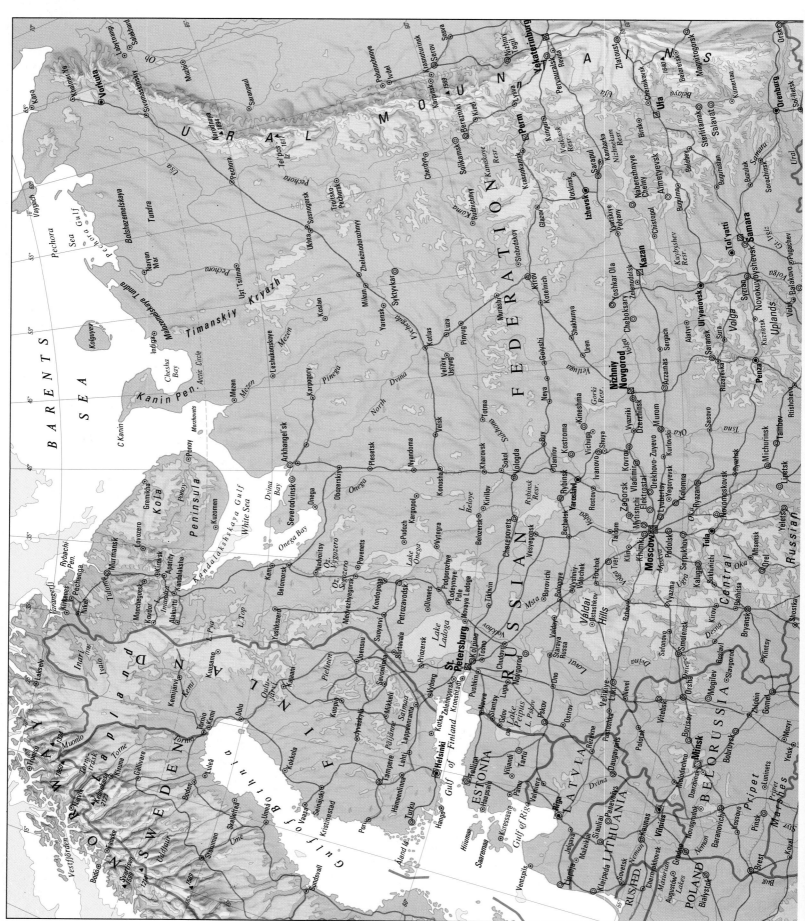

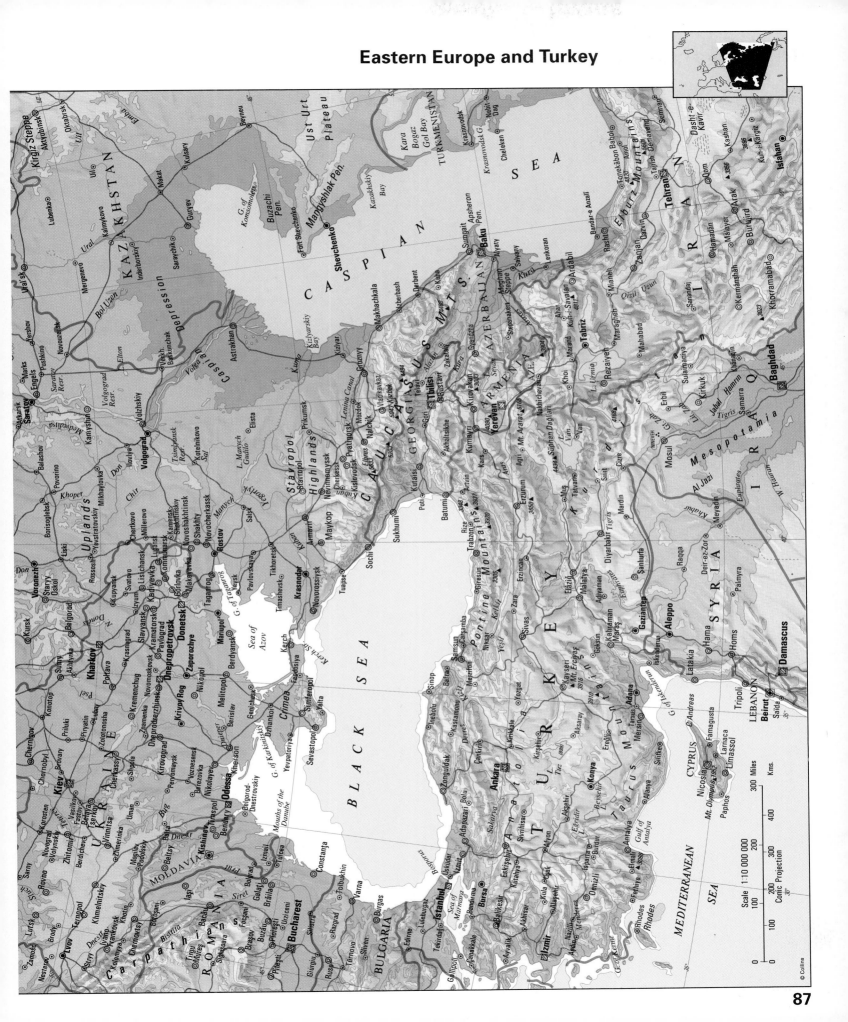

Regions

(Europe)

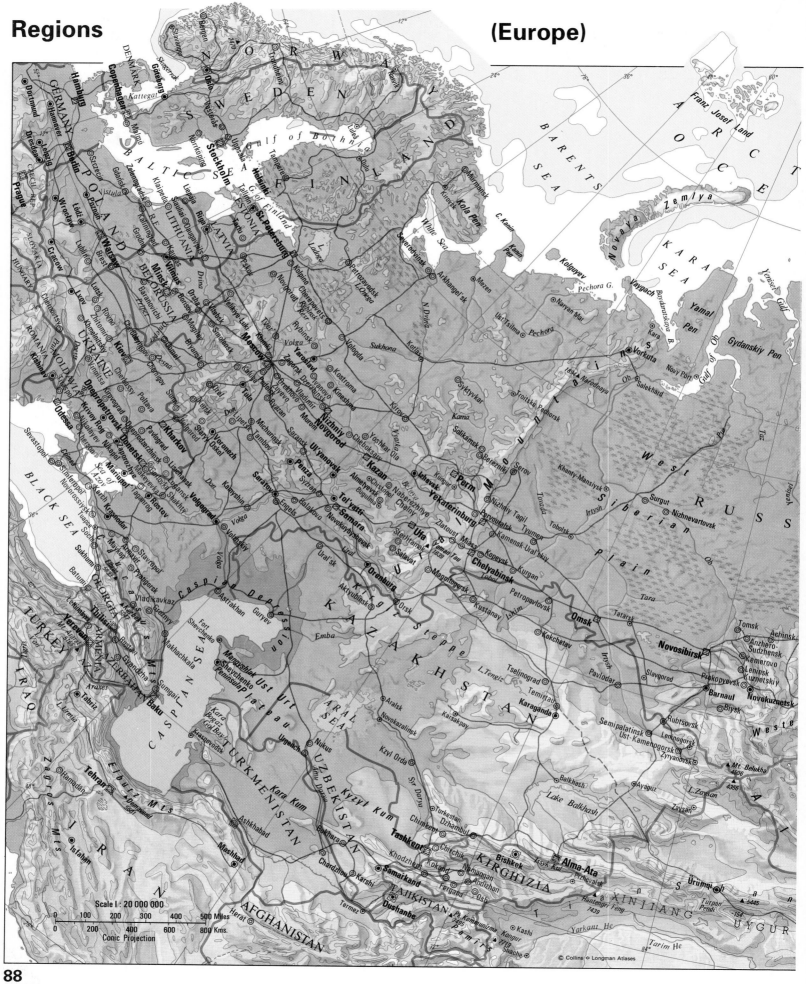

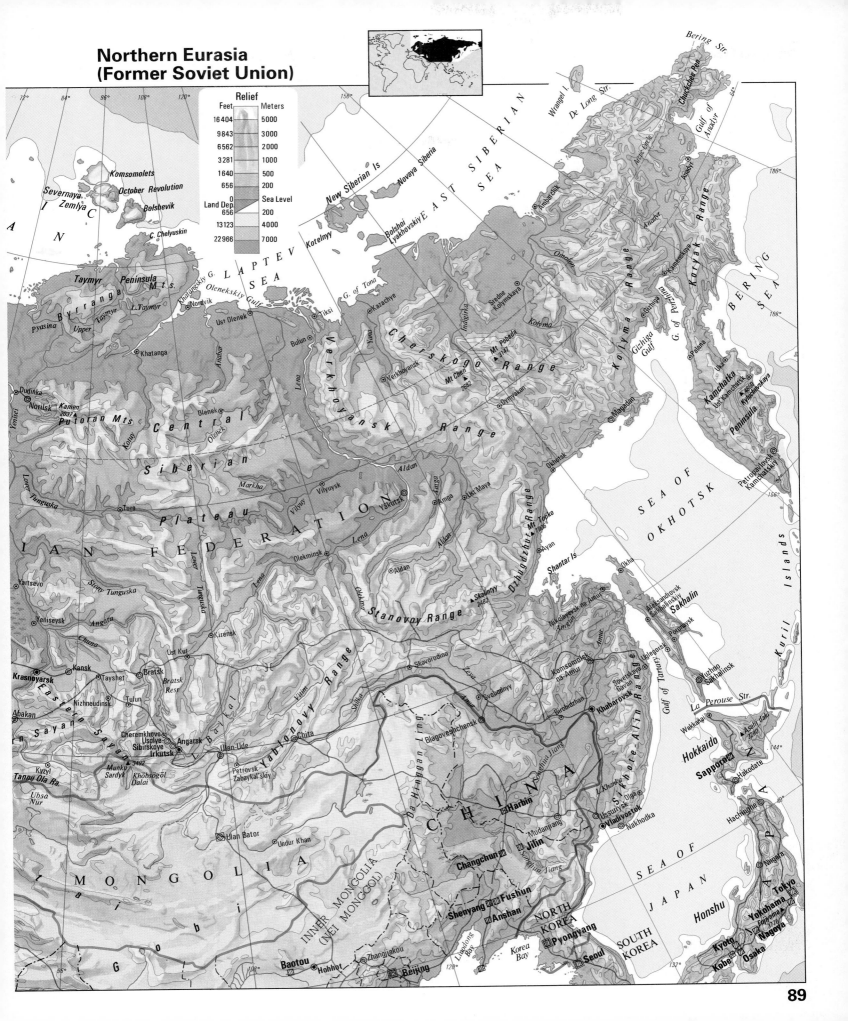

Northern Eurasia
(Former Soviet Union)

Relief

Feet	Meters
16 404	5000
9843	3000
6562	2000
3281	1000
1640	500
656	200
0	Sea Level
Land Dep.	
656	200
13 123	4000
22 966	7000

Bering Str.

Chukchi Pen.

De Long Str.

Wrangel I.

Gulf of Anadyr

Arctic Circle

Anadyr

Komsomolets

October Revolution

Bolshevik

Severnaya Zemlya

C. Chelyuskin

New Siberian Is

Novaya Siberia

EAST SIBERIAN SEA

Bolshoi Lyakhovskiy

Kotelnyy

Ambarchik

Omolon

Kolyma Range

Koryak Range

BERING SEA

Taymyr Peninsula

Byrranga Mts.

L. Taymyr

Upper Taymyr

Khatangskiy G.

Nordvik

Olenekskiy Gulf

LAPTEV SEA

G. of Tona

Tiksi

Bulun

Ust Olenek

Kazachye

Yana

Verkhoyansk

Indigirka

Sredne Kolymskaya

Kolyma

Cherskogo Range

Mt Pobeda 3147

Mt Chen 2682

Oymyakon

Gizhiga

G. of Pertzia

Palana

Uka

Kamchatka Peninsula

Ust Kamchatsk

Klyuchevskaya 4850

Pyasina

Dudinka

Norilsk

Kamen 2037

Putoran Mts

Yenisei

Konu

Khatanga

Anabar

Olenek

Olenek

Markha

Central

Siberian

Plateau

Verkhoyansk Range

Lena

Vilyuy

Vilyuysk

Yakutsk

Aldan

Amga

Ust'Maya

Amga

Okhotsk

Magadan

SEA OF OKHOTSK

Petropavlovsk Kamchatskiy

Yartsevo

Lower Tunguska

Tura

Stony Tunguska

Yeniseysk

Angara

Chuna

Markha

Olekminsk

Lena

Aldan

Aldan

Lower Tunguska

Dzhugdzhur Range

Mt Topko 1906

Ayan

Shantar Is

Okha

Sakhalin

Aleksandrovsk Sakhalinskiy

Poronaysk

Kuril Islands

Abakan

Kansk

Krasnoyarsk

Tayshet

Nizhneudinsk

Tulun

Eastern Sayan

Bratsk

Bratsk Resr

Ust Kut

Kirensk

Lena

Olekma

Skalinyy 2482

Stanovoy Range

Skovorodino

Zeya

Svobodnyy

Komsomolsk na-Amur

Amgun

Sovetskaya Gavan

Nikolayevsk na Amur

Amur

Uglegorsk

Gulf of Tartary

Yuzhno Sakhalinsk

La Perouse Str.

Wakkanai

Asahi dake 2290

Kyzyl

Tannu Ola Ra.

Munku Sardyk 3492

Cheremkhovo

Usolye Sibirskoye

Angarsk

Irkutsk

L. Baikal

Ulan-Ude

Petrovsk Zabaykal'skiy

Yablonovy Range

Vitim

Chita

Shilka

Shilka

Nercha

Blagoveshchensk

Zeya

Birobidzhan

Khabarovsk

Sikhote-Alin Range

Vyazemskiy

Pozharskoye

L. Khanka

Olga

Ussuriysk

Vladivostok

Nakhodka

Yurino Sakhalinsk

Hokkaido

Sapporo

Hakodate

Ubsa Nur

Altai

MONGOLIA

Gobi

Ulan Bator

Undur Khan

Da Hinggan Ling (Khingan)

CHINA

Harbin

Mudanjiang

Jilin

Changchun

Sunghua Jiang

Songhua Jiang

INNER MONGOLIA (NEI MONGGOL)

Shenyang

Fushun

Anshan

NORTH KOREA

Pyongyang

SEA OF JAPAN

JAPAN

Honshu

Hachinohe

Niigata

Fujiyama 3776

Tokyo

Yokohama

Nagoya

Kyoto

Kobe

Osaka

Baotou

Hohhot

Zhangjiakou

Liaodong Bay

Korea Bay

Beijing

Seoul

SOUTH KOREA

RUSSIAN FEDERATION

89

Regions (Asia)

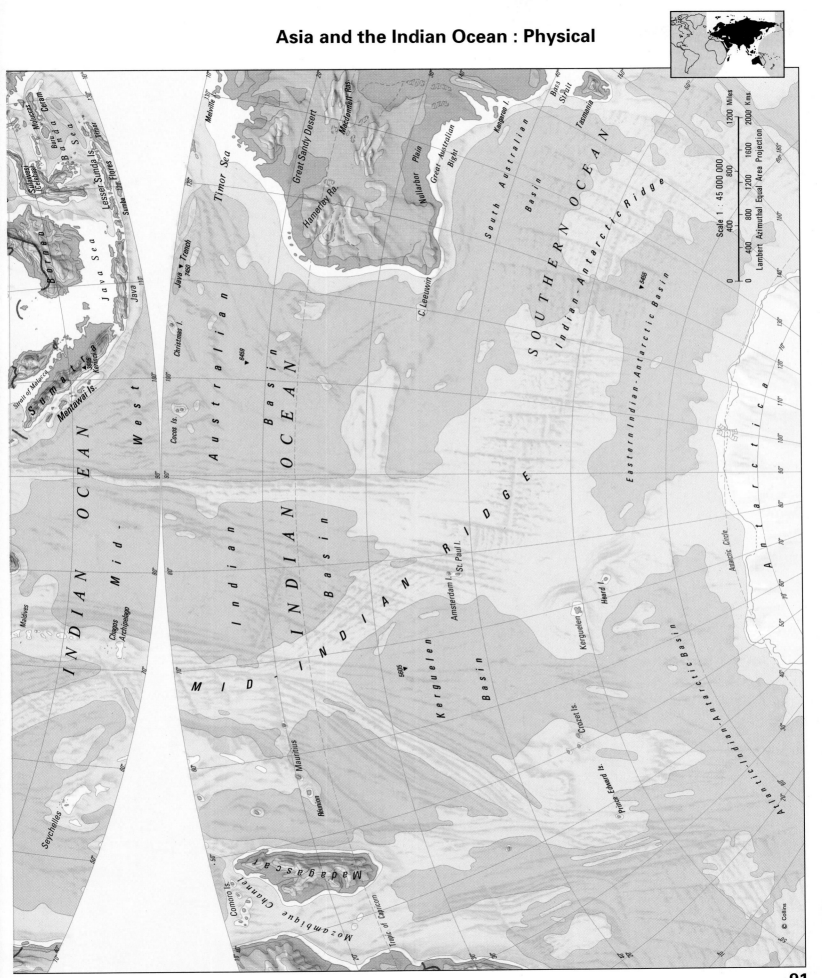

Moluccas

Ceram

Buru

Banda Sea

Sulawesi (Celebes)

Lesser Sunda Is.

Timor

Sumba

Sumbawa

Flores

Borneo

Java Sea

Java

Strait of Malacca

Sumatra

Mentawai Is.

Kerinci 3800

INDIAN OCEAN Mid - West

Maldives

Chagos Archipelago

Seychelles

Mauritius

Réunion

Comoro Is.

Madagascar

Mozambique Channel

Tropic of Capricorn

Melville I.

Timor Sea

Christmas I.

Java Trench 7450

Australian Basin

6459

Cocos Is.

Indian Basin

MID - INDIAN RIDGE

Amsterdam I.

St. Paul I.

5605

Kerguelen Basin

Crozet Is.

Prince Edward Is.

Great Sandy Desert

Macdonnell Ras.

Hamerley Ra.

Nullarbor Plain

Great Australian Bight

C. Leeuwin

Kangaroo I.

Bass Strait

Tasmania

South Australian Basin

SOUTHERN OCEAN

Indian - Antarctic Ridge

Eastern Indian - Antarctic Basin

5465

Heard I.

Kerguelen

Antarctic Circle

Antarctica

Atlantic - Indian - Antarctic Basin

Scale 1 : 45 000 000

0   400   800   1200 Miles

0   400   800   1200   1600   2000 Kms.

Lambert Azimuthal Equal Area Projection

© Collins

91

Regions (Asia)

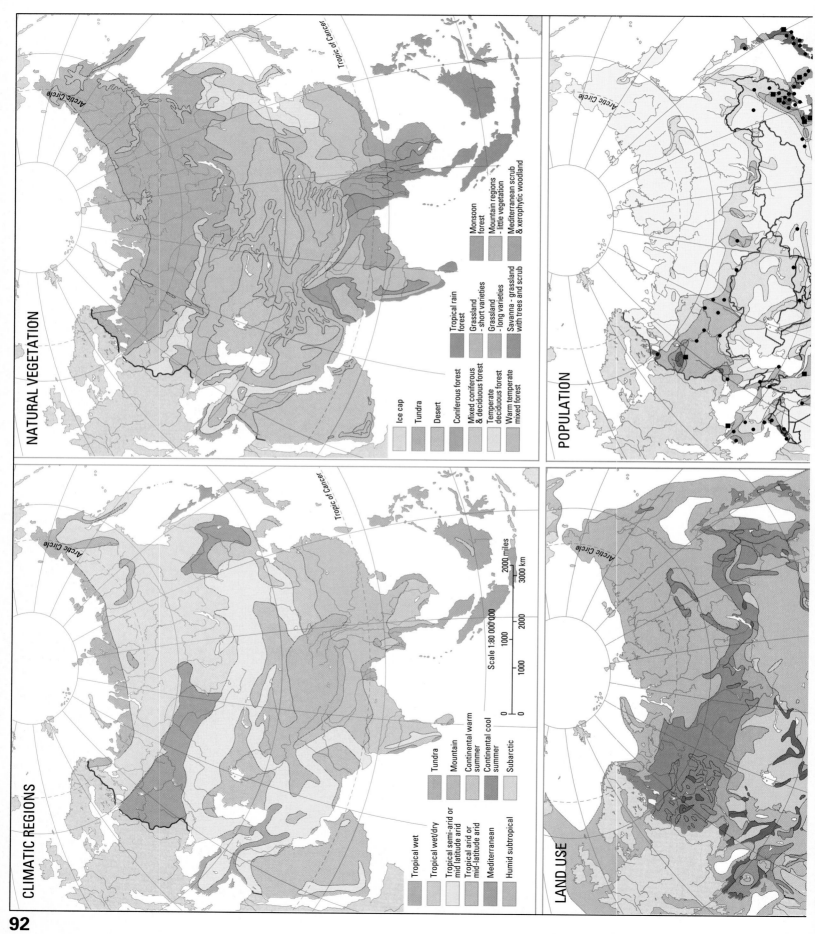

NATURAL VEGETATION

- Ice cap
- Tundra
- Desert
- Coniferous forest
- Mixed coniferous & deciduous forest
- Temperate deciduous forest
- Warm temperate mixed forest
- Tropical rain forest
- Grassland - short varieties
- Grassland - long varieties
- Savanna - grassland with trees and scrub
- Monsoon forest
- Mountain regions - little vegetation
- Mediterranean scrub & xerophytic woodland

CLIMATIC REGIONS

- Tropical wet
- Tropical wet/dry
- Tropical semi-arid or mid latitude arid
- Tropical arid or mid-latitude arid
- Mediterranean
- Humid subtropical
- Tundra
- Mountain
- Continental warm summer
- Continental cool summer
- Subarctic

Scale 1:80 000 000

0 1000 2000

0 1000 2000 3000 km

2000 miles

POPULATION

LAND USE

92

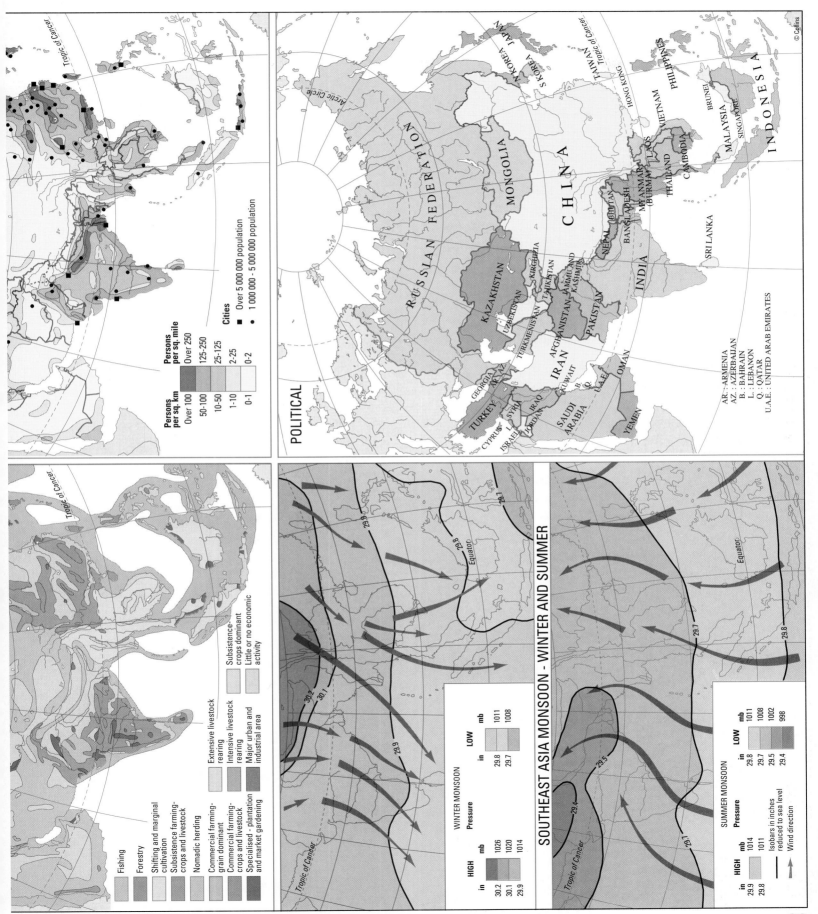

© Collins

Population

Persons per sq. km
- Over 100
- 50–100
- 10–50
- 1–10
- 0–1

Persons per sq. mile
- Over 250
- 125–250
- 25–125
- 2–25
- 0–2

Cities
- ■ Over 5 000 000 population
- ● 1 000 000 – 5 000 000 population

POLITICAL

AR. : ARMENIA
AZ. : AZERBAIJAN
B. : BAHRAIN
L. : LEBANON
Q. : QATAR
U.A.E. : UNITED ARAB EMIRATES

Land Use

- Fishing
- Forestry
- Shifting and marginal cultivation
- Subsistence farming – crops and livestock
- Nomadic herding
- Commercial farming – grain dominant
- Commercial farming – crops and livestock
- Specialised – plantation and market gardening
- Extensive livestock rearing
- Intensive livestock rearing
- Major urban and industrial area
- Subsistence – crops dominant
- Little or no economic activity

SOUTH EAST ASIA MONSOON – WINTER AND SUMMER

WINTER MONSOON

Pressure

HIGH		LOW	
in	mb	in	mb
30.2	1026	29.8	1011
30.1	1020	29.7	1008
29.9	1014		

SUMMER MONSOON

Pressure

HIGH		LOW	
in	mb	in	mb
29.9	1014	29.8	1011
29.8	1011	29.7	1008
		29.5	1002
		29.4	998

Isobars in inches reduced to sea level

Wind direction

Regions (Asia)

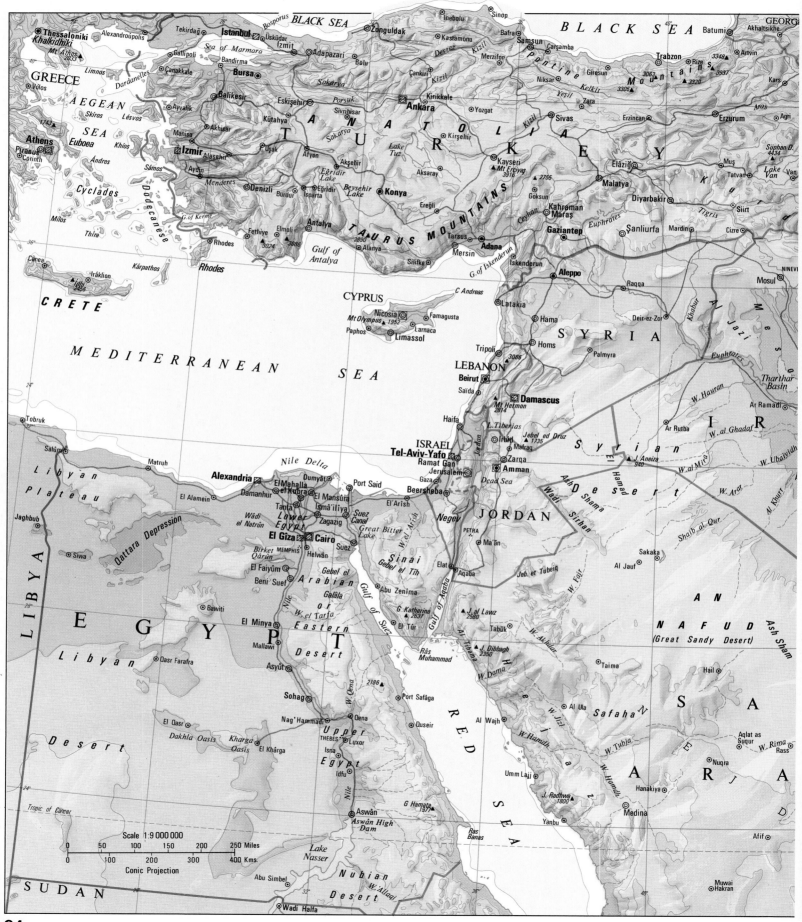

Regions (Asia)

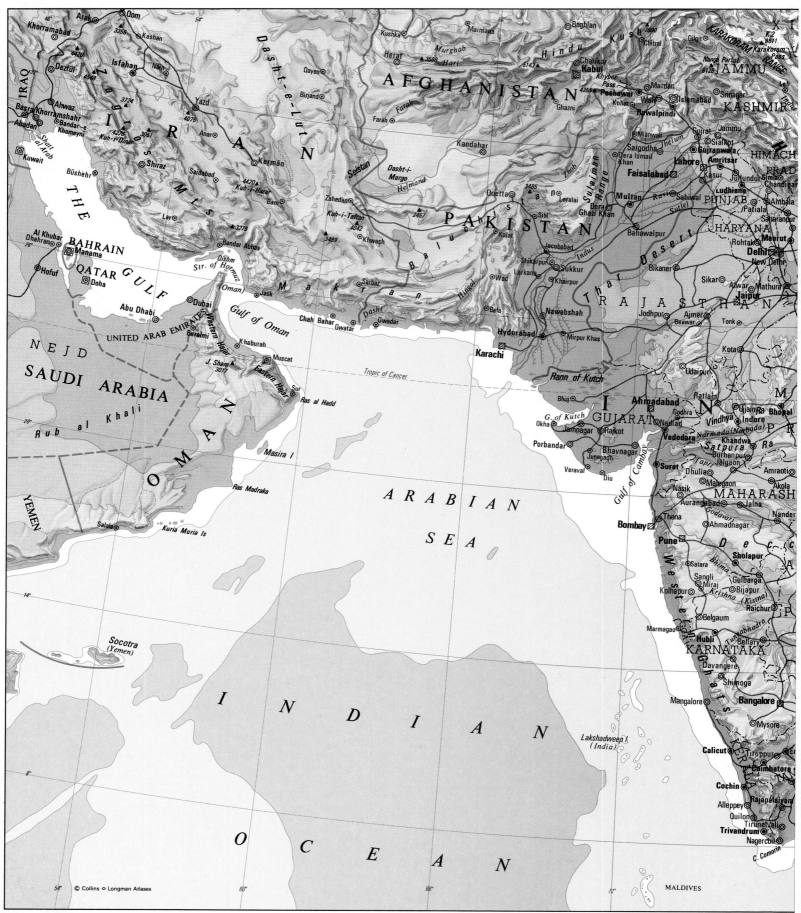

Khorramabad Arak ⊙ Qom
46°   3355
⊙ Kashan
⊙ Isfahan
4420▲
⊙ Dezful 4548▲
IRAQ
Ahwaz ⊙ 3724▲
Khorramshahr 4275▲ Kuh-i-Dinar
Abadan Bandar-e 3061▲
Khomeyni
⊙ Kuwait   Shatt
al Arab   ⊙ Shiraz
Büshehr

THE
BAHRAIN
Al Khubar
Dhahran 26°
⊙ Manama
⊙ Hofuf   QATAR GULF
Doha

NEJD
SAUDI ARABIA
Abu Dhabi
UNITED ARAB EMIRATES
Buraimi
20°   Western Hajar
Rub al Khali
J. Sham Eastern Hajar
3017

YEMEN O
M
A
N

Kashan   DASHT
Nain   Kushka ⊙   ⊙ Maimana
Yazd   Herat   Murghab
4075▲   3585▲ Hari
IRAN   Qayen ⊙   Forah
Anar ⊙   Birjand ⊙

Kermán ⊙   Seistan
4420▲   Dasht-i-
Kuh-i-Hazar   Margo Helmand
Bam ⊙   Zahedan ⊙
Lar ⊙   Kuh-i-Taftan
3279▲   2457▲
3489▲
Bandar Abbas ⊙ Khwash ⊙
Qishm 4042▲
Str. of Hormuz
(Oman)   Jask ⊙   Dasht
Chah Bahar Gwatar Gwadar

Khaburah
Muscat
Sur
Ras al Hadd

Masira I.

Ras Madraka

Salala ⊙   Kuria Muria Is

ARABIAN

SEA

Socotra
(Yemen)

I
N
D
I
A
N

O   C   E   A   N

54°   © Collins ◇ Longman Atlases   60°

AFGHANISTAN

Baghlan ⊙ 7690 ▲
Chatikar
Kabul ⊙ Khyber Mardan ⊙
5143▲ Pass Peshawar
Ghazni ⊙ 4755▲ Kohat
Rawalpindi

Kandahar ⊙

Quetta ⊙ s t a n 3485▲
Loralai Sulaiman Multan
Kalat ⊙ Dera Range
Ghazi Khan
Sibi

Jacobabad ⊙ Indus
Shikarpur ⊙
Sukkur
Larkana ⊙ Khairpur
Wad ⊙
Bela ⊙ Nawabshah ⊙

Hyderabad ⊙
Karachi Mirpur Khas ⊙

Tropic of Cancer

Rann of Kutch

Bhuj ⊙
G. of Kutch
Okha ⊙ Jamnagar ⊙ Rajkot ⊙
GUJARAT
Porbandar ⊙ Bhavnagar ⊙
Junagadh
Veraval ⊙ Diu Gulf of Cambay

Hindu Kush
Gilgit ⊙ KARAKORAM
Chitral ⊙ Nanga Parbat Karakoram
6126▲ Pass
JAMMU
Leh ⊙
Srinagar ⊙ Indus
Islamabad KASHMIR
Wah ⊙ Jammu ⊙
Gujrat ⊙ HIMACH
Sialkot ⊙ PRAD
Gujranwala Simla ⊙
Lahore Amritsar Chandigar
Faisalabad Kasur ⊙ Ludhiana
Jullundur Ambala ⊙
PUNJAB Patiala ⊙
Ravi Sahiwal ⊙ Saharanpur
Bahawalpur Sutlej HARYANA
Meerut ⊙
Bikaner ⊙ Rohtak ⊙ Delhi
Thar Desert New Delhi
Sikar ⊙ Alwar ⊙ Mathura
RAJASTHAN Jaipur
Jodhpur ⊙ Ajmer Tonk ⊙
Beawar
Kota ⊙
Udaipur ⊙
M
Ratlam ⊙
I Ahmadabad Ujjain ⊙ Ra Bhopal
Nadiad Godhra ⊙ N
Vindhya Indore
Vadodara Narmada (Narboda) P R
Khandwa ⊙ Satpura Ra
Burhanpur ⊙
Jalgaon ⊙ Tapti
Surat Dhulia ⊙ Amraoti ⊙
Mategaon ⊙ Akola ⊙
Nasik ⊙ MAHARASH
Aurangabad ⊙ Jalna ⊙
Thana Godavari
Bombay Ahmadnagar ⊙ Nander ⊙
D
Pune e c
Bhima c
Sholapur A
Satara ⊙ Krishna (Kistna)
Sangli N
Mirai Bijapur ⊙
Kolhapur ⊙ Gulbarga Raichur ⊙
Belgaum ⊙ Tungabhadra Bellary ⊙
Marmagao ⊙
Hubli
KARNATAKA
Davangere ⊙
Shimoga ⊙
Mangalore ⊙ Bangalore
Mysore ⊙

Lakshadweep I.
(India)

Calicut Tiruppur ⊙
K Coimbatore
Cochin
Alleppey Rajapalaiyam
Quilon Tirunelveli
Trivandrum
Nagercoil
C. Comorin

66°   72°   MALDIVES

96

South Asia

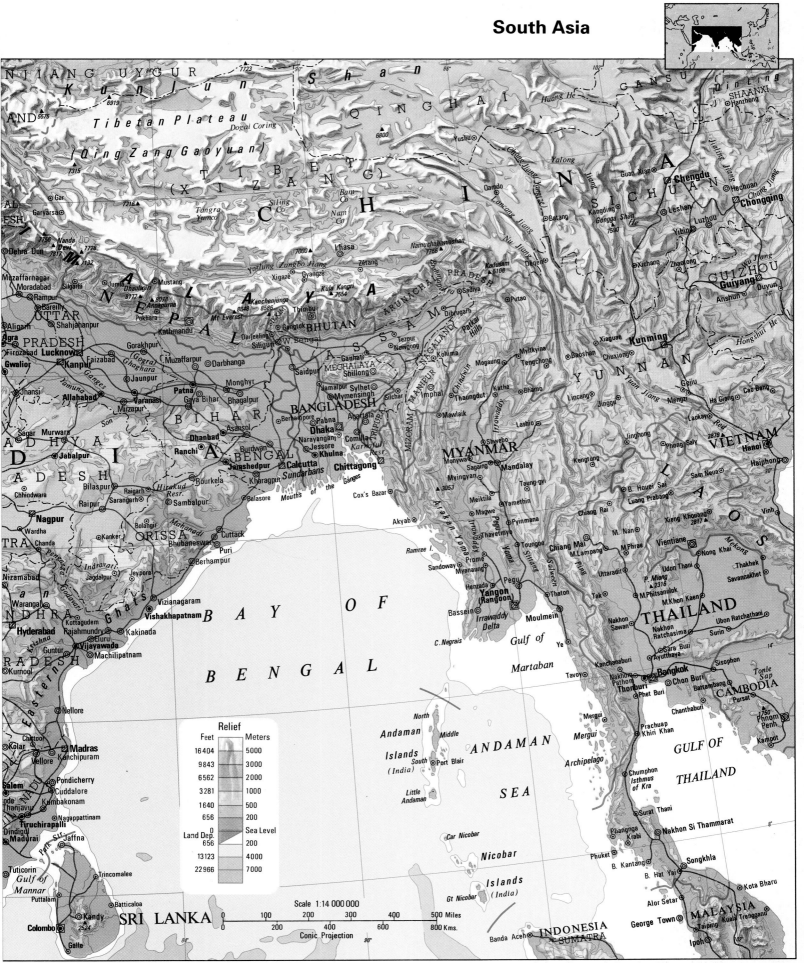

Regions (Asia)

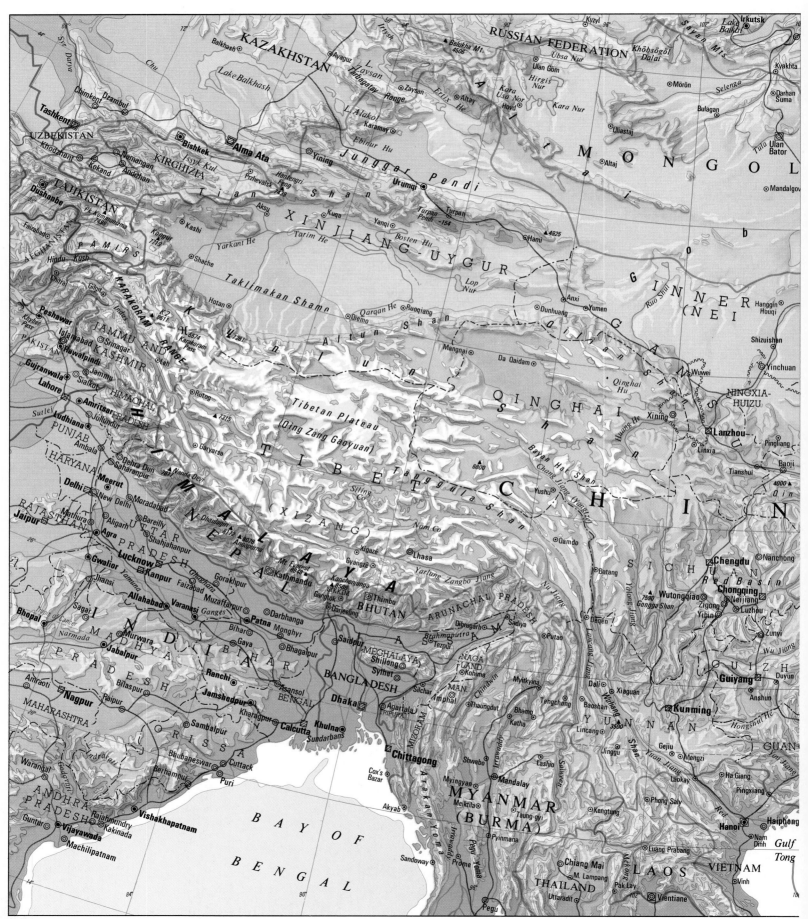

China and East Asia

Regions (Asia)

Japan and Korea

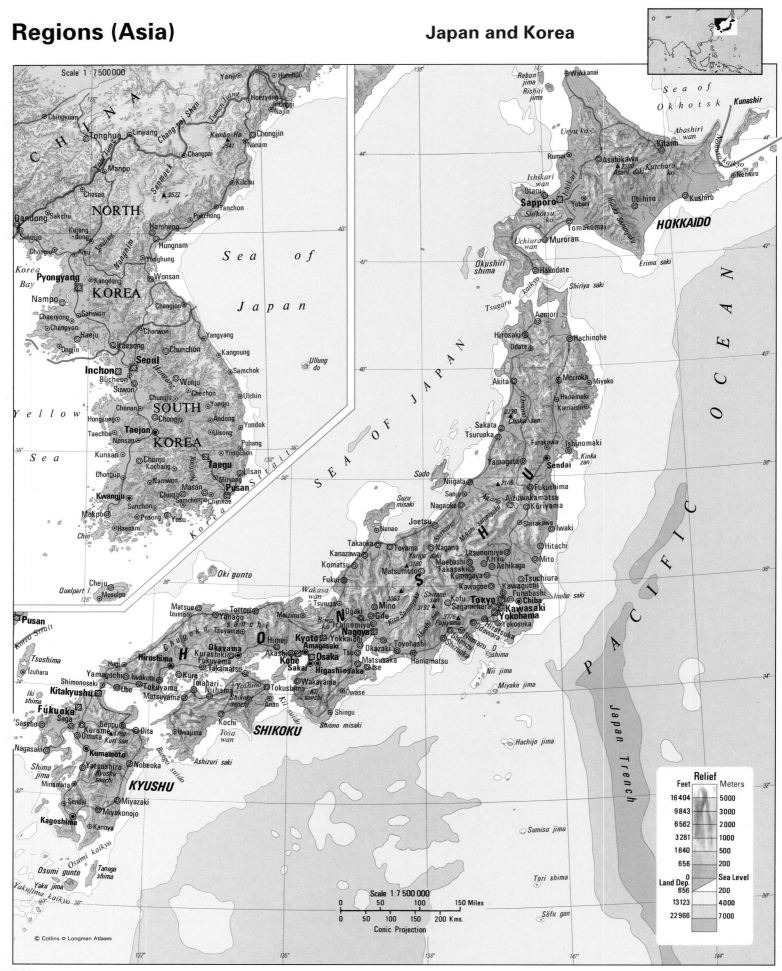

Scale 1 : 7 500 000

Scale 1:7 500 000

Conic Projection

© Collins ◇ Longman Atlases

Relief		
Feet		Meters
16 404		5000
9843		3000
6562		2000
3281		1000
1640		500
656		200
0	Sea Level	
Land Dep.		
656		200
13123		4000
22 966		7000

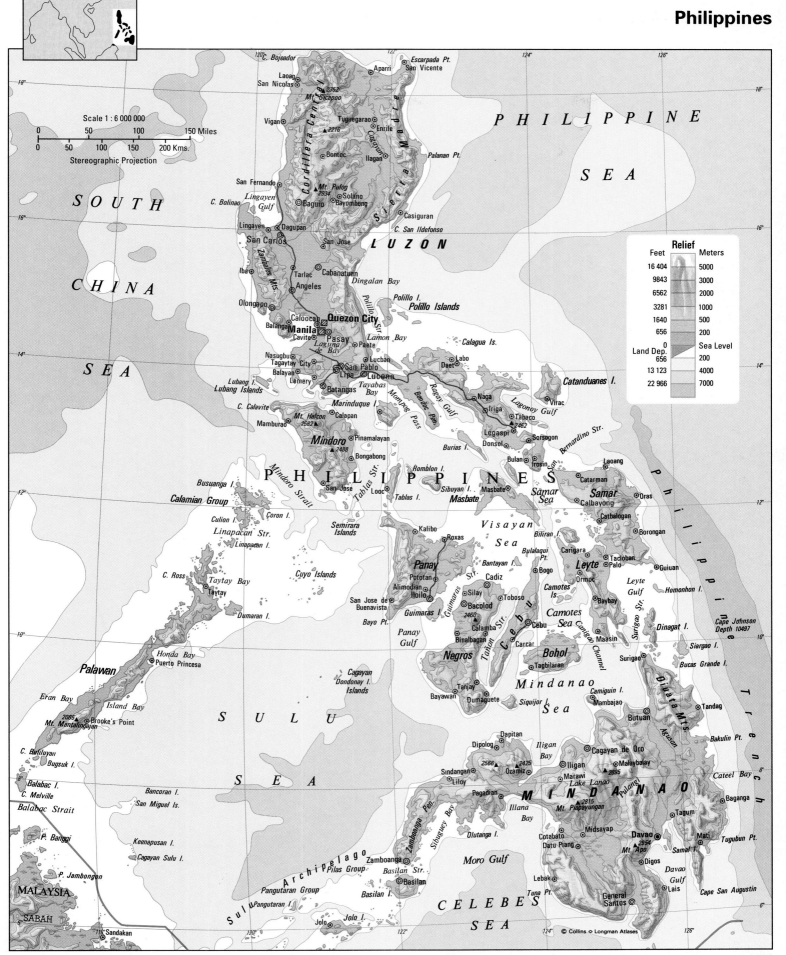

Relief

Feet	Meters
16 404	5000
9843	3000
6562	2000
3281	1000
1640	500
656	200
0	Sea Level
Land Dep.	
656	200
13 123	4000
22 966	7000

Scale 1 : 6 000 000

50   100   150 Miles

50   100   150   200 Kms.

Stereographic Projection

PHILIPPINE SEA

SOUTH CHINA SEA

LUZON

Cordillera Central
Sierra Madre

C. Bojeador
Laoag
San Nicolas
Mt. Sicapoo 2352
Vigan
2216
Tuguegarao
Enrile
Cagayan
Bontoc
Ilagan
San Fernando
Mt. Pulog 2934
Solano
Baguio
Bayombong
Lingayen Gulf
C. Bolinao
Lingayen
Dagupan
San Carlos
San Jose
Zambales Mts.
Iba
Tarlac
Cabanatuan
Angeles
Dingalan Bay
Olongapo
Polillo I.
Caloocan
Quezon City
Balanga
Manila
Pasay
Cavite
Paete
Nasugbu
Laguna de Bay
Tagaytay City
Lucban
Balayan
San Pablo
Lipa
Lucena
Lemery
Batangas
Tayabas Bay
Lubang I.
Lubang Islands
C. Calavite
Marinduque I.
Mt. Helcon 2582
Calapan
Mamburao
Mindoro
Pinamalayan
2488
Bongabong

Aparri
Escarpada Pt.
San Vicente

Palanan Pt.

Casiguran

C. San Ildefonso

Polillo Str.
Polillo Islands
Lamon Bay
Calagua Is.
Labo
Daet
Naga
Iriga
Lagonoy Gulf
Virac
Catanduanes I.
Tabaco 2462
Legaspi
Sorsogon
Donsol
San Bernardino Str.
Bulan
Irosin

Ragay Gulf
Mompog Pass
Burias I.

PHILIPPINES

Mindoro Strait
Mindoro Str.
Busuanga I.
Calamian Group
Culion I.
Coron I.
Linapacan Str.
Linapacan I.
Semirara Islands
San Jose
Tablas Str.
Tablas I.
Looc
Tablas
Romblon I.
Sibuyan I.
Masbate
Masbate
Samar Sea
Laoang
Catarman
Samar
Calbayong
Oras
Catbalogan
Borongan

Cuyo Islands
C. Ross
Taytay Bay
Taytay
Dumaran I.
San Jose de Buenavista
Kalibo
Roxas
Panay
Pototan
Alimodian
Iloilo
Guimaras I.
Bayo Pt.
Panay Gulf
Visayan Sea
Biliran I.
Bulalaqui Pt.
Bantayan I.
Cadiz
Bogo
Silay
Toboso
Bacolod
2460
Calamba
Binalbagan
Guimaras Str.
Tañon Str.
Cebu
Carcar
Camotes Is.
Leyte
Carigara
Tacloban
Palo
Ormoc
Camotes Sea
Baybay
Leyte Gulf
Homonhon I.
Guiuan

Palawan
Honda Bay
Puerto Princesa
Eran Bay
Island Bay
Mt. Mantalingajan 2085
Brooke's Point
C. Buliluyan
Bugsuk I.
Balabac I.
C. Melville
Balabac Strait
P. Banggi
Keenapusan I.
Cagayan Sulu I.
MALAYSIA
SABAH
Sandakan

Cagayan Dondonay I. Islands

SULU SEA

Negros
Tanjay
Bayawan
Dumaguete
Siquijor I.
Mindanao Sea
Bohol
Tagbilaran
Camiguin I.
Mambajao
Dapitan
Dipolog
Iligan Bay
Cagayan de Oro
Sindangan
2566
Ozamiz
2425
Iligan
Malaybalay
2895
Liloy
Marawi
Lake Lanao
Pagadian
Mt. Piapayungan
Pulangi
MINDANAO
2815
Illana Bay
Midsayap
Cotabato
Zamboanga Pen.
Datu Piang
Sibuguey Bay
Olutanga I.
Lebak
Moro Gulf
Agusan
Dinagat I.
Surigao
Maasin
Canigao Channel
Siargao I.
Bucas Grande I.
Butuan
Diuata Mts.
Bakulin Pt.
Tandag
Cateel Bay
Baganga
Tagum
Davao
2954
Mt. Apo
Digos
Samal I.
Davao Gulf
Lais
Cape San Augustin
Mati
Tugubun Pt.
General Santos
Tuna Pt.

SULU ARCHIPELAGO

Zamboanga
Pilas Group
Pangutaran Group
Basilan
Basilan I.
Basilan Str.
Pangutaran
Jolo
Jolo I.
P. Jambongan
San Miguel Is.
Bancoran I.
Pangutaran Group

CELEBES SEA

Cape Johnson Depth 10497

Philippine Trench

© Collins ○ Longman Atlases

101

Regions (Asia)

MYANMAR (BURMA)

THAILAND

LAOS

VIETNAM

CAMBODIA

CHINA

SOUTH CHINA SEA

Gulf of Tongking

Hainan

Gulf of Thailand

Gulf of Martaban

ANDAMAN SEA

INDIAN OCEAN

MALAYSIA

SUMATRA

BORNEO

KALIMANTAN

SARAWAK

BRUNEI

SABAH

JAVA SEA

JAVA

INDONESIA

Palawan

Gejiu Mengzi Mei Xian Chao'an
Nanning Wuzhou Xi Jiang Guangzhou Shantou
Laokay Ha Giang Pingxiang Foshan Kowloon Macau (Port.) HONG KONG Gaoxiong
Phong Saly Bac Can Lang Son Mon Cai Maoming Zhanjiang
Sam Neua Nam Dinh Beihai Haikou
B. Houei Sai Hanoi Haiphong
Ramree I Luang Prabang Thanh Hoa Ninh Binh
Sandoway Pyinmana Chiang Rai Xieng Khouang Ninh Binh Dongfang Yacheng Ya Xian
Prome Chiang Mai Vinh
Myanaung M. Lampang M. Nan Vientiane Ha Tinh
Henzada M. Phrae Nong Khai Thakhek Dong Hoi
Insein Pegu Uttaradit Udon Thani M. Nakhon Phanom Quang Tri
Thaton Tak M. Phitsanulok Savannakhet Hué
Yangon Moulmein M. Khon Kaen Mekong Da Nang
Bassein Gulf of Martaban M. Nakhon Sawan Ayutthaya Nakhon Ratchasima Ubon Ratchathani 2598 Quang Ngai
Ye Nakhon Pathom Sara Buri Surin Pakse Attopeu VIETNAM Kontum
Andaman Thonburi Bangkok Sisophon Samrong Qui Nhon
Tavoy Rat Buri Chon Buri Angkor Battambang
Port Blair Mergui Phet Buri Battambang Tonle Sap CAMBODIA Kratie B. Me Thuot Nha Trang
Islands (India) Tenasserim Chanthaburi Pursat Kompong Chhnang Da Lat Cam Ranh
Little Andaman Mergui Range Kampot Phnom Penh Kompong Cham Loc Ninh Phan Rang
Ten Degree Channel Chumphon Gia Dinh Ho Chi Minh City Cholon
Car Nicobar Long Xuyen My Tho Vung Tau
Nicobar Phu Quoc Rach Gia Mekong Delta
Little Nicobar Phangnga Ko Phangan Can Tho Vinh Loi
Islands (India) Phuket Ko Samui Pte. de Ca Mau Con Son Is
Great Nicobar Nakhon Si Thammarat
Trang Thale Luang
B. Hat Yai Songkhla
Langkawi Kota Bharu
Banda Aceh Alor Setar
Lhokseumawe George Town Butterworth
Meulaboh Langsa Ipoh Kuala Trengganu
Leuser 3381 Binjai Kuala Lipis
Medan Tebingtinggi Teluk Intan Kuantan
Pematangsiantar Kelang Kuala Lumpur Seremban
Sibolga Tanjungbalai Melaka Mersing P. Tioman Anambas Is
Padangsidempuan Rantauparapat Muar Keluang
Nias Toba Batu Pahat Johor Bahru Singapore Bintan Riau Is
Natal Pini Pakanbaru SINGAPORE
Batu Is Bukittinggi Kampar
Siberut Padangpandjang
Mentawai Padang Inderagiri Rengat Lingga
Sipora Singkep
Islands Pagai Utara G. Kerinci 3805 Sungaipenuh Hari Jambi
Pagai Selatan Musi Muntok Bangka Tanjungpandan
Bengkulu Palembang Perabumulih Toboali Belitung
Lahat Baturaja
Kotabumi
Enggano Telukbetung Tanjungkarang
Serang Jakarta Bawean JAVA SEA
Bogor Bandung Cirebon Tegal Pekalongan Kudus
Sukabumi Garut Slamet Semarang Madura
Tasikmalaya Magelang Surakarta Madiun Surabaya
Cilacap Yogyakarta Kediri Malang
Christmas I (Austl.)

South China Sea: Paracel Is, Thitu Is, Nanshan Is, Spratly I, Balabac Str., Kudat, Kota Kinabalu, Kinabalu 4101, Sandakan, Lahad Datu, Bandar Seri Begawan, Miri, Seria, Limbang, Marudi, Murud 2438, Tawau, Tarakan, Mukah, Bintulu, Pegunungan Iran, SARAWAK, Sibu, Rajang, Hose Mts, Kuching, Simanggang, Kayan, Tanjungredeb, G. Niut 1701, Serian, G. Menyapa 2000, BORNEO, Singkawang, Tanjung Datu, Kapuas, Pontianak, Sintang, Raja 2278, Schwaner Mts, Samarinda, Sukadana, Mendawai, Balikpapan, Ketapang, Sukaraja, Palangkaraya, Sampit, Amuntai, Kandangan, Donggala, Tanjung Puting, Banjarmasin, Tanjung Selatan, Makassar Strait, Laut, Ujung Pandang

Calamian Group, Puerto Princesa, Brookes Point 2084, Taytay, SULU SEA, Mindoro, Cali

Mamuju, Makale 3455, Majene, Parepare, Sengkang, Watampone, SULAWESI, CELEBES

Kangean Is, Bali, Singaraja, 3726, Lesser Sunda, FLORES, Denpasar, Mataram, Lombok, Raba, Sumbawa, Sumba

Scale 1:15 000 000

| 0 | 100 | 200 | 300 | 400 | 500 Miles |

| 0 | 200 | 400 | 600 | 800 Kms |

Bonne Projection

© Collins ◇ Longman Atlases

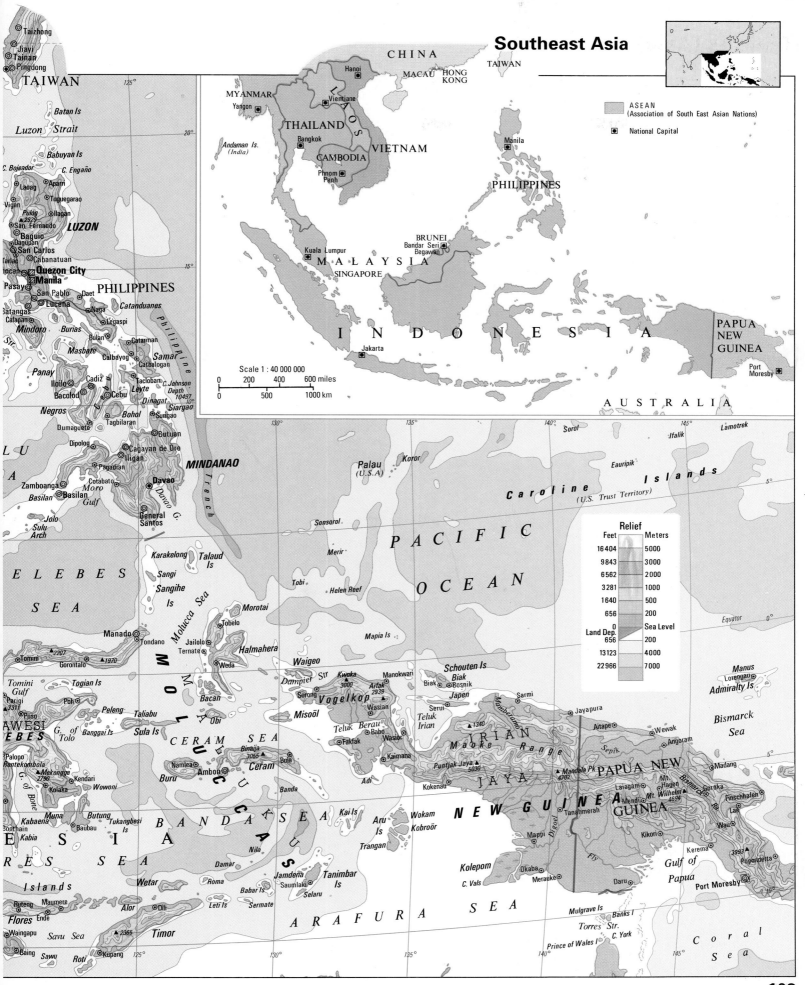

Southeast Asia

TAIWAN

Taizhong
Jiayi
Tainan
Pingdong

Luzon Strait

Batan Is.

Babuyan Is.

C. Bojeador
C. Engaño
Aparri
Laoag
Tuguegarao
Vigan
Ilagan
Pulag
2929
San Fernando
Baguio
Dagupan
San Carlos
Tarlac
Cabanatuan
Quezon City
Manila
Pasay
San Pablo
Daet
Lucena
Naga
Catanduanes
Batangas
Legaspi
Calapan
Mindoro
Burias
Bulan
Catarman
Masbate
Calbayog
Samar
Catbalogan
Panay
Cadiz
Tacloban
Iloilo
Cebu
Leyte
Bacolod
Dinagat
Negros
Bohol
Siargao
Tagbilaran
Surigao
Dumaguete
Butuan
Dipolog
Cagayan de Oro
Iligan
Pagadian
Zamboanga
Cotabato
Basilan
Moro
Davao
Basilan
Gulf
Jolo
Sulu Arch.
General Santos

PHILIPPINES

Luzon

C. Johnson
Depth 10497

MINDANAO

Davao G.

Davao Trench

ASEAN (Association of South East Asian Nations)

National Capital

CHINA

MACAU HONG KONG

TAIWAN

MYANMAR
Yangon

Hanoi

LAOS
Vientiane

THAILAND
Bangkok

Andaman Is. (India)

CAMBODIA
Phnom Penh

VIETNAM

Manila

PHILIPPINES

MALAYSIA
Kuala Lumpur
SINGAPORE

BRUNEI
Bandar Seri Begawan

INDONESIA

Jakarta

PAPUA NEW GUINEA

Port Moresby

Scale 1 : 40 000 000

0   200   400   600 miles

0   500   1000 km

AUSTRALIA

Sorol

Ifalik

Lamotrek

Palau (U.S.A)
Koror

Eauripik

Caroline Islands
(U.S. Trust Territory)

Sonsorol

Merir

PACIFIC

Tobi

OCEAN

Helen Reef

Equator

Karakelong
Talaud Is.

Sangi

Sangihe Is.

Morotai

Mapia Is.

CELEBES SEA

Tobelo

Manado
Tondano

Tomini
2207
Gorontalo
1970

Jailolo
Ternate

Halmahera

Weda

Waigeo

Dampier Str.
Kwoka
3000
Sorong

Manokwari

Biak

Schouten Is.
Biak
Bosnik

Sarmi

Japen

Serui

Manus
Lorengau
Admiralty Is.

MOLUCCA SEA

Arfak
2939
Wasian

Vogelkop

Teluk Irian

Jayapura

Bismarck Sea

Relief

Feet	Meters
16 404	5000
9843	3000
6562	2000
3281	1000
1640	500
656	200
Land Dep.	Sea Level
656	200
13 123	4000
22 966	7000

Tomini Gulf
Parigi
Poh
3311
Poso

Togian Is.

Peleng

Taliabu

Sula Is.

Obi

Misoöl

Teluk Berau
Babo
Fakfak

Wasior

IRIAN

Maoke Range

1340

Aitape

Wewak

Angoram

SULAWESI
CELEBES

G. of Tolo

Banggai Is.

CERAM SEA

Binaija
3065

Bula

Adi

Kaimana

JAYA

Puntjak Jaya
5030

Mandela Pk.
4702

Sepik

PAPUA NEW

Madang

Palopo
Rantekombola
Mekongga
2790
Kolaka

Kendari

Wowoni

Namlea
Ambon

Buru

Ceram

Banda

Kokenau

Laiagam
Mendi
Tanahmerah

Mt. Hagen

Mt. Wilhelm
4694

GUINEA

Goroka

Finschhafen

Lae

Wau

Muna
Butung
Baubau

Tukangbesi Is.

Kai Is.

Wokam
Kobroör

Aru Is.

Trangan

NEW GUINEA

Mappi

Digoel

Fly

Kikori

Kerema

3993
Popondetta

Bonthain
Kabia
Kabaena

BANDA SEA

Nila

Damar

Babar Is.

Jamdena
Saumlaki
Selaru

Tanimbar Is.

Kolepom
C. Vals

Okaba
Merauke

Daru

Gulf of Papua

Port Moresby

INDONESIA

FLORES SEA

Ruteng

Maumere

Ende

Flores

Waingapu

Savu Sea

Baing

Sawu

Wetar

Roma

Alor

Leti Is.

Sermate

Dili

Timor

2365

Roti

Kupang

ARAFURA SEA

Mulgrave Is.

Torres Str.
Prince of Wales I.

Banks I
C. York

CORAL Sea

C. Finisterre
Pyrenees
Douro
Ebro
Corsica
Apennines
Adriatic Sea
Danube
▲2548 Negoiu
Black Sea
Caucasus Mts.
Caspian Sea
Tagus
Balearic Is.
Sardinia
Mt. Olympus 2911▲
Anatolia
Mt. Ararat 5165▲
Pontine Mts.
Elburz Mts.
C. St. Vincent
Sierra Nevada
Sicily
Crete
Taurus Mts.
Cyprus
Euphrates
Mesopotamia
Zagros Mts.
Dasht-e-Kavir
Madeira
Str. of Gibraltar
Tell Atlas
High Atlas
Atlas Mts.
Saharan Atlas

M e d i t e r r a n e a n   S e a
Gulf of Sirte
Tripolitania
Libyan Desert
Qattara Depression –133
Suez Canal
Sinai
Hejaz Asir
Red Sea
An Nafud
The Gulf
Tropic of Cancer

Canary Is.
Tenerife
Toubkal 4165▲

El Djouf
S A H A R A
Ahaggar Mountains
Mt. Tahat 2918▲
Djado Plateau
Tibesti Mountains
Emi Koussi 3415▲
Nubian Desert
Rub al Khali

Aïr or Azbine
Mt. Gréboun ▲1800
Bodélé Depression
Gulf of Aden

Sénégal
Niger
L. Chad
Darfur
J. Gimbala 3071
Blue Nile
Gezira
Ras Dashan 4620▲
Danakil

Gambia
Niger
Bani
White Volta
Black Volta
Chari
Logone
Bahr Aouk
Kotto
White Nile
Bahr el Arab
Bahr el Jebel
Akobo
Sobat
Ethiopian Highlands
Birhan 4154▲

Futa Jalon
Mt. Nimba 1768▲
L. Volta
Jos Plateau
Benue
Adamawa Highlands
Bomu
Uele
Sudd
L. Turkana
Shebelle
Juba

C. Palmas
Bight of Benin
Niger Delta
Mt. Cameroon 4070▲
Bioko
Sangha
Ubangi
Uele
Aruwimi
L. Albert
Mt. Stanley 5119▲
Mt. Elgon 4321▲
Mt. Kenya 5200▲

Gulf of Guinea
São Tomé
Zaïre Basin
Zaïre
Lake Victoria
Mt. Kilimanjaro 5895▲
Equator

ATLANTIC OCEAN
Kasai
Lukenie
Lualaba
Mitumba Mts.
Great Rift Valley
Masai Steppe
Pemba I.
Zanzibar I.
INDIAN OCEAN

Kwilu
Lubilash
Lake Tanganyika
Rufiji
Aldabra Is.

Serra Môco 2610
Bié Plateau
Kasai
Lomami
L. Mweru
Comoro Is.
C. d'Ambre

Cuanza
Chango
Luangwa
L. Malawi
Ruvuma
Madagascar

Cunene
Cuando
Zambezi
Muchinga Mts.
Ankaratra Mts.

Cubango
L. Kariba
Zambezi
Mozambique Channel

Etosha Pan
Okavango Basin
Victoria Falls
Matabele Upland
Save

Namib Desert
Kalahari Desert
Limpopo
Tropic of Capricorn

Great Fish
Vaal
High Veld
Thabana Ntlenyana 3482
Drakensberg

Orange
Orange
Great Karoo
C. of Good Hope
C. Agulhas

Inset political map

MOROCCO
TUNISIA
WESTERN SAHARA
ALGERIA
LIBYA
EGYPT
MAURITANIA
MALI
NIGER
CHAD
SUDAN
ERITREA
DJIBOUTI
SENEGAL
G.B.
GUINEA
BISSAU
GUINEA
BURKINA FASO
BENIN
NIGERIA
CAMEROON
CENTRAL AFRICAN REP.
ETHIOPIA
SIERRA LEONE
CÔTE D'IVOIRE
GHANA
TOGO
LIBERIA
EQUATORIAL GUINEA
GABON
CONGO
ZAÏRE
UGANDA
KENYA
SOMALIA
B.
R.
TANZANIA
ANGOLA
ZAMBIA
MALAWI
MOZAMBIQUE
ZIMBABWE
MADAGASCAR
NAMIBIA
BOTSWANA
SWAZILAND
SOUTH AFRICA
LESOTHO

B. : BURUNDI
G. : GAMBIA
G.B. : GUINEA BISSAU
M. : MALAWI
R. : RWANDA

Climate : Natural Vegetation : Land Use : Population

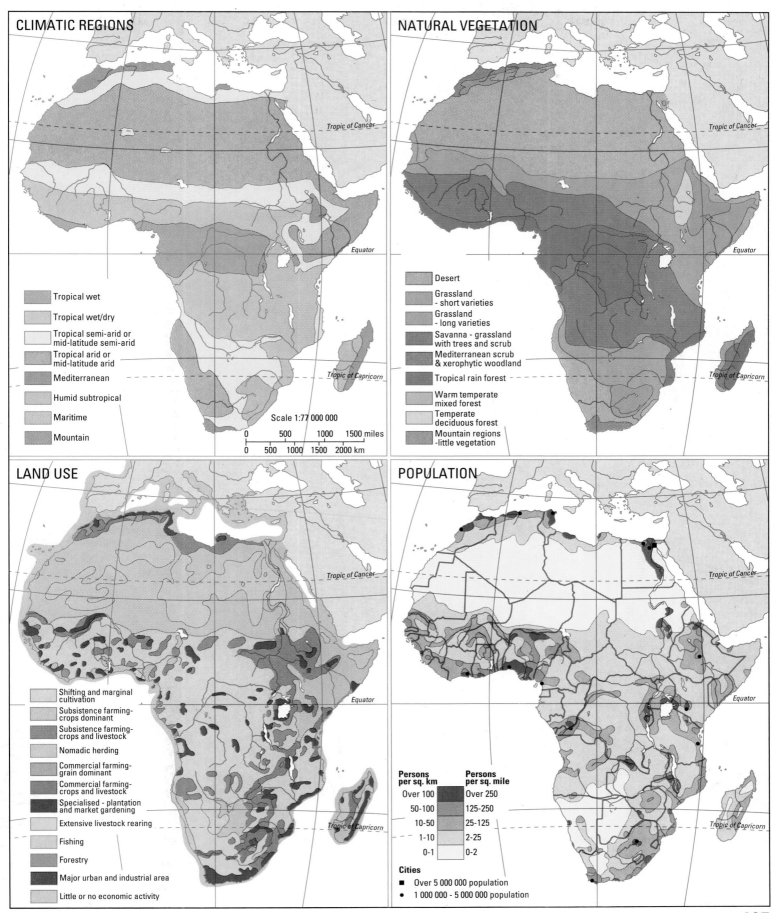

CLIMATIC REGIONS

- Tropical wet
- Tropical wet/dry
- Tropical semi-arid or mid-latitude semi-arid
- Tropical arid or mid-latitude arid
- Mediterranean
- Humid subtropical
- Maritime
- Mountain

Scale 1:77 000 000

0   500   1000   1500 miles
0 500 1000 1500 2000 km

NATURAL VEGETATION

- Desert
- Grassland - short varieties
- Grassland - long varieties
- Savanna - grassland with trees and scrub
- Mediterranean scrub & xerophytic woodland
- Tropical rain forest
- Warm temperate mixed forest
- Temperate deciduous forest
- Mountain regions - little vegetation

LAND USE

- Shifting and marginal cultivation
- Subsistence farming- crops dominant
- Subsistence farming- crops and livestock
- Nomadic herding
- Commercial farming- grain dominant
- Commercial farming- crops and livestock
- Specialised - plantation and market gardening
- Extensive livestock rearing
- Fishing
- Forestry
- Major urban and industrial area
- Little or no economic activity

POPULATION

Persons per sq. km	Persons per sq. mile
Over 100	Over 250
50-100	125-250
10-50	25-125
1-10	2-25
0-1	0-2

Cities
- ■ Over 5 000 000 population
- • 1 000 000 - 5 000 000 population

105

Regions (Africa)

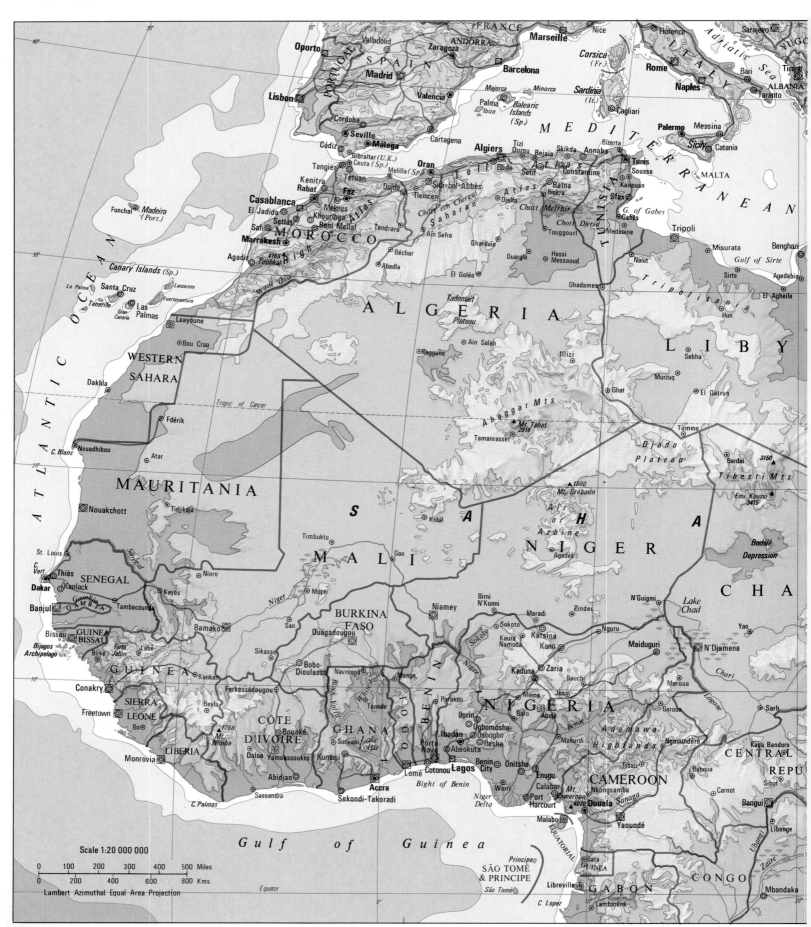

Scale 1:20 000 000

| 0 | 100 | 200 | 300 | 400 | 500 Miles |

| 0 | 200 | 400 | 600 | 800 Kms. |

Lambert Azimuthal Equal Area Projection

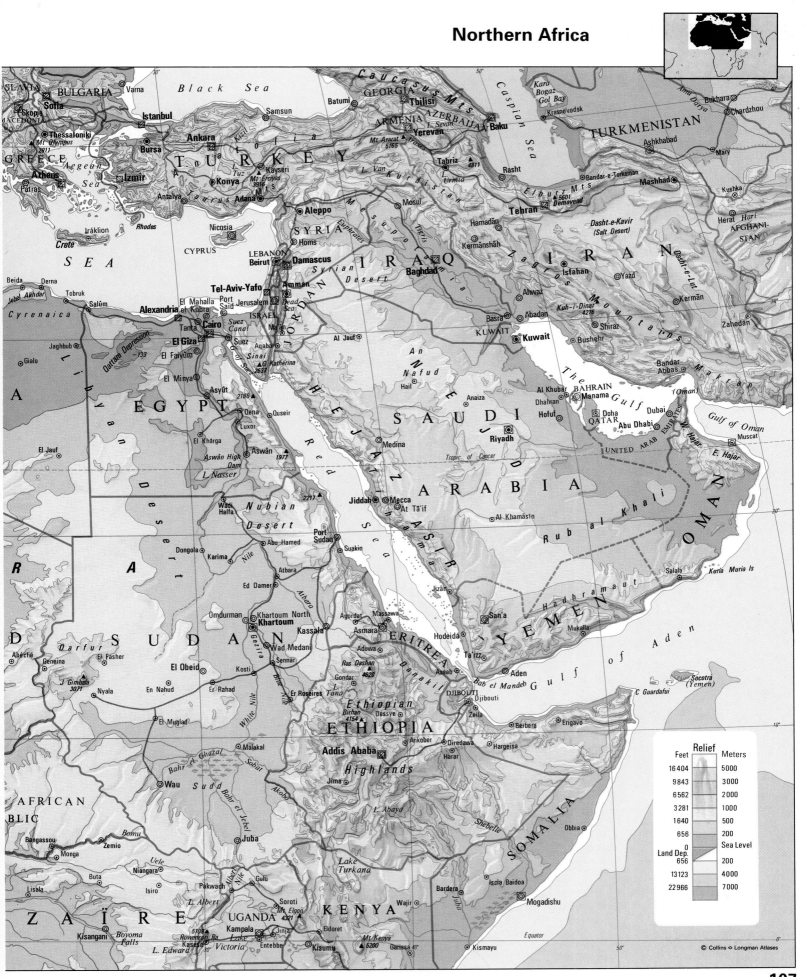

Regions (Africa)

Central and Southern Africa

NIGERIA
CHAD
Makurdi
Adamawa Highlands
Tibati
Ngaoundéré
Kaga Bandoro
Wau
Sudd
Jimma
Ethiopian Highlands
CAMEROON
Calabar
Mt. Cameroon 4070
Nkongsamba
Douala
Malabo
Bata
Yaoundé
Sanaga
CENTRAL AFRICAN REPUBLIC
Baboua
Carnot
Sibut
Bangassou
Bangui
Monga
Zemio
Bomu
Uele
Niangara
SUDAN
Bahr el Jebel
Akobo
Juba
L. Abaya
ETHIOPIA
SOMALIA
Wajir
Bardera
EQUATORIAL GUINEA
Libenge
Lisala
Buta
Isiro
Albert Nile
Gulu
Pakwach
L. Albert
Soroti
Mt. Elgon 4321
Eldoret
KENYA
Libreville
GABON
C. Lopez
Lambaréné
Ogooué
CONGO
Mbandaka
Equator
Boyoma Falls
Kisangani
ZAÏRE
Ruwenzori Range 5109
Kampala
Jinja
Kasese
Entebbe
L. Edward
Mbarara
UGANDA
Kisumu
Nakuru
Mt. Kenya 5200
Garissa
Tana
Kismayu
Mai Ndombe
Bandundu
Mt. Karisimbi 4507
RWANDA
Kigali
L. Kivu
Bukavu
Kindu
Lualaba
BURUNDI
Bujumbura
Lake Victoria
Mwanza
Nairobi
L. Natron
Kilimanjaro 5895
Arusha
Moshi
Mombasa
Brazzaville
Pointe Noire
ANGOLA
Boma
Cabinda
Matadi
Kinshasa
Kwango
Kasai
Ilebo
Kikwit
Kananga
Mbuji Mayi
Kabalo
Kalemie
Kigoma
Tabora
TANZANIA
Lake Tanganyika
Dodoma
Morogoro
Pemba I.
Zanzibar I.
Zanzibar
Tanga
Luanda
Malange
Cuango
Lulua
Kasai
Mwene Ditu
Kamina
Luvua
Luapula
L. Mweru
Iringa
Dar es Salaam
Mafia I.
2959
ANGOLA
Lobito
Benguela
Huambo
Kolwezi
Tenke
Likasi
Lubumbashi
L. Bangweulu
MALAWI
Ruvuma
Mtwara
COMOROS
Pemba
Cuanza
Menongue
Chingola
Kitwe
Ndola
ZAMBIA
Kabwe
Lilongwe
Lichinga
Nacala
Moçambique
Namibe
Lubango
Cubango
Cuito
Zambezi
Cuando
Kafue
Lusaka
Cahora Bassa Dam
Salima
Zomba
Blantyre
Shire
Nampula
MOZAMBIQUE
Mozambique Channel
Cunene
Okavango
Maramba (Livingstone)
Victoria Falls
L. Kariba
Harare
Quelimane
Etosha Pan
Tsumeb
Grootfontein
Okavango Basin
ZIMBABWE
Hwange
Kwekwe
Gweru
Mutare
Save
Beira
Makgadikgadi Salt Pan
Francistown
Bulawayo
Namib Desert
NAMIBIA
Gobabis
Walvis Bay (R.S.A.)
Windhoek
BOTSWANA
Kalahari Desert
Serowe
Selebi Pikwe
Beitbridge
Limpopo
Inhambane
Tanjona Bobaomby
Antsiranana
Massif de Tsaratanana 2886
Mahajanga
Gaborone
Pietersburg
Tropic of Capricorn
Lüderitz
Keetmanshoop
Oranje
Olifants
Nossob
Molopo
Pretoria
Krugersdorp
Johannesburg
Springs
Mbabane
Maputo
MADAGASCAR
Ambatondrazaka
Toamasina
Potchefstroom
Vereeniging
SWAZILAND
Antananarivo
Andevoranto
Sishen
Welkom
Kroonstad
Kimberley
Maseru
3482
LESOTHO
Ladysmith
Pietermaritzburg
Durban
Mangoky
Fianarantsoa
Augrabies Falls
Bloemfontein
Bitterfontein
Calvinia
SOUTH AFRICA
De Aar
Orange
Umtata
INDIAN OCEAN
Toliara
St. Helena B.
Great Karoo
Queenstown
Grahamstown
East London
Cape Town
Worcester
Oudtshoorn
Port Elizabeth
Cape of Good Hope
C. Agulhas
Tanjona Vohimena
Tôlanaro
Tropic of Capricorn
ATLANTIC OCEAN
INDIAN OCEAN

Relief

Feet	Meters
16 404	5000
9843	3000
6562	2000
3281	1000
1640	500
656	200
0	Sea Level

Land Dep.

| 656 | 200 |
| 13 123 | 4000 |

Scale 1 : 20 000 000

0   100   200   300   400   500 Miles
0   200   400   600   800 Kms.

Lambert Azimuthal Equal Area Projection

© Collins ◇ Longman Atlases

Same scale

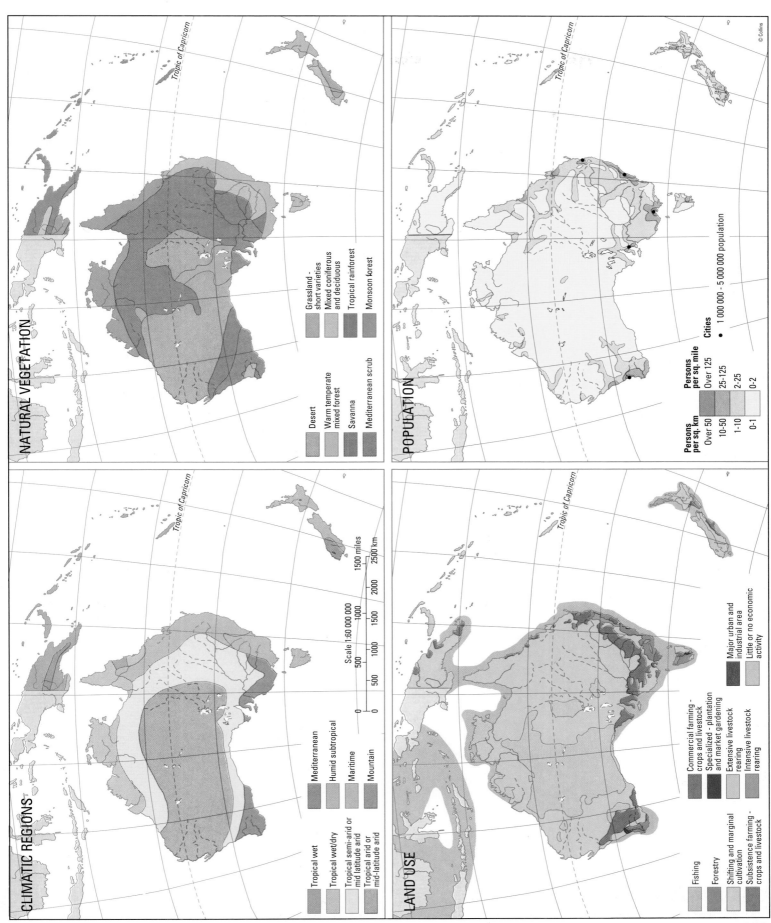

© Collins

NATURAL VEGETATION

Desert

Warm temperate mixed forest

Savanna

Mediterranean scrub

Grassland - short varieties

Mixed coniferous and deciduous

Tropical rainforest

Monsoon forest

POPULATION

Persons per sq. km
- Over 50
- 10-50
- 1-10
- 0-1

Persons per sq. mile
- Over 125
- 25-125
- 2-25
- 0-2

Cities
- ● 1 000 000 - 5 000 000 population

CLIMATIC REGIONS

Tropical wet

Tropical wet/dry

Tropical semi-arid or mid latitude arid

Tropical arid or mid-latitude arid

Mediterranean

Humid subtropical

Maritime

Mountain

Scale 1:60 000 000

0   500   1000   1500 miles

0   500   1000   1500   2000   2500 km

LAND USE

Fishing

Forestry

Shifting and marginal cultivation

Subsistence farming - crops and livestock

Commercial farming - crops and livestock

Specialized - plantation and market gardening

Extensive livestock rearing

Intensive livestock rearing

Major urban and industrial area

Little or no economic activity

Scale 1:20 000 000

0   100   200   300   400   500 Miles

0   200   400   600   800 Kms.

Lambert Azimuthal Equal Area Projection

© Collins ◇ Longman Atlases

New Zealand

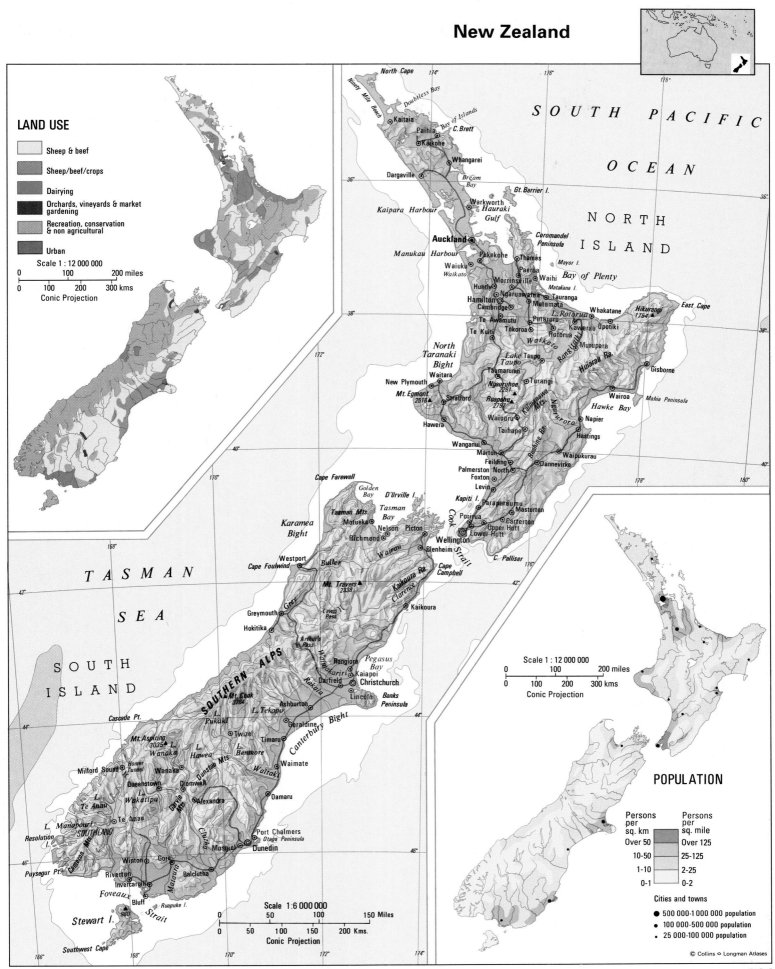

LAND USE

- Sheep & beef
- Sheep/beef/crops
- Dairying
- Orchards, vineyards & market gardening
- Recreation, conservation & non agricultural
- Urban

Scale 1 : 12 000 000

| 0 | 100 | 200 miles |
| 0 | 100 | 200 | 300 kms |

Conic Projection

NORTH ISLAND

North Cape
Ninety Mile Beach
Doubless Bay
Kaitaia
Paihia
Bay of Islands
C. Brett
Kaikohe
Whangarei
Dargaville
Bream Bay
Gt. Barrier I.
Kaipara Harbour
Warkworth
Hauraki Gulf
Auckland
Manukau Harbour
Pukekohe
Thames
Coromandel Peninsula
Waiuku
Paeroa
Mayor I.
Bay of Plenty
Waikato
Morrinsville
Waihi
Huntly
Ngaruawahia
Tauranga
Matakana I.
Hamilton
Matamata
Whakatane
Hikurangi 1754
East Cape
Cambridge
L. Rotorua
Te Awamutu
Putaruru
Kawerau
Opotiki
Te Kuiti
Tokoroa
Rotorua
Murupara
Waikato
Rangitaiki
Huiarau Ra.
North Taranaki Bight
Lake Taupo
Taumarunui
Ngauruhoe 2291
Turangi
Waitara
Kaimanawa Mts.
Gisborne
New Plymouth
Ruapehu 2797
Mt. Egmont 2518
Stratford
Ngaruroro
Wairoa
Mahia Peninsula
Hawera
Waiouru
Hawke Bay
Taihape
Napier
Rangitikei
Wanganui
Hastings
Marton
Waipukurau
Feilding
Dannevirke
Palmerston North
Foxton
Levin
Kapiti I.
Paraparaumu
Masterton
Porirua
Carterton
Upper Hutt
Wellington
Lower Hutt
C. Palliser

SOUTH PACIFIC OCEAN

TASMAN SEA

Cape Farewell
Golden Bay
D'Urville I.
Tasman Mts.
Tasman Bay
Karamea Bight
Motueka
Nelson
Picton
Richmond
Wairau
Blenheim
Westport
Butler
Cook Strait
Cape Foulwind
Cape Campbell
Mt. Travers 2338
Kaikoura Ra.
Clarence
Greymouth
Grey
Lewis Pass
Kaikoura
Hokitika
Arthur's Pass
Waimakariri
Pegasus Bay
Rangiora
SOUTHERN ALPS
Kaiapoi
Christchurch
Rakaia
Darfield
Banks Peninsula
Mt. Cook 3764
Ashburton
Lincoln
L. Tekapo
Geraldine
Canterbury Bight
L. Pukaki
Twizel
Mt. Aspiring 3035
Timaru
L. Wanaka
L. Hawea
L. Benmore
Waimate
Milford Sound
Dunstan Mts.
Waitaki
Homer Tunnel
Wanaka
Queenstown
Cromwell
Oamaru
L. Te Anau
L. Wakatipu
Garvie Mts.
Alexandra
SOUTHLAND
Te Anau
Port Chalmers
L. Manapouri
Otago Peninsula
Resolution I.
Clutha
Mosgiel
Dunedin
Cameron Mts.
Winton
Gore
Puysegur Pt.
Riverton
Balclutha
Mataura
Invercargill
Foveaux
Bluff
980
Ruapuke I.
Stewart I.
Strait
Southwest Cape

SOUTH ISLAND

Cascade Pt.

Scale 1:6 000 000

| 0 | 50 | 100 | 150 Miles |
| 0 | 50 | 100 | 150 | 200 Kms. |

Conic Projection

POPULATION

Scale 1 : 12 000 000

| 0 | 100 | 200 miles |
| 0 | 100 | 200 | 300 kms |

Conic Projection

Persons per sq. km	Persons per sq. mile
Over 50	Over 125
10-50	25-125
1-10	2-25
0-1	0-2

Cities and towns

- 500 000-1 000 000 population
- 100 000-500 000 population
- 25 000-100 000 population

© Collins ◇ Longman Atlases

Regions

The 34 countries surrounding the Pacific Ocean and the 23 island states scattered across it have become a region of great economic and political importance. Approximately 2.4 billion people live in the region - more than half of the world's population. The region produces half of the world's total wealth (GNP) and has an abundance of natural resources, including 21% of the world's oil resources, 63% of its wool, 67% of its cotton, 87% of its natural rubber and 94% of its natural silk.

The graphs on these two pages show the importance of the trade between the major countries in the region. (The graphs show the trade between countries as a percentage of total trade for each selected country).

CANADA
Total Imports $105 965 million
Total Exports $114 845 million

% of total trade
IMPORTS: U.S.A., Japan
EXPORTS: U.S.A., Japan

U.S.A.
Total Imports $446 460 million
Total Exports $319 680 million

% of total trade
IMPORTS: Japan, Canada, Mexico, Taiwan, South Korea
EXPORTS: Canada, Japan, Mexico, South Korea, Taiwan

JAPAN
Total Imports $164 770 million
Total Exports $259 760 million

% of total trade
IMPORTS: U.S.A., South Korea, Australia, China, Indonesia, Taiwan, Canada, Malaysia
EXPORTS: U.S.A., South Korea, Taiwan, Hong Kong, Singapore, China, Australia, Canada

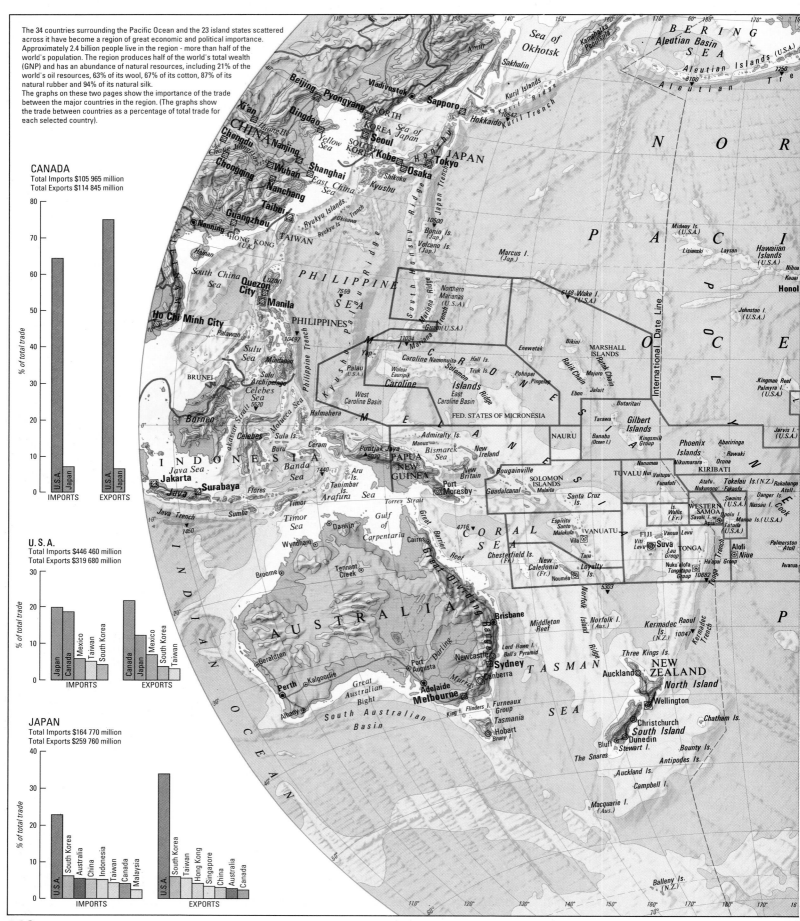

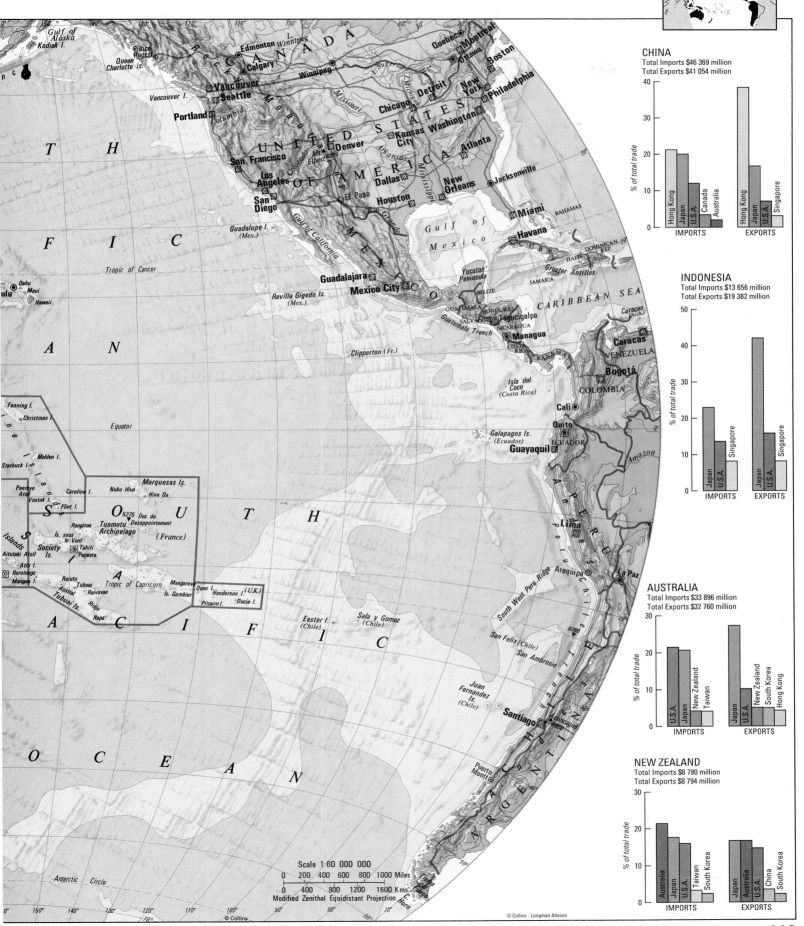

Pacific Ocean

CHINA
Total Imports $46 369 million
Total Exports $41 054 million

% of total trade

IMPORTS: Hong Kong, Japan, U.S.A., Canada, Australia
EXPORTS: Hong Kong, Japan, U.S.A., Singapore

INDONESIA
Total Imports $13 656 million
Total Exports $19 382 million

% of total trade

IMPORTS: Japan, U.S.A., Singapore
EXPORTS: Japan, U.S.A., Singapore

AUSTRALIA
Total Imports $33 896 million
Total Exports $32 760 million

% of total trade

IMPORTS: U.S.A., Japan, New Zealand, Taiwan
EXPORTS: Japan, U.S.A., New Zealand, South Korea, Hong Kong

NEW ZEALAND
Total Imports $6 780 million
Total Exports $8 794 million

% of total trade

IMPORTS: Australia, Japan, U.S.A., Taiwan, South Korea
EXPORTS: Japan, Australia, U.S.A., China, South Korea

Scale 1:60 000 000

0 200 400 600 800 1000 Miles

0 400 800 1200 1600 Kms.

Modified Zenithal Equidistant Projection

© Collins - Longman Atlases

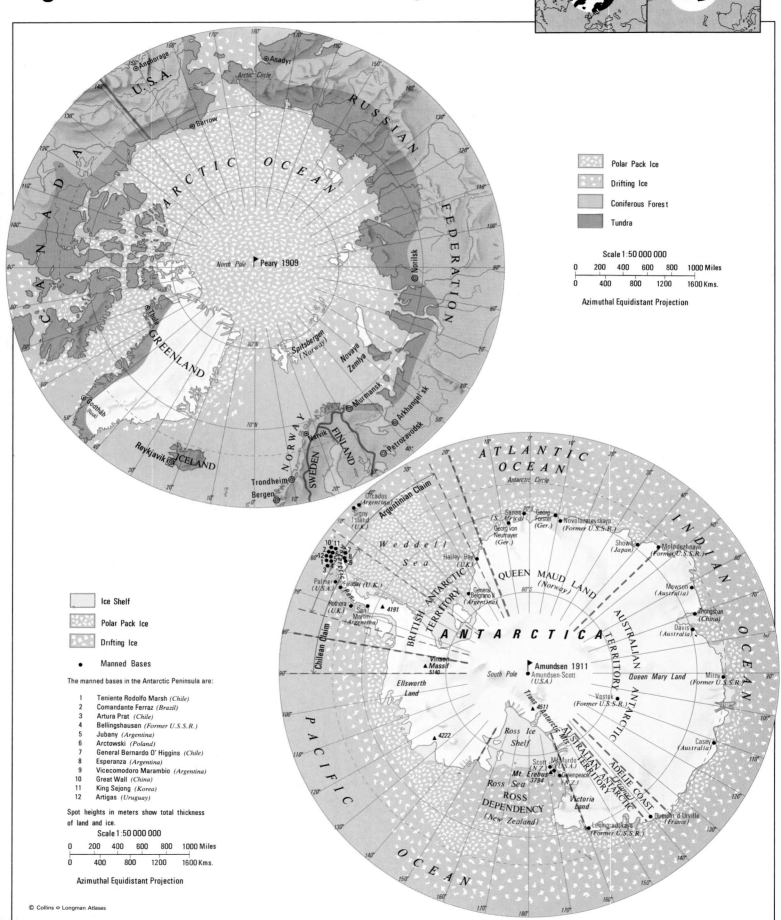

Polar Pack Ice

Drifting Ice

Coniferous Forest

Tundra

Scale 1:50 000 000

| 0 | 200 | 400 | 600 | 800 | 1000 Miles |

| 0 | 400 | 800 | 1200 | 1600 Kms. |

Azimuthal Equidistant Projection

Ice Shelf

Polar Pack Ice

Drifting Ice

● Manned Bases

The manned bases in the Antarctic Peninsula are:

1   Teniente Rodolfo Marsh (Chile)
2   Comandante Ferraz (Brazil)
3   Artura Prat (Chile)
4   Bellingshausen (Former U.S.S.R.)
5   Jubany (Argentina)
6   Arctowski (Poland)
7   General Bernardo O' Higgins (Chile)
8   Esperanza (Argentina)
9   Vicecomodoro Marambio (Argentina)
10 Great Wall (China)
11 King Sejong (Korea)
12 Artigas (Uruguay)

Spot heights in meters show total thickness of land and ice.

Scale 1:50 000 000

| 0 | 200 | 400 | 600 | 800 | 1000 Miles |

| 0 | 400 | 800 | 1200 | 1600 Kms. |

Azimuthal Equidistant Projection

© Collins ◇ Longman Atlases

Countries of the World[1]

Flag	Country	Capital[2]	Area[2] (sq. mi) (sq. km)	Population[3]	Major or[2] Official Languages	Important[3] Products
	Afghanistan	Kabul	260,000 647,497	16,560,000	Pushtu, Dari	karakul skins, cotton, fruit, natural gas
	Albania	Tirana (Tiranë)	11,097 28,489	3,200,000	Albanian, Greek	minerals, sugar beets, livestock, electricity, wheat
	Algeria	Algiers	918,497 2,400,000	25,360,000	Arabic, Berber dialects, French	wheat, barley, petroleum, fruit, natural gas
	Andorra	Andorra	185 466	53,000	Catalan, French, Spanish	livestock, tobacco
	Angola	Luanda	481,351 1,246,700	10,020,000	Portuguese, Bantu languages	petroleum, diamonds, coffee, sugar, bananas
	Antigua and Barbuda	St. John's	108 281	85,000	English	cotton, clothing, rum, livestock, bananas
	Argentina	Buenos Aires	1,100,000 2,766,890	32,690,000	Spanish, Italian	meat, wool, sugar cane, iron ore, sunflower seeds
	Armenia	Yerevan	11,490 29,800	3,290,000	Armenian, Russian	almonds, cotton, grain, minerals, machinery
	Australia	Canberra	3,000,000 7,700,000	17,200,000	English	wheat, wool, livestock, metal ores, coal, bauxite
	Austria	Vienna	32,377 83,857	7,800,000	German	lumber, metal products, paper, wheat, barley
	Azerbaijan	Baku	33,430 86,600	7,130,000	Azerbaijani, Russian	cotton, fruit, grain, oil, steel, iron ore, rice
	Bahamas	Nassau	5,380 13,934	255,000	English, Creole	pharmaceuticals, chemicals, lobsters, rum, livestock
	Bahrain	Manama	268 693	486,000	Arabic, English, Farsi	petroleum products, aluminum processing
	Bangladesh	Dhaka	55,813 143,998	108,000,000	Bengali, English	jute goods, tea, fish, newsprint, hides and skins
	Barbados	Bridgetown	166 430	257,000	English	clothing, rum, sugar, fish, electronic components
	Belarus (Belorussia)	Minsk	80,134 207,600	10,260,000	Byelorussian, Russian	flax, grain, livestock, potatoes, peat, machinery
	Belgium	Brussels	11,799 30,519	9,980,000	Dutch, French, German	precious stones, metals, chemical products
	Belize	Belmopan	8,866 22,963	193,000	English, Spanish, Mayan	lumber, sugar, livestock, fish, fruit, clothing, molases
	Benin	Porto-Novo	43,483 112,622	4,760,000	French, Fon	palm oil, cotton, cocoa, sugar
	Bhutan	Thimphu (Thimbu)	18,000 46,620	600,000	Dzongkha, Sharchop, Nepali, English	lumber, fruit, vegetables, cement
	Bolivia	La Paz, Sucre	425,000 1,100,000	6,410,000	Spanish, Quechua, Aymara	petroleum, tin, gold, silver, zinc, coffee
	Bosnia and Herzegovina	Sarajevo	19,736 51,129	4,355,000	Serbo Croatian	wheat, corn, plums, potatoes, textiles
	Botswana	Gaborone	224,710 600,372	1,350,000	English, Setswana	livestock, diamonds, copper, nickel, salt

[1]Includes Independent Countries; flags are based on most recent information available at time of publication.

[2]Source: *Background Notes*, United States Department of State

[3]Source: *Statesman's* Year-Book 1991-1992

Countries of the World[1]

Flag	Country	Capital[2]	Area[2] (sq. mi) (sq. km)	Population[3]	Major or[2] Official Languages	Important[3] Products
	Brazil	Brasilia	3,290,000 8,511,965	155,600,000	Portuguese	iron ore, steel, coffee, soybeans, shoes
	Brunei	Bandar Seri Begawan	2,227 5,769	256,500	Malay, Chinese, English	petroleum, rubber, lumber, rice, pepper
	Bulgaria	Sofia	44,365 110,987	8,900,000	Bulgarian	farm products, minerals, machinery, equipment
	Burkina Faso	Ouaga-dougou	106,000 274,200	8,760,000	French, others	livestock, cotton, rice, peanuts, sesame, grains
	Burundi	Bujumbura	10,747 27,834	5,460,000	Kirundi, French, Swahili	cotton, tea, coffee, bananas, grain, cattle
	Cambodia	Phnom Penh	69,900 181,040	8,300,000	Khmer, French	fish, rubber, maize, beans
	Cameroon	Yaoundé	183,568 475,439	11,540,000	English, French, African languages	cotton, coffee, cocoa, sugar, rubber, palm oil
	Canada	Ottawa	3,800,000 9,970,000	27,000,000	English, French	food products, machinery, lumber, metal ores
	Cape Verde	Praia	1,557 4,033	369,000	Portuguese, Crioulo	tuna, shellfish, salt, bananas, coffee, sugar
	Central African Republic	Bangui	242,000 623,000	3,040,000	French, Sangho	coffee, diamonds, peanuts, lumber, cotton
	Chad	N'Djaména	496,000 1,284,634	5,540,000	French, Arabic, Chadian languages	livestock, cotton, millet, fish, sugar
	Chile	Santiago	302,778 756,945	13,700,000	Spanish	paper, lumber, copper, nitrates, fish meal, gold
	China	Beijing	3,700,000 9,600,000	1,114,000,000	Mandarin Chinese	petroleum, minerals, grain, tea, raw silk
	Colombia	Bogotá	440,000 1,140,000	33,000,000	Spanish	petroleum, coffee, bananas, textiles
	Comoros	Moroni	838 2,171	503,000	Comoran, French	vanilla, copra, cloves, perfume essences, coffee
	Congo	Brazzaville	132,000 342,000	2,260,000	French, Lingala, Monokutuba	lumber, petroleum, cassava, bananas, plantains
	Costa Rica	San José	19,652 51,032	2,910,000	Spanish	livestock, sugar, cocoa, coffee, palm oil, bananas
	Côte d'Ivoire (Ivory Coast)	Yamous-soukro	124,500 322,500	12,100,000	French, tribal dialects	lumber, coffee, cocoa, sugar, petroleum products
	Croatia	Zagreb	21,829 56,538	4,690,000	Croato-Serbian	grain, livestock, timber, coal, petroleum, cement
	Cuba	Havana	44,200 110,860	10,580,000	Spanish	sugar, citrus fruit, tobacco, minerals, fish
	Cyprus	Nicosia	3,572 9,251	702,100	Greek, Turkish, English	citrus fruits, grapes, potatoes, copper, cement
	Czech Republic	Prague	30,442 78,864	10,000,000	Czech	iron and steel, machinery, timber, wheat, potatoes
	Denmark	Copenhagen	16,632 43,076	5,150,000	Danish, English	machinery, meat, fish, dairy products, metals
	Djibouti	Djibouti	9,000 23,310	510,000	French, Arabic, Afar, Somali	livestock, hides, fish
	Dominica	Roseau	290 754	108,812	English, French patois	fruit juices, bananas, soap, coconuts, fruit
	Dominican Republic	Santo Domingo	18,704 48,442	7,200,000	Spanish	coffee, bananas, bauxite, nickel, sugar, rice

Countries of the World[1]

Flag	Country	Capital[2]	Area[2] (sq. mi) (sq. km)	Population[3]	Major or[2] Official Languages	Important[3] Products
	Ecuador	Quito	109,000 271,000	9,620,000	Spanish, Quechua	bananas, coffee, cocoa beans, shrimp, petroleum
	Egypt	Cairo	386,650 1,001,450	56,000,000	Arabic, English, French	cotton, textiles, aluminum, oranges, crude oil
	El Salvador	San Salvador	8,260 21,476	5,380,000	Spanish	cotton, coffee, sugar, livestock, lumber, maize
	Equatorial Guinea	Malabo	10,820 28,023	417,000	Spanish, Fang, Bubi, English	lumber, coffee, cocoa beans, bananas, fish
	Estonia	Tallinn	17,413 45,100	1,580,000	Estonian, Russian	peat, grain, livestock, vegetables, paper, potatoes
	Eritrea	Asmara	45,405 117,600	2,614,700	Semitic languages	salt, sesame seeds, lentils
	Ethiopia	Addis Ababa	426,400 1,104,300	45,000,000	Amharic, Tiqrinya, Arabic	hides, coffee, sugar, maize
	Fiji	Suva	7,055 18,376	747,000	Fijian, Hindustani, English	copra, sugar, gold, ginger, canned fish
	Finland	Helsinki	130,160 337,113	4,970,000	Finnish, Swedish, Lappish	lumber, paper, manufactured goods, wood pulp
	France	Paris	220,668 551,670	56,610,000	French	machinery, sugar, grapes, livestock, wheat, clothing
	Gabon	Libreville	102,317 266,024	1,220,000	French, Bantu languages	coffee, petroleum, lumber, manganese, metals
	Gambia	Banjul	4,361 11,300	875,000	English, Mandinka, Wolof, Fula	fish, peanuts, cotton, livestock
	Georgia	Tbilisi	26,900 69,700	5,460,000	Georgian, Russian	grain, tea, coal, manganese, steel, fruit
	Germany	Berlin	137,838 357,000	79,110,000	German	precision instruments, chemicals, cars
	Ghana	Accra	92,100 238,538	14,900,000	English, Akan, Mole-Dagbani	lumber, gold, tobacco, cocoa beans, coffee
	Greece	Athens	51,146 131,957	10,260,000	Greek	textiles, olive oil, fruit, tobacco
	Grenada	St. George's	133 344	91,000	English, French-African Patois	cocoa beans, mace, fish, nutmeg, bananas, sugar
	Guatemala	Guatemala City	42,000 108,700	9,000,000	Spanish, Mayan languages	cotton, chicle gum, bananas, coffee, lumber
	Guinea	Conakry	95,000 246,048	6,710,000	French, Fulani, others	bauxite, sugar, cassava, rice, bananas, alumina
	Guinea-Bissau	Bissau	13,948 36,125	966,000	Portuguese, Crioulo	peanuts, palm oil, fish, coconuts, rice
	Guyana	Georgetown	83,000 215,000	990,000	English, Creole	bauxite, aluminum, sugar, rice, shrimp, rum
	Haiti	Port-au-Prince	10,714 27,750	5,690,000	French, Creole	coffee, sugar, rice, cotton, sisal
	Honduras	Tegucigalpa	43,277 112,088	4,440,000	Spanish, Indian languages	bananas, coffee, sugar, lumber, shrimp, lobster
	Hungary	Budapest	35,919 93,030	10,450,000	Hungarian (Magyar)	consumer goods, tools, machinery, wheat, wine
	Iceland	Reykjavik	39,709 102,845	255,000	Icelandic	fish, marine products, metals
	India	New Delhi	1,268,884 3,287,263	844,320,000	Hindi, English others	clothing, textiles, leather, jems, chemicals, tea

Countries of the World[1]

Flag	Country	Capital[2]	Area[2] (sq. mi) (sq. km)	Population[3]	Major or[2] Official Languages	Important[3] Products
	Indonesia	Jakarta	736,000 2,000,000	179,100,000	Bahasa Indonesia, Dutch	petroleum, lumber, coffee, manufactured goods
	Iran	Tehran	636,294 1,648,000	53,920,000	Farsi, Kurdish, Azerbaijani	wheat, petroleum, rice, sugar, tobacco
	Iraq	Baghdad	167,924 434,934	17,800,000	Arabic, Kurdish	petroleum, dates, wheat, rice
	Ireland	Dublin	27,136 70,282	3,520,000	Irish, English	chemicals, dairy products, machinery, peat, barley
	Israel	Jerusalem	7,850 20,325	4,980,000	Hebrew, Arabic, English	citrus, chemicals, textiles, machinery, diamonds
	Italy	Rome	116,303 301,225	57,700,000	Italian	clothing, shoes, textiles, machinery, cars, fruit
	Jamaica	Kingston	4,244 10,991	2,400,000	English, Creole	bauxite, bananas, sugar, citrus, molasses, cocoa
	Japan	Tokyo	145,856 377,765	123,610,000	Japanese	cars, metal products, textiles, electronics
	Jordan	Amman	35,000 91,000	3,170,000	Arabic	phosphates, citrus fruits, olives, chemicals, grapes
	Kazakhstan	Alma-Ata	1,049,155 2,717,300	16,690,000	Kazakh, Russian	cotton, grain, livestock, metal ores, oil, coal
	Kenya	Nairobi	244,960 582,646	24,030,000	Kiswahili, Bantu languages, English	coffee, tea, textiles, sugar, chemicals, leather
	Kiribati	Tarawa	276 717	72,298	English, Gilbertese	copra, tuna, coconuts, poultry
	Korea, North	Pyongyang	47,000 121,730	22,420,000	Korean	chemicals, fertilizers, minerals, rice, maize
	Korea, South	Seoul	38,000 98,500	42,790,000	Korean	machinery, steel, rice, fish, electronics
	Kuwait	Kuwait	6,880 17,818	2,040,000	Arabic, Kurdish, English	petroleum, shrimp, fertilizer
	Kyrgyzstan (Kirghizia)	Bishkek	76,640 198,500	4,370,000	Kirghiz, Russian	livestock, sugar beets, wheat, hemp, fruit, tobacco
	Laos	Vientiane	91,430 236,804	4,050,000	Lao, French, English	lumber, coffee, maize, textiles, rice, sugar
	Latvia	Riga	24,595 63,700	2,690,000	Latvian, Russian	barley, oats, livestock, electric railway cars
	Lebanon	Beirut	4,015 10,452	3,000,000	Arabic, French, English	citrus fruits, grapes, wheat, olives
	Lesotho	Maseru	11,718 30,350	1,720,000	English	diamonds, mohair, wool, wheat
	Liberia	Monrovia	43,000 111,370	2,440,000	English, Mande, Kwa, West Atlantic	lumber, iron ore, gold, cocoa, coffee, rubber
	Libya	Tripoli	679,536 1,758,610	4,000,000	Arabic	petroleum, olives, dates, barley, wheat
	Liechtenstein	Vaduz	62 160	28,877	German	textiles, steel screws, precision instruments
	Lithuania	Vilnius	25,170 65,200	3,720,000	Lithuanian, Russian	grain, potatoes, sugar beets, timber, machinery
	Luxembourg	Luxembourg	1,034 2,586	378,400	Luxembourgish, German, French	steel, maize, barley, potatoes, wheat, wine
	Macedonia[4]	Skopje	9,925 25,713	1,909,136	Macedonian, Albanian	wheat, cotton, corn, livestock, steel

[4]Macedonia declared independence from Yugoslavia in November 1991. It has not been widely recognized as an independent state by the international community.

Countries of the World[1]

Flag	Country	Capital[2]	Area[2] (sq. mi) (sq. km)	Population[3]	Major or[2] Official Languages	Important[3] Products
	Madagascar	Antananarivo	228,880 592,800	11,440,000	Malagasy, French	chromium, graphite, cloves, vanilla, coffee
	Malawi	Lilongwe	45,747 118,484	7,980,000	Chichewa, English	tobacco, peanuts, maize, tea
	Malaysia	Kuala Lumpur	127,316 329,749	17,810,000	Bahasa Malaysia, Chinese, Tamil	petroleum, lumber, tin, rubber, palm oil, fruit
	Maldives	Malé	115 298	213,215	Divehi, English	coconuts, fish, millet, tropical fruits
	Mali	Bamako	474,764 1,240,278	9,090,000	Bambara, French	fish, livestock, cotton, peanuts, rice, millet
	Malta	Valletta	121 316	355,910	Maltese, English	manufactured goods, chemicals, fish
	Marshall Islands	Majuro	70 181	45,563	English, Marshallese	coconuts, fruit, phosphates
	Mauritania	Nouakchott	419,212 1,085,760	1,970,000	Arabic, Pulaar, Wolot, Soninke	iron ore, dates, cereals, vegetables, fish
	Mauritius	Port Louis	720 1,865	1,091,682	English, Creole, French, Hindi	molasses, sugar, tea, fish, clothing, plastics
	Mexico	Mexico City	764,000 2,000,000	81,400,000	Spanish, Indian languages	cotton, petroleum, maize, livestock, coffee, minerals
	Micronesia	Palikir	271 701	107,900	English, others	copra, fish
	Moldova (Moldovia)	Kishinev	13,000 33,700	4,360,000	Moldavian (Romanian), Russian	grain, sugar beets, steel, clothing, fish
	Monaco	Monaco	0.8 1.95	26,000	French, English, Italian	plastics, electronics, chemicals, perfume
	Mongolia	Ulan Baatar	604,103 1,566,500	2,150,000	Mongolian	livestock, wheat, oats, footwear, minerals
	Morocco	Rabat	172,413 446,550	24,370,000	Arabic, Berber, French, Spanish	phosphates, citrus, cereals, sugar
	Mozambique	Maputo	303,769 789,800	16,110,000	Portuguese, Bantu languages	cashews, shrimp, sugar, copra, petroleum products
	Myanmar (Burma)	Yangon (Rangoon)	261,228 676,577	40,780,000	Burmese	teak, rice, sugar, cement, rubber
	Namibia	Windhoek	320,827 823,145	1,290,000	English, Afrikaans, German	livestock, diamonds, uranium, fertilizers
	Nauru	Yaren	8 21	8,100	Nauruan, English	phosphates
	Nepal	Kathmandu	56,136 147,181	18,900,000	Nepali, Bihari	lumber, grain, cattle, jute, potatoes, oil seeds
	Netherlands	Amsterdam, The Hague	16,464 41,473	15,010,000	Dutch	manufactured goods, wheat, flower bulbs
	New Zealand	Wellington	103,886 269,063	3,420,000	English, Maori	meat, dairy products, wool, manufactured goods
	Nicaragua	Managua	57,000 148,000	3,870,000	Spanish, Indian languages	coffee, cotton, sugar, chemicals, meat
	Niger	Niamey	490,000 1,267,000	8,040,000	French, Hausa, Djerma	coal, phosphates, uranium, peanuts, livestock
	Nigeria	Abuja	356,700 923,768	88,500,000	English, Hausa, Ibo, Yoruba	petroleum, lumber, tin, cocoa, palm oil
	Norway	Oslo	150,000 386,000	4,240,000	Norwegian, Lapp	petroleum, lumber, fish, ships, chemicals

Countries of the World[1]

Flag	Country	Capital[2]	Area[2] (sq. mi) (sq. km)	Population[3]	Major or[2] Official Languages	Important[3] Products
	Oman	Muscat	82,030 212,457	1,500,000	Arabic, English	petroleum, fish, dates, cement
	Pakistan	Islamabad	310,527 803,943	114,000,000	Urdu, English, Punjabi	cotton, rice, garments, sugar, leather
	Panama	Panama City	29,762 77,381	2,300,000	Spanish, English	bananas, sugar, rice, coffee, lumber, fruit
	Papua New Guinea	Port Moresby	178,260 461,693	3,700,000	Melanesian languages, English	coffee, copra, lumber, copper, rubber
	Paraguay	Asunción	157,047 406,750	4,160,000	Guarani, Spanish	meat, tobacco, cotton, soybeans, lumber
	Peru	Lima	496,222 1,280,000	21,550,000	Spanish, Quechua	coffee, cotton, sugar, fish, copper, petroleum
	Philippines	Manila	117,187 300,000	60,900,000	Pilipino, English	copper, sugar, garments, coconuts, electronics
	Poland	Warsaw	120,725 312,680	37,930,000	Polish	grains, textiles, coal, copper, ships
	Portugal	Lisbon	36,390 94,276	10,390,000	Portuguese	cork, fish, wine, chemicals, textiles, manufactured goods
	Qatar	Doha	4,427 11,437	371,863	Arabic, English	petroleum, fish, steel
	Romania	Bucharest	91,699 237,499	23,000,000	Romanian, Hungarian, German	petroleum, grains, machinery, minerals, cement
	Russia	Moscow	6,592,800 17,075,000	148,040,000	Russian	petroleum, coal, iron ore, grain, machinery, metals
	Rwanda	Kigali	10,169 26,338	6,710,000	Kinyarwanda, French	coffee, tea, pyrethrom, potatoes, tin
	St. Kitts and Nevis	Basseterre	68 168	44,380	English	sugar, cotton, fish, coconuts
	St. Lucia	Castries	238 619	146,600	English, French patois	bananas, coconuts, citrus fruit, cocoa beans, spices
	St. Vincent and the Grenadines	Kingstown	150 388	113,950	English	bananas, eddoes, copra, coconuts
	San Marino	San Marino	24 62	23,200	Italian	tiles, chemicals, wheat, textiles, wine
	São Tomé and Príncipe	São Tomé	387 1,001	124,000	Portuguese, Fang	copra, palm oil, cocoa beans, coffee, bananas
	Saudi Arabia	Riyadh	830,000 2,331,000	12,000,000	Arabic	petroleum, dates, chemicals, livestock, wheat
	Senegal	Dakar	76,000 196,840	7,330,000	French, Wolof, others	phosphates, fertilizer, petroleum products
	Seychelles	Victoria	171 444	67,378	Creole, English, French	copra, fish, coconuts, cinnamon bark
	Sierra Leone	Freetown	27,925 72,325	4,140,000	English, Mende, Krio	coffee, cocoa beans, fish, ginger, peanuts
	Singapore	Singapore	239 620	2,690,000	Malay, English, Chinese, Tamil	machinery, textiles, fish, optical instruments
	Slovakia	Bratislava	18,928 49,035	5,000,000	Slovak	iron ore, livestock, timber, wheat, potatoes

Countries of the World[1]

Flag	Country	Capital[2]	Area[2] (sq. mi) (sq. km)	Population[3]	Major or[2] Official Languages	Important[3] Products
	Slovenia	Ljubljana	7,819 20,251	1,950,000	Slovenian	wheat, maize, potatoes, timber, lignite, machinery
	Solomon Islands	Honiara	11,599 27,556	325,600	Melanesian languages, English	fish, copra, rice, palm oil, rattan furniture
	Somalia	Mogadishu	246,000 686,803	7,560,000	Somali, Arabic, English, Italian	livestock, bananas, fruit, hides and skins
	South Africa	Capetown, Pretoria	472,359 1,233,404	33,000,000	Afrikaans, English, Bantu languages	gold, diamonds, coal, fruits, textiles, cotton
	Spain	Madrid	194,884 504,750	38,420,000	Spanish, Catalan, Galician, Basque	fruit, grain, wine, cars, clothing, cotton
	Sri Lanka	Colombo	25,332 65,610	16,900,000	Sinhala, Tamil, English	rubber, tea, gems, fish, copra, textiles
	Sudan	Khartoum	967,500 2,500,000	25,560,000	Arabic, English, tribal languages	peanuts, sugar, cotton, sesame seeds, gum arabic
	Suriname	Paramaribo	63,037 163,265	416,839	Dutch, English, Surinamese	aluminum, bauxite, lumber, shrimp, bananas
	Swaziland	Mbabane	6,704 17,363	681,059	Siswati, English	citrus, canned fruit, sugar, asbestos, wood pulp
	Sweden	Stockholm	173,731 449,964	8,600,000	Swedish	lumber, cars, chemicals, machinery, paper
	Switzerland	Bern	15,941 41,288	6,750,000	German, French, Italian, Romansch	precision instruments, dairy products, chemicals
	Syria	Damascus	71,500 185,170	11,300,000	Arabic, English, French, Kurdish	textiles, grains, olives, cotton, petroleum
	Taiwan[5]	Taipei (Taibei)	14,000 35,981	20,400,000	Mandarin Chinese	electrical machinery, footwear, textiles, toys
	Tajikistan	Dushanbe	55,240 143,100	5,250,000	Tajik, Russian	grain, livestock, textiles, coal, lead, oil, zinc
	Tanzania	Dodoma	363,950 942,623	25,090,000	Kiswahill, English	diamonds, cashews, sisal, cloves, coffee, tea, cotton
	Thailand	Bangkok	198,114 513,115	55,900,000	Thai	rubber, tapioca, jewelry, rice, textiles, lumber
	Togo	Lomé	21,853 56,600	3,400,000	Ewe, French, Kabre	coffee, cocoa beans, phosphates, cotton
	Tonga	Nuku'alofa	288 747	103,000	Tongan, English	coconuts, bananas, vanilla, tapa cloth, footwear, fish
	Trinidad and Tobago	Port-of-Spain	1,980 5,128	1,240,000	English	ammonia, fertilizer, petroleum, sugar, cement
	Tunisia	Tunis	63,378 164,149	8,180,000	Arabic, French	textiles, phosphates, olive oil, cereals
	Turkey	Ankara	296,000 766,640	56,470,000	Turkish, Kurdich, Arabic	textiles, iron and steel, chemicals, cotton, nuts
	Turkmenistan	Ashkhabad	186,400 488,100	3,620,000	Turkmen, Russian	minerals, cotton, livestock, clothing, carpets
	Tuvalu	Funafuti	10 26	8,229	Tuvaluan, English	coconuts, handicrafts, copra, postage stamps
	Uganda	Kampala	94,354 235,885	18,440,000	English, Swahili, Bantu languages	cotton, coffee, tea, tobacco, sugar, cement
	Ukraine	Kiev	171,770 445,000	51,840,000	Ukrainian, Russian	grain, sugar beets, coal, steel, chemicals

[5]Both Taiwan and China claim to be the sole legitimate government of all of China. In 1971 Taiwan lost its UN seat to mainland China, and in 1979 the United States changed its diplomatic recognition from Taipei to Beijing. Taiwan has diplomatic relations with about two dozen countries.

Countries of the World[1]

Flag	Country	Capital[2]	Area[2] (sq. mi) (sq. km)	Population[3]	Major or[2] Official Languages	Important[3] Products
	United Arab Emirates	Abu Dhabi	30,000 82,880	1,840,000	Arabic, English, Hindi, Urdu	petroleum, fish, chemicals, dates, fertilizers
	United Kingdom	London	94,251 244,111	57,410,000	English, Welsh, Gaelic	chemicals, foods, iron and steel, machinery
	United States of America	Washington, D.C.	3,615,105 9,363,123	253,600,000	English, Spanish	aircraft, chemicals, machinery, grain, fruits
	Uruguay	Montevideo	68,037 176,215	3,110,000	Spanish	livestock, wool, leather, textiles, wheat, rice
	Uzbekistan	Tashkent	172,741 447,400	20,320,000	Uzbek, Russian	cotton, livestock, rice, coal, cement, clothing, oil
	Vanuatu	Port-Vila	4,706 12,189	142,630	Bislama, English, French	fish, copra, cocoa beans, livestock, timber
	Vatican City	Vatican City	109 acres 0.439	1,000	Italian, Latin, French	coins, postage stamps
	Venezuela	Caracas	352,143 912,050	19,250,000	Spanish	petroleum, iron ore, coffee, cocoa beans
	Vietnam	Hanoi	127,330 329,707	65,000,000	Vietnamese, French, Chinese, Khmer	coal, minerals, fish, vegetables, rice, rubber
	Western Samoa	Apia	1,133 2,934	157,158	Samoan, English	coconuts, cocoa beans, lumber, bananas, fruit
	Yemen	Sanaa (Sana'a)	203,796 527,970	12,000,000	Arabic	cotton, fish, salt, fruit, grains
	Yugoslavia[6]	Belgrade	39,438 102,173	9,900,000	Serbo-Croatian, Slovenian	wheat, lumber, sheep, sugar, fabrics
	Zaire	Kinshasa	905,063 2,350,000	38,550,000	French, Bantu languages	copper, diamonds, cobalt, petroleum, coffee
	Zambia	Lusaka	290,585 752,614	8,500,000	English, Bantu languages	cobalt, copper, emeralds, cotton, sugar
	Zimbabwe	Harare	151,000 391,090	9,600,000	English, Shona, Sindebele	cotton, fruits, tobacco, coal, chrome, nickel

[6]Yugoslavia, formerly comprised of six replublics, now consists of the two republics of Serbia and Montenegro.

Outlying Territories of the United States

Flag	Country	Capital[2]	Area[2] (sq. mi) (sq. km)	Population[3]	Major or[2] Official Languages	Important[3] Products
	American Samoa (US)	Pago Pago	76 198	39,500	Samoan, English	tuna, pet food, fish meal, handicrafts
	Guam (US)	Agaña	209 541	133,000	Chamorro, English	fruits, vegetables, fish, shrimp, livestock
	Northern Marianas (US)	Saipan	185 480	21,200	Chamorro, English	copra, livestock, fish, fruits, vegetables, sugar
	Palau (US)	Koror	188 488	14,208	English, Palauan	bauxite, yams, copra, fruits, fish, handicrafts
	Puerto Rico (US)	San Juan	3,435 8,897	3,291,000	Spanish, English	chemicals, clothing, fish, electronic goods, sugar
	Virgin Islands (US)	Charlotte Amalie	133 344	103,200	English	manufacturing, petroleum refining, fruits, sugar

How to Use the Index

The number in dark type which precedes each name in the index refers to the number of the page where that feature or place will be found.

The geographical coordinates which follow the place name are sometimes only approximate but are close enough for the place name to be located.

The alphabetical order of names composed of two or more words is governed primarily by the first word and then by the second. This is an example of the rule:

White Nile   Whitehorse
White Sea   Whitney, Mt,

Latitude and Longitude

In the index each place name is followed by its geographical coordinates which allow the reader to find the place on the map. These coordinates give the latitude and longitude of a particular place.

The latitude (or parallel) is the distance of a point north or south of the Equator measured as an angle with the center of the earth. The Equator is latitude 0°, the North Pole is 90°N and the South Pole 90°S. On a globe the lines could be drawn as concentric circles parallel to the Equator, decreasing in diameter from the Equator until they become a point at the Poles. On the maps these lines of latitude are usually represented as lines running across the map from East to West in smooth curves. They are numbered on the sides of the map; north of the Equator the numbers increase southwards. The degree interval between them depends on the scale of the map. On a large scale map (for example, 1:2 000 000) the interval is one degree, but on a small scale (for example 1:50 000 000) it will be ten degrees.

Lines of longitude (or meridians) cut the latitude lines at right angles on the globe and intersect with one another at the Poles. Longitude is measured by the angle at the center of the earth between it and the meridian of origin which runs through Greenwich, London, U.K. (0°). It may be a measurement East or West of this line and from 0° to 180° in each direction. The longitude line of 180° runs North-South through the Pacific Ocean. On a particular map the interval between the lines of longitude is always the same as that between the lines of latitude and normally they are drawn vertically. They are numbered in the top and bottom margins and a note states East or West from Greenwich.

The unit of measurement for latitude and longitude is the degree. It is subdivided into 60 minutes. An index entry states the position of a place in degrees and minutes, a space being left between the degrees and minutes. The latitude is followed by N(orth) or S(outh) and the longitude by E(ast) or W(est).

The following is a list of the principal abbreviations used in the index:

Afghan.	Afghanistan	est.	estuary	Miss.	Mississippi	Resr.	Reservoir
Ala.	Alabama	f.	physical feature eg. valley, plain	Mo.	Missouri	Russian Fed.	Russian Federation
Ark.	Arkansas			Mt.	Mount	S.C.	South Carolina
b., B.	bay, Bay	Fla.	Florida	mtn., Mtn.	mountain, Mountain	Sd.	Sound
Bangla.	Bangladesh	g., G.	gulf, Gulf	mts., Mts.	mountains, Mountains	S.Korea	South Korea
Bosnia.	Bosnia-Herzegovina	Ga.	Georgia	N.C.	North Carolina	str., Str.	strait, Strait
c., C.	cape, Cape	i., I., is., Is.	island, Island, islands, Islands	Neth.	Netherlands	Switz.	Switzerland
C.A.R.	Central African Republic			N.Korea	North Korea	Tenn.	Tennessee
		Ill.	Illinois	N.Y	New York State	Tex.	Texas
Calif.	California	Ind.	Indiana	Oreg.	Oregon	U.A.E.	United Arab Emirates
Colo.	Colorado	l., L.	lake, Lake	pen., Pen.	peninsula, Peninsula	U.K.	United Kingdom
d.	internal division eg. county, state	La.	Louisiana	Phil.	Philippines	U.S.A.	United States of America
		Liech.	Liechtenstein	P.N.G.	Papua New Guinea	Vt.	Vermont
Del.	Delaware	Lux.	Luxembourg	Pt.	Point	Wash.	Washington
des.	desert	Mass.	Massachusetts	r., R.	river, River	W. Sahara	Western Sahara
Dom. Rep.	Dominican Republic	Mich.	Michigan	Rep. of Ire.	Republic of Ireland	W. Va.	West Virginia
Equat. Guinea	Equatorial Guinea	Minn.	Minnesota			Yugo.	Yugoslavia

PAGE	PLACENAME	LATITUDE	LONGITUDE
59	Fort Pierce, *U.S.A.*	27 28N	80 20W
52	Fort Smith, *d., Canada*	63 30N	118 0W
61	Fort Smith, *U.S.A.*	35 23N	94 25W
58	Fort Wayne, *U.S.A.*	41 5N	85 8W
61	Fort Worth, *U.S.A.*	32 45N	97 20W
71	Fortaleza, *Brazil*	3 45S	38 35W
65	Fort-de-France, *Martinique*	14 36N	61 5W
99	Foshan, *China*	23 3N	113 8E
53	Foxe Channel, *Canada*	65 0N	80 0W
84	France, *Europe*	47 0N	2 0E
82	Frankfurt, *Germany*	50 6N	8 41E
88	Franz Josef Land, *is., Russian Fed.*	81 0N	54 0E
52	Fraser, *r., Canada*	49 5N	123 0W
81	Frederikshavn, *Denmark*	57 28N	10 33E
60	Freeport, *U.S.A.*	42 17N	89 38W
106	Freetown, *Sierra Leone*	8 30N	13 17W
82	Freiburg, *Germany*	48 0N	7 52E
62	Fremont, *U.S.A.*	37 34N	122 1W
71	French Guiana, *S. America*	3 40N	53 0W
62	Fresno, *U.S.A.*	36 45N	119 45W
53	Frobisher B., *Canada*	63 0N	66 45W
100	Fujiyama, *mtn., Japan*	35 23N	138 42E
100	Fukui, *Japan*	36 4N	136 12E
100	Fukuoka, *Japan*	33 39N	130 21E
100	Fukushima, *Japan*	37 44N	140 28E
100	Fukuyama, *Japan*	34 29N	133 21E
55	Fundy, B. of, *N. America*	44 30N	66 30W
81	Funen, *i., Denmark*	55 15N	10 30E
112	Furneaux Group, *is., Australia*	40 10S	148 5E
99	Fushun, *China*	41 51N	123 53E
99	Fuxin, *China*	42 8N	121 39E
99	Fuzhou, *China*	26 1N	119 20E

G

PAGE	PLACENAME	LATITUDE	LONGITUDE
84	Gabès, *Tunisia*	33 53N	10 7E
108	Gabon, *Africa*	0 00	12 0E
108	Gaborone, *Botswana*	24 45S	25 55E
59	Gadsden, *U.S.A.*	34 0N	86 0W
59	Gainesville, *U.S.A.*	29 37N	82 21W
113	Galapagos Is., *Pacific Oc.*	0 30S	90 30W
83	Galati, *Romania*	45 27N	27 59E
60	Galesburg, *U.S.A.*	40 57N	90 22W
97	Galle, *Sri Lanka*	6 1N	80 13E
81	Gällivare, *Sweden*	67 10N	20 40E
61	Galveston, *U.S.A.*	29 18N	94 48W
79	Galway B., *Rep. of Ire.*	53 12N	9 7W
106	Gambia, *Africa*	13 30N	15 0W
97	Ganges, *r., India*	23 30N	90 25E
106	Gao, *Mali*	16 19N	0 9W
99	Gaoxiong, *Taiwan*	22 36N	120 17E
84	Garonne, *r., France*	45 0N	0 37W
106	Garoua, *Cameroon*	9 17N	13 22E
58	Gary, *U.S.A.*	41 34N	87 20W
58	Gaspé Pen., *Canada*	48 30N	65 0W
59	Gastonia, *U.S.A.*	35 14N	81 12W
65	Gatun L., *Panama*	9 20N	80 0W
81	Gävle, *Sweden*	60 41N	17 10E
97	Gaya, *India*	24 48N	85 0E
94	Gaza, *Egypt*	31 30N	34 28E
94	Gaziantep, *Turkey*	37 4N	37 21E
83	Gdańsk, *Poland*	54 22N	18 38E
83	Gdańsk, G. of, *Poland*	54 45N	19 15E
83	Gdynia, *Poland*	54 31N	18 30E
110	Geelong, *Australia*	38 10S	144 26E
80	Gelsenkirchen, *Germany*	51 30N	7 5E
101	General Santos, *Phil.*	6 5N	125 15E
82	Geneva, *Switz.*	46 13N	6 9E
82	Geneva, L., *Switz.*	46 30N	6 30E
82	Genoa, *Italy*	44 24N	8 54E
80	Gent, *Belgium*	51 2N	3 42E
102	George Town, *Malaysia*	5 30N	100 16E
70	Georgetown, *Guyana*	6 46N	58 10W
87	Georgia, *Asia*	42 0N	43 30E
59	Georgia, *d., U.S.A.*	32 50N	83 15W
58	Georgian B., *Canada*	45 15N	80 45W
82	Gera, *Germany*	50 51N	12 11E
82	Germany, *Europe*	52 0N	10 0E
97	Ghaghara, *r., India*	25 45N	84 50E
106	Ghana, *Africa*	8 0N	1 0W
84	Gibraltar, *Europe*	36 7N	5 22W
84	Gibraltar, Str. of, *Africa/Europe*	36 0N	5 25W
110	Gibson Desert, *Australia*	24 30S	124 0E
100	Gifu, *Japan*	35 27N	136 50E
84	Gijón, *Spain*	43 32N	5 40W
63	Gila, *r., U.S.A.*	32 43N	114 33W
84	Gironde, *r., France*	45 35N	1 0W
111	Gisborne, *New Zealand*	38 41S	178 2E
89	Gizhiga G., *Russian Fed.*	61 0N	158 0E
110	Gladstone, *Australia*	23 52S	151 16E
79	Glasgow, *U.K.*	55 52N	4 15W
63	Glendale, *U.S.A.*	34 10N	118 17W
58	Glens Falls, *town, U.S.A.*	43 19N	73 39W
83	Gliwice, *Poland*	50 17N	18 40E
79	Gloucester, *U.K.*	51 52N	2 15W
98	Gobi, *des., Asia*	43 30N	103 30E
97	Godavari, *r., India*	16 40N	82 15E
53	Godthåb, *Greenland*	64 10N	51 40W
71	Goiânia, *Brazil*	16 43S	49 18W
59	Goldsboro, *U.S.A.*	35 23N	78 0W
83	Gomel, *Belorussia*	52 25N	31 0E
61	Gómez Palacio, *Mexico*	25 34N	103 30W
107	Gondar, *Ethiopia*	12 39N	37 29E
108	Good Hope, C. of, *South Africa*	34 20S	18 25E
110	Goondiwindi, *Australia*	28 30S	150 17E
97	Gorakhpur, *India*	26 45N	83 23E
81	Göteborg, *Sweden*	57 45N	12 0E
81	Gotland, *i., Sweden*	57 30N	18 30E
82	Göttingen, *Germany*	51 32N	9 57E
80	Gouda, *Neth.*	52 1N	4 43E
75	Gough I., *Atlantic Oc.*	40 20S	10 0W
74	Governador Valadares, *Brazil*	18 51S	42 0W
84	Gozo, *i., Malta*	36 3N	14 16E
79	Grampian Highlands, *U.K.*	56 55N	4 0W
75	Gran Canaria, *i., Canary Is.*	28 0N	15 30W
72	Gran Chaco, *f., S. America*	22 0S	60 0W
84	Granada, *Spain*	37 10N	3 35W
65	Grand Bahama I., *Bahamas*	26 35N	78 0W
63	Grand Canyon, *f., U.S.A.*	36 10N	112 45W
65	Grand Cayman, *i., Cayman Is.*	19 20N	81 30W
60	Grand Forks, *U.S.A.*	47 55N	97 3W
60	Grand Island, *town, U.S.A.*	40 55N	98 21W
58	Grand Rapids, *town, U.S.A.*	42 57N	85 40W
62	Grand Teton, *mtn., U.S.A.*	43 44N	110 48W
52	Grande Prairie, *town, Canada*	55 10N	118 52W
60	Granite City, *U.S.A.*	38 43N	90 4W
82	Graz, *Austria*	47 5N	15 22E
65	Great Abaco I., *Bahamas*	26 30N	77 0W
110	Great Artesian Basin, *f., Australia*	26 30S	143 2E
110	Great Australian Bight, *Australia*	33 20S	130 0E
110	Great Barrier Reef, *f., Australia*	16 30S	146 30E
62	Great Basin, *f., U.S.A.*	40 35N	116 0W
52	Great Bear L., *Canada*	66 0N	120 0W
110	Great Dividing Range, *mts., Australia*	29 0S	152 0E
62	Great Falls, *town, U.S.A.*	47 30N	111 17W
65	Great Inagua I., *Bahamas*	21 0N	73 20W
12	Great Lakes, *N. America*	47 0N	83 0W
50	Great Plains, *f., N. America*	45 0N	107 0W
104	Great Rift Valley, *f., Africa*	7 0S	33 0E
62	Great Salt L., *U.S.A.*	41 10N	112 30W
62	Great Salt Lake Desert, *U.S.A.*	40 40N	113 30W
110	Great Sandy Desert, *Australia*	22 0S	125 0E
52	Great Slave L., *Canada*	61 30N	114 20W
110	Great Victoria Desert, *Australia*	29 0S	127 30E
66	Greater Antilles, *is., C. America*	17 0N	70 0W
85	Greece, *Europe*	39 0N	22 0E
62	Greeley, *U.S.A.*	40 25N	104 42W
62	Green, *r., U.S.A.*	38 11N	109 53W
60	Green Bay, *town, U.S.A.*	44 30N	88 1W
53	Greenland, *N. America*	68 0N	45 0W
79	Greenock, *U.K.*	55 57N	4 45W
59	Greensboro, *U.S.A.*	36 4N	79 47W
61	Greenville, *Miss., U.S.A.*	33 25N	91 5W
59	Greenville, *N.C., U.S.A.*	35 36N	77 23W
59	Greenville, *S.C., U.S.A.*	34 52N	82 25W
67	Grenada, *C. America*	12 15N	61 45W
82	Grenoble, *France*	45 11N	5 43E
110	Grey Range, *mts., Australia*	28 30S	142 15E
111	Greymouth, *New Zealand*	42 28S	171 12E
83	Grodno, *Belorussia*	53 40N	23 50E
80	Groningen, *Neth.*	53 13N	6 35E
110	Groote Eylandt, *i., Australia*	14 0S	136 30E
87	Groznyy, *Russian Fed.*	43 21N	45 42E
64	Guadalajara, *Mexico*	20 30N	103 20W
84	Guadalquivir, *r., Spain*	36 50N	6 20W
67	Guadeloupe, *C. America*	16 20N	61 40W
84	Guadiana, *r., Portugal*	37 10N	7 24W
56	Guam, *i., Mariana Is.*	13 30N	144 40E
99	Guangzhou, *China*	23 20N	113 30E
65	Guantánamo, *Cuba*	20 9N	75 14W
72	Guaporé, *r., Bolivia/Brazil*	12 0S	65 15W
64	Guatemala, *C. America*	15 40N	90 0W
64	Guatemala City, *Guatemala*	14 38N	90 22W
70	Guayaquil, *Ecuador*	2 13S	79 54W
70	Guiana Highlands, *S. America*	4 0N	59 0W
99	Guilin, *China*	25 21N	110 11E
106	Guinea, *Africa*	10 30N	10 30W
106	Guinea Bissau, *Africa*	12 0N	15 30W
106	Guinea, G. of, *Africa*	2 0N	1 0W
98	Guiyang, *China*	26 35N	106 40E
96	Gujranwala, *Pakistan*	32 6N	74 11E
96	Gujrat, *Pakistan*	32 35N	74 6E
96	Gulbarga, *India*	17 22N	76 47E
97	Guntur, *India*	16 20N	80 27E
87	Guryev, *Kazakhstan*	47 8N	51 59E
70	Guyana, *S. America*	4 40N	59 0W
97	Gwalior, *India*	26 12N	78 9E
108	Gweru, *Zimbabwe*	19 25S	29 50E
95	Gyandzha, *Azerbaijan*	40 39N	46 20E
83	Györ, *Hungary*	47 41N	17 40E

H

PAGE	PLACENAME	LATITUDE	LONGITUDE
80	Haarlem, *Neth.*	52 22N	4 38E
100	Hachinohe, *Japan*	40 30N	141 30E
100	Haeju, *N. Korea*	38 4N	125 40E
81	Hafnarfjördhur, *town, Iceland*	64 4N	21 58W
80	Hagen, *Germany*	51 22N	7 27E
58	Hagerstown, *U.S.A.*	39 39N	77 43W
94	Haifa, *Israel*	32 49N	34 59E
99	Haikou, *China*	20 5N	110 25E
94	Hail, *Saudi Arabia*	27 31N	41 45E
99	Hailar, *China*	49 15N	119 41E
99	Hainan, *i., China*	18 30N	109 40E
102	Haiphong, *Vietnam*	20 58N	106 41E
65	Haiti, *C. America*	19 0N	73 0W
100	Hakodate, *Japan*	41 46N	140 44E
53	Halifax, *Canada*	44 38N	63 35W
82	Halle, *Germany*	51 28N	11 58E
103	Halmahera, *i., Indonesia*	0 45N	128 0E
81	Hälsingborg, *Sweden*	56 5N	12 45E
94	Hama, *Syria*	35 9N	36 44E
95	Hamadān, *Iran*	34 47N	48 33E
100	Hamamatsu, *Japan*	34 42N	137 42E
82	Hamburg, *Germany*	53 33N	10 0E
100	Hamhung, *N. Korea*	39 54N	127 35E
75	Hamilton, *Bermuda*	32 18N	64 48W
58	Hamilton, *Canada*	43 15N	79 50W
111	Hamilton, *New Zealand*	37 46S	175 18E
80	Hamm, *Germany*	51 40N	7 49E
81	Hammerfest, *Norway*	70 40N	23 44E
59	Hampton, *U.S.A.*	37 2N	76 23W
99	Hangzhou, *China*	30 10N	120 7E
82	Hannover, *Germany*	52 23N	9 44E
102	Hanoi, *Vietnam*	21 1N	105 52E
108	Harare, *Zimbabwe*	17 43S	31 5E
99	Harbin, *China*	45 45N	126 41E
81	Hardangerfjorden, *est., Norway*	60 15N	6 25E
80	Harlingen, *Neth.*	53 10N	5 25E
61	Harlingen, *U.S.A.*	26 11N	97 42W
62	Harney Basin, *f., U.S.A.*	43 15N	120 40W
58	Harrisburg, *U.S.A.*	40 35N	76 59W
58	Hartford, *U.S.A.*	41 40N	72 51W
60	Harvey, *U.S.A.*	41 37N	87 39W
79	Harwich, *U.K.*	51 56N	1 18E
111	Hastings, *New Zealand*	39 39S	176 52E
59	Hatteras, C., *U.S.A.*	35 13N	75 32W
61	Hattiesburg, *U.S.A.*	31 19N	89 16W
65	Havana, *Cuba*	23 7N	82 25W
57	Hawaii, *d., U.S.A.*	21 0N	156 0W
111	Hawke B., *New Zealand*	39 18S	177 15E
52	Hay River, *town, Canada*	60 51N	115 42W
91	Heard I., *Indian Oc.*	53 0S	74 0E
80	Heerlen, *Neth.*	50 53N	5 59E
99	Hefei, *China*	31 55N	117 18E
99	Hegang, *China*	47 36N	130 30E
82	Heidelberg, *Germany*	49 25N	8 42E
82	Heilbronn, *Germany*	49 8N	9 14E
81	Hekla, Mt., *Iceland*	64 0N	19 45W
82	Heligoland B., *Germany*	54 0N	8 15E
80	Helmond, *Neth.*	51 28N	5 40E
81	Helsingör, *Denmark*	56 3N	12 38E
81	Helsinki, *Finland*	60 8N	25 0E
99	Henan, *d., China*	33 45N	113 0E
99	Hengyang, *China*	26 58N	112 31E
97	Henzada, *Myanmar*	17 38N	95 35E
95	Herat, *Afghan.*	34 21N	62 10E
63	Hermosillo, *Mexico*	29 4N	110 58W
80	Herne, *Germany*	51 32N	7 12E
81	Herning, *Denmark*	56 8N	9 0E
59	Hickory, *U.S.A.*	35 44N	81 23W
100	Higashiosaka, *Japan*	34 34N	135 45E
84	High Atlas, *mts., Morocco*	31 30N	6 0W
59	High Point, *town, U.S.A.*	35 58N	80 0W
82	Hildesheim, *Germany*	52 9N	9 58E
57	Hilo, *U.S.A.*	19 42N	155 4W
80	Hilversum, *Neth.*	52 14N	5 12E
97	Himalaya, *mts., Asia*	29 0N	84 0E
100	Himeji, *Japan*	34 50N	134 40E
96	Hindu Kush, *mts., Asia*	36 40N	70 0E
100	Hiroshima, *Japan*	34 30N	132 27E
65	Hispaniola, *i., C. America*	19 0N	71 0W
102	Ho Chi Minh City, *Vietnam*	10 46N	106 43E
110	Hobart, *Australia*	42 54S	147 18E
107	Hodeida, *Yemen*	14 50N	42 58E
95	Hofuf, *Saudi Arabia*	25 20N	49 34E
99	Hohhot, *China*	40 49N	111 37E
100	Hokkaido, *i., Japan*	43 0N	144 0E
65	Holguín, *Cuba*	20 54N	76 15W
79	Holyhead, *U.K.*	53 18N	4 38W
94	Homs, *Syria*	34 44N	36 43E
65	Honduras, *C. America*	14 30N	87 0W
65	Honduras, G. of, *Carib. Sea*	16 20N	87 30W
99	Hong Kong, *Asia*	22 30N	114 10E
57	Honolulu, *U.S.A.*	21 19N	157 50W
100	Honshu, *i., Japan*	36 0N	138 0E

PAGE	PLACENAME	LATITUDE	LONGITUDE
62	Hood, Mt., *U.S.A.*	45 23 N	121 41 W
80	Hoorn, *Neth.*	52 38 N	5 3 E
63	Hoover Dam, *U.S.A.*	36 0 N	114 27 W
95	Hormuz, Str. of, *Asia*	26 35 N	56 20 E
73	Horn, C., *S. America*	56 0 S	67 16 W
84	Hospitalet, *Spain*	41 20 N	2 6 E
61	Hot Springs, *town, U.S.A.*	34 30 N	93 2 W
98	Hotan, *China*	37 7 N	79 57 E
61	Houma, *U.S.A.*	29 36 N	90 43 W
61	Houston, *U.S.A.*	29 46 N	95 22 W
98	Hovd, *Mongolia*	48 0 N	91 45 E
82	Hradec Králové, *Czech Rep.*	50 13 N	15 50 E
83	Hron, *r., Slovakia*	47 49 N	18 45 E
99	Huainan, *China*	32 41 N	117 6 E
99	Huaiyan, *China*	33 31 N	119 10 E
108	Huambo, *Angola*	12 47 S	15 44 E
70	Huancayo, *Peru*	12 5 S	75 12 W
99	Huang He, *r., China*	37 55 N	118 46 E
99	Huangshi, *China*	30 13 N	115 5 E
70	Huanta, *Peru*	12 54 S	74 13 W
70	Huánuco, *Peru*	9 55 S	76 11 W
96	Hubli, *India*	15 20 N	75 14 E
79	Huddersfield, *U.K.*	53 38 N	1 49 W
58	Hudson, *r., U.S.A.*	40 45 N	74 0 W
53	Hudson B., *Canada*	58 0 N	86 0 W
53	Hudson Str., *Canada*	62 0 N	70 0 W
102	Hué, *Vietnam*	16 28 N	107 35 E
84	Huelva, *Spain*	37 15 N	6 56 W
110	Hughenden, *Australia*	20 50 S	144 10 E
79	Humber, *r., U.K.*	53 40 N	0 12 W
62	Humboldt, *r., U.S.A.*	40 2 N	118 31 W
81	Húnaflói, *b., Iceland*	65 45 N	20 50 W
83	Hungary, *Europe*	47 30 N	19 0 E
100	Hungnam, *N. Korea*	39 49 N	127 40 E
59	Huntington, *U.S.A.*	38 25 N	82 26 W
63	Huntington Beach, *town, U.S.A.*	33 39 N	118 1 W
59	Huntsville, *U.S.A.*	34 44 N	86 35 W
58	Huron, L., *Canada/U.S.A.*	45 0 N	82 30 W
81	Húsavík, *Iceland*	66 3 N	17 17 W
61	Hutchinson, *U.S.A.*	38 5 N	97 56 W
97	Hyderabad, *India*	17 22 N	78 26 E
96	Hyderabad, *Pakistan*	25 23 N	68 24 E

I

PAGE	PLACENAME	LATITUDE	LONGITUDE
83	Iaşi, *Romania*	47 9 N	27 38 E
106	Ibadan, *Nigeria*	7 23 N	3 56 E
70	Ibagué, *Colombia*	4 25 N	75 20 W
84	Ibiza, *i., Spain*	39 0 N	1 23 E
70	Ica, *Peru*	14 2 S	75 48 W
81	Iceland, *Europe*	64 45 N	18 0 W
100	Ichinomiya, *Japan*	35 18 N	136 48 E
62	Idaho, *d., U.S.A.*	44 58 N	115 56 W
62	Idaho Falls, *town, U.S.A.*	43 30 N	112 2 W
80	IJsselmeer, *l., Neth.*	52 45 N	5 20 E
71	Ilhéus, *Brazil*	14 50 S	39 6 W
101	Iligan, *Phil.*	8 15 N	124 15 E
60	Illinois, *d., U.S.A.*	40 30 N	89 30 W
101	Iloilo, *Phil.*	10 45 N	122 32 E
106	Ilorin, *Nigeria*	8 32 N	4 34 E
97	Imphal, *India*	24 47 N	93 55 E
100	Inchon, *S. Korea*	37 30 N	126 38 E
60	Independence, *U.S.A.*	39 5 N	94 24 W
97	India, *Asia*	23 0 N	78 30 E
91	Indian Ocean,		
58	Indiana, *d., U.S.A.*	40 0 N	86 15 W
58	Indianapolis, *U.S.A.*	39 45 N	86 10 W
102	Indonesia, *Asia*	6 0 S	118 0 E
96	Indore, *India*	22 42 N	75 54 E
96	Indus, *r., Pakistan*	24 0 N	67 33 E
82	Inn, *r., Europe*	48 33 N	13 26 E
79	Inner Hebrides, *is., U.K.*	56 50 N	6 45 W
82	Innsbruck, *Austria*	47 17 N	11 25 E
82	Interlaken, *Switz.*	46 42 N	7 52 E
52	Inuvik, *d., Canada*	65 0 N	128 0 W
111	Invercargill, *New Zealand*	46 26 S	168 21 E
79	Inverness, *U.K.*	57 27 N	4 15 W
85	Ionian Sea, *Med. Sea*	38 30 N	18 45 E
60	Iowa, *d., U.S.A.*	42 0 N	93 30 W
60	Iowa City, *U.S.A.*	41 40 N	91 32 W
102	Ipoh, *Malaysia*	4 36 N	101 2 E
79	Ipswich, *U.K.*	52 4 N	1 9 E
72	Iquique, *Chile*	20 13 S	70 10 W
70	Iquitos, *Peru*	3 51 S	73 13 W
85	Iráklion, *Greece*	35 20 N	25 8 E
95	Iran, *Asia*	32 0 N	54 30 E
64	Irapuato, *Mexico*	20 40 N	101 40 W
94	Iraq, *Asia*	33 0 N	44 0 E
103	Irian, Teluk, *b., Indonesia*	2 30 S	135 20 E
101	Iriga, *Phil.*	13 26 N	123 24 E
108	Iringa, *Tanzania*	7 49 S	35 39 E
79	Irish Sea, *U.K./Rep. of Ire.*	53 40 N	4 30 W
98	Irkutsk, *Russian Fed.*	52 18 N	104 15 E
97	Irrawaddy, *r., Myanmar*	17 45 N	95 25 E
88	Irtysh, *r., Asia*	61 0 N	68 40 E
81	Ísafjördhur, *Iceland*	66 5 N	23 6 W
95	Isfahan, *Iran*	32 42 N	51 40 E
88	Ishim, *r., Asia*	57 50 N	71 0 E
94	Iskenderun, *Turkey*	36 37 N	36 8 E
96	Islamabad, *Pakistan*	33 40 N	73 8 E
94	Ismâ'ilîya, *Egypt*	30 36 N	32 15 E
94	Israel, *Asia*	32 0 N	34 50 E
94	Istanbul, *Turkey*	41 2 N	28 58 E
102	Isthmus of Kra, *Thailand*	9 40 N	99 30 E
71	Itabuna, *Brazil*	14 48 S	39 18 W
84	Italy, *Europe*	43 0 N	12 0 E
83	Ivano-Frankovsk, *Ukraine*	48 55 N	24 42 E
86	Ivanovo, *Russian Fed.*	57 0 N	41 0 E
53	Ivigtut, *Greenland*	61 10 N	48 0 W
100	Iwaki, *Japan*	36 58 N	140 58 E
86	Izhevsk, *Russian Fed.*	56 49 N	53 11 E
94	Izmir, *Turkey*	38 24 N	27 9 E

J

PAGE	PLACENAME	LATITUDE	LONGITUDE
97	Jabalpur, *India*	23 10 N	79 59 E
58	Jackson, *Mich., U.S.A.*	42 15 N	84 24 W
61	Jackson, *Miss., U.S.A.*	32 18 N	90 12 W
61	Jackson, *Tenn., U.S.A.*	35 37 N	88 49 W
59	Jacksonville, *Fla., U.S.A.*	30 20 N	81 40 W
59	Jacksonville, *N.C., U.S.A.*	34 45 N	77 26 W
97	Jaffna, *Sri Lanka*	9 38 N	80 2 E
96	Jaipur, *India*	26 53 N	75 50 E
102	Jakarta, *Indonesia*	6 8 S	106 45 E
64	Jalapa, *Mexico*	19 45 N	96 48 W
112	Jaluit, *i., Pacific Oc.*	6 0 N	169 35 E
65	Jamaica, *C. America*	18 0 N	77 0 W
102	Jambi, *Indonesia*	1 36 S	103 39 E
60	James, *r., U.S.A.*	42 55 N	97 28 W
53	James B., *Canada*	53 0 N	80 0 W
58	Jamestown, *U.S.A.*	42 6 N	79 14 W
96	Jammu, *Jammu & Kashmir*	32 44 N	74 52 E
96	Jammu & Kashmir, *Asia*	33 30 N	76 0 E
96	Jamnagar, *India*	22 28 N	70 6 E
97	Jamshedpur, *India*	22 47 N	86 12 E
60	Janesville, *U.S.A.*	42 42 N	89 2 W
100	Japan, *Asia*	36 0 N	138 0 E
99	Japan, Sea of, *Asia*	40 0 N	135 0 E
70	Japurá, *r., Brazil*	3 0 S	64 50 W
102	Java, *i., Indonesia*	7 30 S	110 0 E
102	Java Sea, *Indonesia*	5 0 S	111 0 E
60	Jefferson City, *U.S.A.*	38 34 N	92 10 W
82	Jena, *Germany*	50 56 N	11 35 E
84	Jerez de la Frontera, *Spain*	36 41 N	6 8 W
59	Jersey City, *U.S.A.*	40 40 N	74 4 W
94	Jerusalem, *Israel/Jordan*	31 47 N	35 13 E
97	Jhansi, *India*	25 27 N	78 34 E
96	Jhelum, *r., Pakistan*	31 4 N	72 10 E
99	Jiamusi, *China*	46 50 N	130 21 E
99	Ji'an, *China*	27 8 N	115 0 E
99	Jiayi, *Taiwan*	23 38 N	120 27 E
107	Jiddah, *Saudi Arabia*	21 30 N	39 10 E
99	Jilin, *China*	43 53 N	126 35 E
99	Jilong, *Taiwan*	25 10 N	121 43 E
107	Jimma, *Ethiopia*	7 39 N	36 47 E
99	Jinan, *China*	36 50 N	117 0 E
108	Jinja, *Uganda*	0 27 N	33 14 E
99	Jinzhou, *China*	41 7 N	121 6 E
99	Jixi, *China*	45 17 N	131 0 E
71	João Pessoa, *Brazil*	7 6 S	34 53 W
96	Jodhpur, *India*	26 18 N	73 8 E
108	Johannesburg, *South Africa*	26 10 S	28 2 E
59	Johnson City, *U.S.A.*	36 20 N	82 23 W
58	Johnstown, *U.S.A.*	40 20 N	78 55 W
102	Johor Bahru, *Malaysia*	1 29 N	103 40 E
60	Joliet, *U.S.A.*	41 32 N	88 5 W
61	Jonesboro, *U.S.A.*	35 50 N	90 42 W
81	Jönköping, *Sweden*	57 45 N	14 10 E
61	Joplin, *U.S.A.*	37 6 N	94 31 W
94	Jordan, *Asia*	31 0 N	36 0 E
62	Jordan, *Mont., U.S.A.*	47 19 N	106 55 W
106	Jos, *Nigeria*	9 54 N	8 53 E
110	Joseph Bonaparte G., *Australia*	14 0 S	128 30 E
81	Jotunheimen, *mts., Norway*	61 30 N	9 0 E
62	Juan de Fuca, Str. of, *Canada/U.S.A.*	48 15 N	124 0 W
71	Juàzeiro do Norte, *Brazil*	7 10 S	39 18 W
107	Juba, *r., Somalia*	0 20 S	42 53 E
74	Juiz de Fora, *Brazil*	21 47 S	43 23 W
96	Jullundur, *India*	31 18 N	75 40 E
74	Jundiaí, *Brazil*	23 10 S	46 54 W
57	Juneau, *U.S.A.*	58 20 N	134 20 W
82	Jungfrau, *mtn., Switz.*	46 30 N	8 0 E
98	Junggar Pendi, *f., Asia*	44 20 N	86 30 E
82	Jura Mts., *Europe*	46 55 N	6 45 E
70	Juruá, *r., Brazil*	2 33 S	65 50 W
81	Jyväskylä, *Finland*	62 16 N	25 50 E

K

PAGE	PLACENAME	LATITUDE	LONGITUDE
96	Kabul, *Afghan.*	34 30 N	69 10 E
108	Kabwe, *Zambia*	14 29 S	28 25 E
106	Kaduna, *Nigeria*	10 28 N	7 25 E
100	Kaesong, *N. Korea*	37 59 N	126 30 E
100	Kagoshima, *Japan*	31 37 N	130 32 E
80	Kaiserslautern, *Germany*	49 27 N	7 47 E
81	Kajaani, *Finland*	64 14 N	27 37 E
97	Kakinada, *India*	16 59 N	82 20 E
108	Kalahari Desert, *Botswana*	23 55 S	23 0 E
58	Kalamazoo, *U.S.A.*	42 17 N	85 36 W
108	Kalemie, *Zaïre*	5 57 S	29 10 E
110	Kalgoorlie, *Australia*	30 49 S	121 29 E
102	Kalimantan, *d., Indonesia*	1 0 S	113 0 E
83	Kaliningrad, *Russian Fed.*	54 40 N	20 30 E
86	Kaluga, *Russian Fed.*	54 31 N	36 16 E
89	Kamchatka Pen., *Russian Fed.*	56 0 N	160 0 E
88	Kamensk-Ural'skiy, *Russian Fed.*	56 29 N	61 49 E
108	Kamina, *Zaïre*	8 46 S	25 0 E
52	Kamloops, *Canada*	50 39 N	120 24 W
108	Kampala, *Uganda*	0 19 N	32 35 E
108	Kananga, *Zaïre*	5 53 S	22 26 E
100	Kanazawa, *Japan*	36 35 N	136 40 E
97	Kanchenjunga, *mtn., Asia*	27 44 N	88 11 E
96	Kandahar, *Afghan.*	31 36 N	65 47 E
97	Kandy, *Sri Lanka*	7 18 N	80 43 E
110	Kangaroo I., *Australia*	35 45 S	137 30 E
86	Kanin Pen., *Russian Fed.*	68 0 N	45 0 E
60	Kankakee, *U.S.A.*	41 8 N	87 52 W
106	Kankan, *Guinea*	10 22 N	9 11 W
59	Kannapolis, *U.S.A.*	35 30 N	80 36 W
106	Kano, *Nigeria*	12 0 N	8 31 E
97	Kanpur, *India*	26 27 N	80 14 E
60	Kansas, *d., U.S.A.*	38 30 N	99 0 W
60	Kansas City, *U.S.A.*	39 7 N	94 39 W
89	Kansk, *Russian Fed.*	56 11 N	95 20 E
106	Kaolack, *Senegal*	14 9 N	16 4 W
95	Kara Bogaz Gol B., *Turkmenistan*	41 20 N	53 40 E
95	Kara Kum, *des., Turkmenistan*	38 45 N	58 0 E
88	Kara Sea, *Russian Fed.*	73 0 N	65 0 E
96	Karachi, *Pakistan*	24 51 N	67 2 E
88	Karaganda, *Kazakhstan*	49 53 N	73 7 E
96	Karakoram Range, *mts., Jammu & Kashmir*	35 30 N	76 30 E
81	Karlskrona, *Sweden*	56 10 N	15 35 E
82	Karlsruhe, *Germany*	49 0 N	8 24 E
81	Karlstad, *Sweden*	59 24 N	13 32 E
88	Karsakpay, *Kazakhstan*	47 47 N	66 43 E
98	Kashi, *China*	39 29 N	76 2 E
107	Kassala, *Sudan*	15 24 N	36 30 E
82	Kassel, *Germany*	51 18 N	9 30 E
97	Kathmandu, *Nepal*	27 42 N	85 19 E
83	Katowice, *Poland*	50 15 N	18 59 E
106	Katsina, *Nigeria*	13 0 N	7 32 E
81	Kattegat, *str., Denmark/Sweden*	57 0 N	11 20 E
57	Kauai, *i., U.S.A.*	22 5 N	159 30 W
81	Kaunas, *Lithuania*	54 52 N	23 55 E
100	Kawagoe, *Japan*	35 58 N	139 30 E
100	Kawasaki, *Japan*	35 30 N	139 45 E
106	Kayes, *Mali*	14 26 N	11 28 W
94	Kayseri, *Turkey*	38 42 N	35 28 E
88	Kazakhstan, *Asia*	49 0 N	64 0 E
86	Kazan, *Russian Fed.*	55 45 N	49 10 E
102	Kediri, *Indonesia*	7 55 S	112 1 E
53	Keewatin, *d., Canada*	65 0 N	90 0 W
85	Kefallinía, *i., Greece*	38 15 N	20 33 E
81	Keflavík, *Iceland*	64 1 N	22 35 W
62	Kelowna, *Canada*	49 50 N	119 29 W
88	Kemerovo, *Russian Fed.*	55 25 N	86 10 E
81	Kemi, *r., Finland*	65 47 N	24 28 E
84	Kenitra, *Morocco*	34 20 N	6 34 W
60	Kenora, *Canada*	49 47 N	94 26 W
60	Kenosha, *U.S.A.*	42 35 N	87 49 W
59	Kentucky, *d., U.S.A.*	37 30 N	85 15 W
108	Kenya, *Africa*	0 0 0	38 0 E
96	Kerala, *d., India*	10 30 N	76 30 E
82	Kerch, *Ukraine*	45 22 N	36 27 E
91	Kerguelen, *i., Indian Oc.*	49 30 S	69 30 E
95	Kermān, *Iran*	30 18 N	57 5 E
95	Kermānshāh, *Iran*	34 19 N	47 4 E
57	Ketchikan, *U.S.A.*	55 25 N	131 40 W
58	Keweenaw Pen., *U.S.A.*	47 10 N	88 30 W
99	Khabarovsk, *Russian Fed.*	48 32 N	135 8 E
97	Kharagpur, *India*	22 23 N	87 22 E
87	Kharkov, *Ukraine*	50 0 N	36 15 E
107	Khartoum, *Sudan*	15 33 N	32 35 E
87	Kherson, *Ukraine*	46 39 N	32 38 E
85	Khios, *i., Greece*	38 23 N	26 4 E
98	Khöbsögöl Dalai, *l., Mongolia*	51 0 N	100 30 E
95	Khorramabad, *Iran*	33 29 N	48 21 E
95	Khorramshahr, *Iran*	30 26 N	48 9 E
84	Khouribga, *Morocco*	32 54 N	6 57 W
97	Khulna, *Bangla.*	22 49 N	89 34 E
82	Kiel, *Germany*	54 20 N	10 8 E
83	Kielce, *Poland*	50 52 N	20 37 E
83	Kiev, *Ukraine*	50 28 N	30 29 E
108	Kigali, *Rwanda*	1 59 S	30 5 E
108	Kigoma, *Tanzania*	4 52 S	29 36 E
108	Kikwit, *Zaïre*	5 2 S	18 51 E
108	Kilimanjaro, *mtn., Tanzania*	3 2 S	37 20 E

PAGE	PLACENAME	LATITUDE	LONGITUDE
79	Killarney, Rep. of Ire.	52 4 N	9 32 W
61	Killeen, U.S.A.	31 8 N	97 44 W
108	Kimberley, South Africa	28 45 S	24 46 E
110	Kimberley Plateau, Australia	17 20 S	127 20 E
108	Kindu, Zaïre	3 0 S	25 56 E
110	King I., Australia	39 50 S	144 0 E
59	Kingsport, U.S.A.	36 33 N	82 34 W
58	Kingston, Canada	44 14 N	76 30 W
65	Kingston, Jamaica	17 58 N	76 48 W
79	Kingston upon Hull, U.K.	53 45 N	0 20 W
65	Kingstown, St. Vincent	13 12 N	61 14 W
61	Kingsville, U.S.A.	27 31 N	97 52 W
108	Kinshasa, Zaïre	4 18 S	15 18 E
89	Kirensk, Russian Fed.	57 45 N	108 0 E
98	Kirghizia, Asia	41 30 N	75 0 E
88	Kirgiz Steppe, f., Kazakhstan	50 0 N	57 10 E
112	Kiribati, Pacific Oc.	4 0 S	175 0 E
95	Kirkuk, Iraq	35 28 N	44 26 E
86	Kirov, Russian Fed.	58 38 N	49 38 E
87	Kirovograd, Ukraine	48 31 N	32 15 E
81	Kiruna, Sweden	67 53 N	20 15 E
108	Kisangani, Zaïre	0 33 N	25 14 E
83	Kishinev, Moldavia	47 0 N	28 50 E
107	Kismayu, Somalia	0 25 S	42 31 E
108	Kisumu, Kenya	0 3 S	34 47 E
100	Kitakyushu, Japan	33 50 N	130 50 E
58	Kitchener, Canada	43 27 N	80 30 W
53	Kitikmeot, d., Canada	71 0 N	105 0 W
52	Kitimat, Canada	54 5 N	128 38 W
108	Kitwe, Zambia	12 48 S	28 14 E
82	Klagenfurt, Austria	46 38 N	14 20 E
62	Klamath Mts., U.S.A.	41 40 N	123 20 W
59	Knoxville, U.S.A.	36 0 N	83 57 W
100	Kobe, Japan	34 42 N	135 15 E
80	Koblenz, Germany	50 21 N	7 36 E
57	Kodiak I., U.S.A.	57 0 N	153 50 W
98	Kokand, Uzbekistan	40 33 N	70 55 E
88	Kokchetav, Kazakhstan	53 18 N	69 25 E
81	Kokkola, Finland	63 50 N	23 10 E
58	Kokomo, U.S.A.	40 30 N	86 9 W
86	Kola Pen., Russian Fed.	67 0 N	38 0 E
86	Kolomna, Russian Fed.	55 5 N	38 45 E
89	Kolyma, r., Russian Fed.	68 50 N	161 0 E
89	Kolyma Range, mts., Russian Fed.	63 0 N	160 0 E
98	Kommunizma, Peak, mtn., Tajikistan	38 39 N	72 1 E
89	Komsomolets, i., Russian Fed.	80 20 N	96 0 E
89	Komsomolsk-na-Amur, Russian Fed.	50 32 N	136 59 E
94	Konya, Turkey	37 51 N	32 30 E
100	Korea Str., Japan/S. Korea	35 5 N	129 20 E
100	Kōriyama, Japan	37 23 N	140 22 E
56	Koror, i., Palau	7 30 N	134 30 E
89	Koryak Range, mts., Russian Fed.	62 20 N	171 0 E
110	Kosciusko, Mt., Australia	36 28 S	148 17 E
83	Koăice, Slovakia	48 44 N	21 15 E
86	Kostroma, Russian Fed.	57 46 N	40 59 E
96	Kota, India	25 11 N	75 58 E
102	Kota Bharu, Malaysia	6 7 N	102 15 E
102	Kota Kinabalu, Malaysia	5 59 N	116 4 E
81	Kotka, Finland	60 26 N	26 55 E
99	Kowloon, Hong Kong	22 20 N	114 15 E
83	Kragujevac, Yugo.	44 1 N	20 55 E
87	Krasnodar, Russian Fed.	45 2 N	39 0 E
95	Krasnovodsk, Turkmenistan	40 1 N	53 0 E
89	Krasnoyarsk, Russian Fed.	56 5 N	92 46 E
80	Krefeld, Germany	51 20 N	6 32 E
87	Kremenchug, Ukraine	49 3 N	33 25 E
97	Krishna, r., India	16 0 N	81 0 E
81	Kristiansand, Norway	58 8 N	7 59 E
87	Krivoy Rog, Ukraine	47 55 N	33 24 E
108	Kroonstad, South Africa	27 40 S	27 15 E
102	Kuala Lumpur, Malaysia	3 8 N	101 42 E
102	Kuala Trengganu, Malaysia	5 10 N	103 10 E
102	Kuantan, Malaysia	3 50 N	103 19 E
102	Kuching, Malaysia	1 32 N	110 20 E
100	Kumamoto, Japan	32 50 N	130 42 E
106	Kumasi, Ghana	6 45 N	1 35 W
95	Kumayri, Armenia	40 47 N	43 49 E
98	Kunlun Shan, mts., China	36 40 N	88 0 E
98	Kunming, China	25 4 N	102 41 E
81	Kuopio, Finland	62 51 N	27 30 E
95	Kura, r., Asia	39 18 N	49 22 E
100	Kurashiki, Japan	34 36 N	133 43 E
100	Kure, Japan	34 20 N	132 40 E
88	Kurgan, Russian Fed.	55 20 N	65 20 E
96	Kuria Muria Is., Oman	17 30 N	56 0 E
89	Kuril Is., Russian Fed.	46 0 N	150 30 E
97	Kurnool, India	15 51 N	78 1 E
87	Kursk, Russian Fed.	51 45 N	36 14 E
100	Kurume, Japan	33 20 N	130 29 E
100	Kushiro, Japan	42 58 N	144 24 E
88	Kustanay, Kazakhstan	53 15 N	63 40 E
87	Kutaisi, Georgia	42 15 N	42 44 E
95	Kuwait, Asia	29 20 N	47 40 E
95	Kuwait, town, Kuwait	29 20 N	48 0 E
100	Kwangju, S. Korea	35 7 N	126 52 E
100	Kyoto, Japan	35 4 N	135 50 E
100	Kyushu, i., Japan	32 0 N	130 0 E
88	Kzyl Orda, Kazakhstan	44 52 N	65 28 E

L

PAGE	PLACENAME	LATITUDE	LONGITUDE
84	La Coruña, Spain	43 22 N	8 24 W
60	La Crosse, U.S.A.	43 48 N	91 15 W
80	La Louvière, Belgium	50 29 N	4 11 E
72	La Paz, d., Bolivia	16 0 S	68 10 W
89	La Perouse Str., Russian Fed.	45 50 N	142 30 E
73	La Plata, Argentina	34 58 S	57 55 W
73	La Plata, Río de, est., Argentina/Uruguay	35 15 S	56 46 W
82	La Spezia, Italy	44 7 N	9 49 E
106	Laayoune, W. Sahara	27 10 N	13 11 W
106	Labé, Guinea	11 17 N	12 11 W
53	Labrador, f., Canada	54 0 N	61 30 W
53	Labrador City, Canada	52 54 N	66 50 W
86	Ladoga, L., Russian Fed.	61 0 N	32 0 E
58	Lafayette, Ind., U.S.A.	40 25 N	86 54 W
61	Lafayette, La., U.S.A.	30 14 N	92 1 W
106	Lagos, Nigeria	6 27 N	3 28 E
96	Lahore, Pakistan	31 34 N	74 22 E
81	Lahti, Finland	61 0 N	25 40 E
61	Lake Charles, town, U.S.A.	30 13 N	93 12 W
59	Lakeland, town, U.S.A.	28 2 N	81 59 W
58	Lakewood, U.S.A.	41 29 N	81 48 W
96	Lakshadweep Is., Indian Oc.	11 0 N	72 0 E
59	Lancaster, U.S.A.	40 2 N	76 19 W
53	Lancaster Sd., Canada	74 0 N	85 0 W
79	Land's End, c., U.K.	50 3 N	5 45 W
58	Lansing, U.S.A.	42 44 N	84 34 W
98	Lanzhou, China	36 1 N	103 45 E
102	Laos, Asia	19 0 N	104 0 E
81	Lapland, f., Sweden/Finland	68 10 N	24 0 E
89	Laptev Sea, Russian Fed.	74 30 N	125 0 E
62	Laramie Mts., U.S.A.	42 0 N	105 40 W
61	Laredo, U.S.A.	27 31 N	99 30 W
63	Las Cruces, U.S.A.	32 23 N	106 29 W
75	Las Palmas de Gran Canaria, Canary Is.	28 8 N	15 27 W
63	Las Vegas, U.S.A.	36 11 N	115 8 W
94	Latakia, Syria	35 31 N	35 47 E
81	Latvia, Europe	57 0 N	25 0 E
110	Launceston, Australia	41 25 S	147 7 E
82	Lausanne, Switz.	46 32 N	6 39 E
60	Lawrence, U.S.A.	38 58 N	95 14 W
61	Lawton, U.S.A.	34 37 N	98 25 W
84	Le Havre, France	49 30 N	0 6 E
84	Le Mans, France	48 1 N	0 10 E
60	Leavenworth, U.S.A.	39 19 N	94 55 W
94	Lebanon, Asia	34 0 N	36 0 E
79	Leeds, U.K.	53 48 N	1 34 W
80	Leeuwarden, Neth.	53 12 N	5 48 E
110	Leeuwin, C., Australia	34 0 S	115 0 E
65	Leeward Is., C. America	18 0 N	61 0 W
82	Leghorn, Italy	43 33 N	10 18 E
79	Leicester, U.K.	52 39 N	1 9 W
80	Leiden, Neth.	52 10 N	4 30 E
82	Leipzig, Germany	51 20 N	12 20 E
80	Lek, r., Neth.	51 55 N	4 29 E
89	Lena, r., Russian Fed.	72 0 N	127 10 E
88	Leninsk Kuznetskiy, Russian Fed.	54 44 N	86 13 E
80	Lens, France	50 26 N	2 50 E
64	León, Mexico	21 10 N	101 42 W
84	León, Spain	42 35 N	5 34 W
110	Leonora, Australia	28 54 S	121 20 E
85	Leskovac, Yugo.	43 0 N	21 56 E
108	Lesotho, Africa	29 30 S	28 0 E
65	Lesser Antilles, is., C. America	13 0 N	65 0 W
85	Lésvos, i., Greece	39 10 N	26 16 E
62	Lethbridge, Canada	49 43 N	112 48 W
80	Leverkusen, Germany	51 2 N	6 59 E
79	Lewis, i., U.K.	58 10 N	6 40 W
62	Lewiston, Idaho, U.S.A.	46 25 N	117 1 W
58	Lewiston, Maine, U.S.A.	44 6 N	70 13 W
59	Lexington, Ky., U.S.A.	38 3 N	84 30 W
101	Leyte, i., Phil.	11 0 N	124 45 E
98	Lhasa, China	29 41 N	91 10 E
99	Liaodong B., China	40 20 N	121 0 E
99	Liaoning, d., China	41 30 N	123 0 E
99	Liaoyuan, China	42 53 N	125 10 E
106	Liberia, Africa	6 30 N	9 30 W
108	Libreville, Gabon	0 30 N	9 25 E
106	Libya, Africa	26 30 N	17 0 E
107	Libyan Desert, Africa	25 0 N	26 10 E
108	Lichinga, Mozambique	13 19 S	35 13 E
82	Liechtenstein, Europe	47 8 N	9 35 E
80	Liège, Belgium	50 38 N	5 35 E
81	Liepāja, Latvia	56 30 N	21 0 E
84	Ligurian Sea, Med. Sea	43 30 N	9 0 E
108	Likasi, Zaïre	10 58 S	26 47 E
80	Lille, France	50 39 N	3 5 E
81	Lillehammer, Norway	61 6 N	10 27 E
108	Lilongwe, Malawi	13 58 S	33 49 E
70	Lima, Peru	12 6 S	77 3 W
58	Lima, U.S.A.	40 43 N	84 6 W
94	Limassol, Cyprus	34 40 N	33 3 E
79	Limerick, Rep. of Ire.	52 40 N	8 37 W
85	Límnos, i., Greece	39 54 N	25 21 E
84	Limoges, France	45 50 N	1 15 E
108	Limpopo, r., Mozambique	25 14 S	33 33 E
60	Lincoln, U.S.A.	40 48 N	96 42 W
81	Linköping, Sweden	58 25 N	15 35 E
82	Linz, Austria	48 19 N	14 18 E
84	Lions, G. of, France	43 12 N	4 15 E
101	Lipa, Phil.	13 57 N	121 10 E
86	Lipetsk, Russian Fed.	52 37 N	39 36 E
84	Lisbon, Portugal	38 44 N	9 8 W
81	Lithuania, Europe	55 0 N	23 50 E
61	Little Rock, town, U.S.A.	34 44 N	92 15 W
99	Liuzhou, China	24 17 N	109 15 E
79	Liverpool, U.K.	53 25 N	2 59 W
82	Ljubljana, Slovenia	46 4 N	14 28 E
84	Lleida, Spain	41 37 N	0 38 E
108	Lobito, Angola	12 20 S	13 34 E
62	Lodi, U.S.A.	38 8 N	121 16 W
83	Łódź, Poland	51 49 N	19 28 E
81	Lofoten, is., Norway	68 15 N	13 50 E
52	Logan, Mt., Canada	60 45 N	140 0 W
84	Loire, r., France	47 18 N	2 0 W
81	Lolland, i., Denmark	54 50 N	11 30 E
106	Lomé, Togo	6 10 N	1 21 E
79	Lomond, Loch, U.K.	56 7 N	4 36 W
58	London, Canada	42 58 N	81 15 W
79	London, U.K.	51 32 N	0 6 W
79	Londonderry, U.K.	55 0 N	7 21 W
110	Londonderry, C., Australia	13 58 S	126 55 E
72	Londrina, Brazil	23 30 S	51 13 W
63	Long Beach, town, U.S.A.	33 46 N	118 11 W
58	Long I., U.S.A.	40 50 N	73 0 W
61	Longview, Tex., U.S.A.	32 30 N	94 44 W
62	Longview, Wash., U.S.A.	46 8 N	122 57 W
98	Lop Nur, l., China	40 30 N	90 30 E
58	Lorain, U.S.A.	41 28 N	82 10 W
84	Lorient, France	47 45 N	3 21 W
73	Los Angeles, Chile	37 28 S	72 21 W
63	Los Angeles, U.S.A.	34 0 N	118 17 W
63	Los Mochis, Mexico	25 45 N	108 57 W
61	Louisiana, d., U.S.A.	30 60 N	92 30 W
58	Louisville, U.S.A.	38 13 N	85 48 W
84	Lourdes, France	43 6 N	0 2 W
58	Lowell, U.S.A.	42 39 N	71 18 W
89	Lower Tunguska, r., Russian Fed.	65 50 N	88 0 E
108	Luanda, Angola	8 50 S	13 20 E
61	Lubbock, U.S.A.	33 35 N	101 51 W
82	Lübeck, Germany	53 52 N	10 40 E
83	Lublin, Poland	51 18 N	22 31 E
108	Lubumbashi, Zaïre	11 41 S	27 29 E
97	Lucknow, India	26 50 N	80 54 E
108	Lüderitz, Namibia	26 38 S	15 10 E
96	Ludhiana, India	30 56 N	75 52 E
82	Ludwigshafen, Germany	49 29 N	8 27 E
82	Lugano, Switz.	46 1 N	8 58 E
87	Lugansk, Ukraine	48 35 N	39 20 E
81	Luleå, Sweden	65 35 N	22 10 E
99	Luoyang, China	34 48 N	112 25 E
108	Lusaka, Zambia	15 26 S	28 20 E
79	Luton, U.K.	51 53 N	0 25 W
80	Luxembourg, d., Belgium	49 58 N	5 30 E
82	Luzern, Switz.	47 3 N	8 17 E
101	Luzon, i., Phil.	15 35 N	120 50 E
83	Lvov, Ukraine	49 50 N	24 3 E
59	Lynchburg, U.S.A.	37 24 N	79 10 W
53	Lynn Lake, town, Canada	56 51 N	101 1 W
82	Lyon, France	45 46 N	4 50 E

M

PAGE	PLACENAME	LATITUDE	LONGITUDE
94	Ma'ān, Jordan	30 11 N	35 43 E
80	Maas, r., Neth.	51 44 N	4 42 E
80	Maastricht, Neth.	50 51 N	5 42 E
71	Macapá, Brazil	0 4 N	51 4 W
99	Macau, Asia	22 13 N	113 36 E
110	Macdonnell Ranges, mts., Australia	23 30 S	132 0 E
85	Macedonia, Europe	41 30 N	21 40 E
71	Maceió, Brazil	9 40 S	35 44 W
70	Machala, Ecuador	3 20 S	79 57 W
110	Mackay, L., Australia	22 30 S	128 58 E
52	Mackenzie, r., Canada	69 20 N	134 0 W
52	Mackenzie Mts., Canada	64 0 N	130 0 W
59	Macon, U.S.A.	32 49 N	83 37 W
112	Macquarie I., Pacific Oc.	54 29 S	158 58 E
108	Madagascar, Africa	20 0 S	46 30 E
75	Madeira, i., Madeira Is.	32 45 N	17 0 W
75	Madeira Is., Atlantic Oc.	32 45 N	17 0 W
60	Madison, U.S.A.	43 5 N	89 22 W
102	Madiun, Indonesia	7 37 S	111 33 E
97	Madras, India	13 5 N	80 18 E
61	Madre Lagoon, b., U.S.A.	27 0 N	97 35 W

PAGE	PLACENAME	LATITUDE	LONGITUDE
110	New Britain, *i., P.N.G.*	6 0 S	150 0 E
58	New Britain, *U.S.A.*	41 40 N	72 47 W
59	New Brunswick, *U.S.A.*	40 29 N	74 27 W
112	New Caledonia, *i., Pacific Oc.*	22 0 S	165 0 E
96	New Delhi, *India*	28 37 N	77 13 E
103	New Guinea, *i., Austa.*	5 0 S	140 0 E
58	New Hampshire, *d., U.S.A.*	43 35 N	71 40 W
58	New Haven, *U.S.A.*	41 14 N	72 50 W
110	New Ireland, *i., P.N.G.*	2 30 S	151 30 E
58	New Jersey, *d., U.S.A.*	40 0 N	74 30 W
58	New London, *U.S.A.*	41 21 N	72 7 W
54	New Mexico, *d., U.S.A*	34 0 N	106 0 W
61	New Orleans, *U.S.A.*	29 58 N	90 7 W
89	New Siberian Is., *Russian Fed.*	76 0 N	144 0 E
110	New South Wales, *d., Australia*	32 30 S	146 0 E
59	New York, *U.S.A.*	40 40 N	73 50 W
58	New York, *d., U.S.A.*	43 0 N	75 0 W
111	New Zealand, *Austa.*	41 0 S	175 0 E
59	Newark, *U.S.A.*	40 44 N	74 11 W
59	Newburgh, *U.S.A.*	41 30 N	74 1 W
110	Newcastle, *Australia*	32 55 S	151 46 E
79	Newcastle upon Tyne, *U.K.*	54 58 N	1 36 W
53	Newfoundland, *d., Canada*	55 0 N	60 0 W
79	Newport, *U.K.*	51 34 N	2 59 W
59	Newport News, *U.S.A.*	36 59 N	76 26 W
102	Nha Trang, *Vietnam*	12 15 N	109 10 E
58	Niagara Falls, *town, U.S.A.*	43 6 N	79 4 W
106	Niamey, *Niger*	13 32 N	2 5 E
66	Nicaragua, *C. America*	13 0 N	85 0 W
66	Nicaragua, L., *Nicaragua*	11 30 N	85 30 W
82	Nice, *France*	43 42 N	7 16 E
97	Nicobar Is., *India*	8 0 N	94 0 E
94	Nicosia, *Cyprus*	35 11 N	33 23 E
66	Nicoya Pen., *Costa Rica*	10 30 N	85 30 W
106	Niger, *Africa*	17 0 N	9 30 E
106	Niger, *r., Nigeria*	4 15 N	6 5 E
106	Nigeria, *Africa*	9 0 N	7 30 E
100	Niigata, *Japan*	37 58 N	139 2 E
80	Nijmegen, *Neth.*	51 50 N	5 52 E
87	Nikolayev, *Ukraine*	46 57 N	32 0 E
94	Nile, *r., Egypt*	31 30 N	30 25 E
82	Nîmes, *France*	43 50 N	4 21 E
99	Ningbo, *China*	29 54 N	121 33 E
58	Nipigon, L., *Canada*	49 50 N	88 30 W
85	Niš, *Yugo.*	43 20 N	21 54 E
86	Nizhniy Novgorod, *Russian Fed.*	56 20 N	44 0 E
86	Nizhniy Tagil, *Russian Fed.*	58 0 N	60 0 E
106	Nkongsamba, *Cameroon*	4 59 N	9 53 E
100	Nobeoka, *Japan*	32 36 N	131 40 E
89	Nordvik, *Russian Fed.*	73 40 N	110 50 E
59	Norfolk, *U.S.A.*	36 54 N	76 18 W
112	Norfolk I., *Pacific Oc.*	29 2 S	167 57 E
89	Norilsk, *Russian Fed.*	69 21 N	88 2 E
61	Norman, *U.S.A.*	35 13 N	97 26 W
110	Normanton, *Australia*	17 40 S	141 5 E
81	Norrköping, *Sweden*	58 35 N	16 10 E
50	North America,		
81	North C., *Norway*	71 10 N	25 45 E
59	North Carolina, *d., U.S.A.*	35 30 N	80 0 W
58	North Channel, *str., Canada*	46 2 N	82 50 W
60	North Dakota, *d., U.S.A.*	47 0 N	100 0 W
111	North I., *New Zealand*	39 0 S	175 0 E
100	North Korea, *Asia*	39 35 N	126 40 E
60	North Platte, *r., U.S.A.*	41 15 N	100 45 W
76	North Sea, *Europe*	56 0 N	3 0 E
79	North West Highlands, *U.K.*	57 30 N	5 15 W
79	North York Moors, *hills, U.K.*	54 21 N	0 50 W
79	Northampton, *U.K.*	52 14 N	0 54 W
79	Northern Ireland, *d., U.K.*	54 40 N	6 45 W
56	Northern Marianas, *is., Pacific Oc.*	15 0 N	145 0 E
110	Northern Territory, *d., Australia*	20 0 S	133 0 E
53	Northwest Territories, *d., Canada*	66 0 N	95 0 W
81	Norway, *Europe*	65 0 N	13 0 E
76	Norwegian Sea, *Europe*	66 0 N	2 0 E
79	Norwich, *U.K.*	52 38 N	1 17 E
79	Nottingham, *U.K.*	52 57 N	1 10 W
106	Nouadhibou, *Mauritania*	20 54 N	17 1 W
106	Nouakchott, *Mauritania*	18 9 N	15 58 W
112	Nouméa, *N. Cal.*	22 16 S	166 27 E
53	Nova Scotia, *d., Canada*	45 0 N	64 0 W
88	Novaya Zemlya, *i., Russian Fed.*	74 0 N	56 0 E
83	Novi Sad, *Yugo.*	45 16 N	19 52 E
87	Novocherkassk, *Russian Fed.*	47 25 N	40 5 E
88	Novokuznetsk, *Russian Fed.*	53 45 N	87 12 E
86	Novomoskovsk, *Russian Fed.*	54 6 N	38 15 E
87	Novorossiysk, *Russian Fed.*	44 44 N	37 46 E
88	Novosibirsk, *Russian Fed.*	55 4 N	82 55 E
107	Nubian Desert, *Sudan*	21 0 N	34 0 E
61	Nuevo Laredo, *Mexico*	27 30 N	99 31 W
110	Nullarbor Plain, *f., Australia*	31 30 S	128 0 E
57	Nunivak I., *U.S.A.*	60 0 N	166 30 W
82	Nürnberg, *Germany*	49 27 N	11 5 E
108	Nyasa, L., *Africa*	12 0 S	34 30 E
83	Nyíregyháza, *Hungary*	47 59 N	21 43 E

O

PAGE	PLACENAME	LATITUDE	LONGITUDE
57	Oahu, *i., Hawaiian Is.*	21 30 N	158 0 W
59	Oak Ridge, *town, U.S.A.*	36 2 N	84 12 W
62	Oakland, *U.S.A.*	37 47 N	122 13 W
64	Oaxaca, *Mexico*	17 5 N	96 41 W
86	Ob, *r., Russian Fed.*	66 50 N	69 0 E
80	Oberhausen, *Germany*	51 28 N	6 51 E
59	Ocala, *U.S.A.*	29 11 N	82 9 W
63	Oceanside, *U.S.A.*	33 12 N	117 23 W
81	Odense, *Denmark*	55 24 N	10 25 E
82	Oder, *r., Poland/Germany*	53 30 N	14 36 E
83	Odessa, *Ukraine*	46 30 N	30 46 E
61	Odessa, *U.S.A.*	31 51 N	102 22 W
82	Offenbach, *Germany*	50 6 N	8 46 E
106	Ogbomosho, *Nigeria*	8 5 N	4 11 E
62	Ogden, *U.S.A.*	41 14 N	111 58 W
58	Ohio, *d., U.S.A.*	40 15 N	82 45 W
58	Ohio, *r., U.S.A.*	36 59 N	89 8 W
100	Oita, *Japan*	33 15 N	131 40 E
62	Okanogan, *r., U.S.A.*	48 22 N	119 35 W
108	Okavango Basin, *f., Botswana*	19 30 S	23 0 E
100	Okayama, *Japan*	34 40 N	133 54 E
100	Okazaki, *Japan*	34 58 N	137 10 E
59	Okeechobee, L., *U.S.A.*	26 55 N	80 45 W
59	Okefenokee Swamp, *f., U.S.A.*	30 42 N	82 20 W
89	Okhotsk, *Russian Fed.*	59 20 N	143 15 E
89	Okhotsk, Sea of, *Russian Fed.*	55 0 N	150 0 E
61	Oklahoma, *d., U.S.A.*	35 20 N	98 0 W
61	Oklahoma City, *U.S.A.*	35 28 N	97 32 W
80	Oldenburg, *Germany*	53 8 N	8 13 E
89	Olekminsk, *Russian Fed.*	60 25 N	120 0 E
71	Olinda, *Brazil*	8 0 S	34 51 W
83	Olomouc, *Czech Rep.*	49 36 N	17 16 E
83	Olsztyn, *Poland*	53 48 N	20 29 E
62	Olympia, *U.S.A.*	47 3 N	122 53 W
62	Olympic Mts., *U.S.A.*	47 50 N	123 45 W
85	Olympus, Mt., *Greece*	40 4 N	22 20 E
60	Omaha, *U.S.A.*	41 16 N	95 57 W
96	Oman, *Asia*	22 30 N	57 30 E
95	Oman, G. of, *Asia*	25 0 N	58 0 E
107	Omdurman, *Sudan*	15 37 N	32 59 E
88	Omsk, *Russian Fed.*	55 0 N	73 22 E
100	Omuta, *Japan*	33 2 N	130 26 E
86	Onega, *r., Russian Fed.*	63 59 N	38 11 E
86	Onega, L., *Russian Fed.*	62 0 N	35 30 E
106	Onitsha, *Nigeria*	6 10 N	6 47 E
53	Ontario, *d., Canada*	52 0 N	86 0 W
58	Ontario, L., *N. America*	43 40 N	78 0 W
84	Oporto, *Portugal*	41 9 N	8 37 W
83	Oradea, *Romania*	47 3 N	21 55 E
84	Oran, *Algeria*	35 45 N	0 38 W
108	Orange, *r., South Africa*	28 43 S	16 30 E
101	Oras, *Phil.*	12 10 N	125 26 E
81	Örebro, *Sweden*	59 17 N	15 13 E
62	Oregon, *d., U.S.A.*	43 49 N	120 36 W
86	Orekhovo-Zuyevo, *Russian Fed.*	55 47 N	39 0 E
86	Orel, *Russian Fed.*	52 58 N	36 4 E
86	Orenburg, *Russian Fed.*	51 50 N	55 0 E
70	Orinoco, *r., Venezuela*	9 0 N	61 30 W
64	Orizaba, *Mexico*	18 51 N	97 8 W
59	Orlando, *U.S.A.*	28 33 N	81 21 W
84	Orléans, *France*	47 54 N	1 54 E
86	Orsk, *Russian Fed.*	51 13 N	58 35 E
72	Oruro, *Bolivia*	17 59 S	67 9 W
100	Osaka, *Japan*	34 40 N	135 30 E
58	Oshawa, *Canada*	43 53 N	78 51 W
106	Oshogbo, *Nigeria*	7 50 N	4 35 E
83	Osijek, *Croatia*	45 35 N	18 43 E
81	Oslo, *Norway*	59 56 N	10 45 E
80	Osnabrück, *Germany*	52 17 N	8 3 E
80	Ostend, *Belgium*	51 13 N	2 55 E
83	Ostrava, *Czech Rep.*	49 50 N	18 15 E
58	Oswego, *U.S.A.*	43 27 N	76 31 W
100	Otaru, *Japan*	43 14 N	140 59 E
58	Ottawa, *Canada*	45 25 N	75 43 W
58	Ottawa, *r., Canada*	45 23 N	73 55 W
60	Ottumwa, *U.S.A.*	41 1 N	92 25 W
61	Ouachita Mts., *U.S.A.*	34 40 N	94 25 W
106	Ouagadougou, *Burkina Faso*	12 20 N	1 40 W
84	Oujda, *Morocco*	34 41 N	1 45 W
79	Outer Hebrides, *is., U.K.*	57 40 N	7 35 W
84	Oviedo, *Spain*	43 21 N	5 50 W
110	Owen Stanley Range, *mts., P.N.G.*	9 30 S	148 0 E
62	Owyhee, *r., U.S.A.*	43 46 N	117 2 W
79	Oxford, *U.K.*	51 48 N	1 15 W
63	Oxnard, *U.S.A.*	34 12 N	119 11 W
61	Ozark Plateau, *U.S.A.*	37 0 N	93 0 W

P

PAGE	PLACENAME	LATITUDE	LONGITUDE
64	Pachuca, *Mexico*	20 10 N	98 44 W
113	Pacific Ocean,		
102	Padang, *Indonesia*	0 55 S	100 21 E
82	Paderborn, *Germany*	51 43 N	8 44 E
82	Padua, *Italy*	45 27 N	11 52 E
61	Paducah, *U.S.A.*	37 5 N	88 36 W
101	Pagadian, *Phil.*	7 50 N	123 24 E
96	Pakistan, *Asia*	30 0 N	70 0 E
56	Palau, *Pacific Oc.*	7 0 N	134 25 E
101	Palawan, *i., Phil.*	9 40 N	118 30 E
102	Palembang, *Indonesia*	2 59 S	104 50 E
84	Palermo, *Italy*	38 9 N	13 22 E
61	Palestine, *U.S.A.*	31 46 N	95 38 W
97	Palk Str., *India/Sri Lanka*	10 0 N	79 40 E
63	Palm Springs, *town, U.S.A.*	33 50 N	116 33 W
84	Palma, *Spain*	39 36 N	2 39 E
111	Palmerston North, *New Zealand*	40 20 S	175 39 E
70	Palmira, *Colombia*	3 33 N	76 17 W
98	Pamirs, *mts., Tajikistan*	37 50 N	73 30 E
59	Pamlico Sd., *U.S.A.*	35 20 N	75 55 W
61	Pampa, *U.S.A.*	35 32 N	100 58 W
73	Pampas, *f., Argentina*	34 0 S	64 0 W
84	Pamplona, *Spain*	42 49 N	1 39 W
66	Panama, *C. America*	9 0 N	80 0 W
66	Panama Canal, *Panama*	9 21 N	79 54 W
66	Panama City, *Panama*	8 57 N	79 30 W
66	Panama, G. of, *Panama*	8 30 N	79 0 W
101	Panay, *i., Phil.*	11 10 N	122 30 E
103	Papua, G. of, *P.N.G.*	8 50 S	145 0 E
110	Papua New Guinea, *Austa.*	6 0 S	144 0 E
71	Para, *d., Brazil*	4 0 S	53 0 W
74	Paraguay, *r., Argentina*	27 30 S	58 50 W
74	Paraguay, *S. America*	23 0 S	57 0 W
71	Paramaribo, *Suriname*	5 52 N	55 14 W
72	Paraná, *Argentina*	31 45 S	60 30 W
71	Paranã, *Brazil*	12 33 S	47 48 W
102	Parepare, *Indonesia*	4 3 S	119 40 E
82	Paris, *France*	48 52 N	2 20 E
61	Paris, *U.S.A.*	33 40 N	95 33 W
62	Park Range, *mts., U.S.A.*	40 0 N	106 30 W
58	Parkersburg, *U.S.A.*	39 17 N	81 32 W
82	Parma, *Italy*	44 48 N	10 18 E
71	Parnaíba, *r., Brazil*	2 58 S	41 47 W
63	Pasadena, *Calif., U.S.A.*	34 9 N	118 9 W
61	Pasadena, *Tex., U.S.A.*	29 42 N	95 13 W
61	Pascagoula, *U.S.A.*	30 23 N	88 31 W
62	Pasco, *U.S.A.*	46 14 N	119 6 W
70	Pasto, *Colombia*	1 12 N	77 17 W
73	Patagonia, *f., Argentina*	42 20 S	67 0 W
59	Paterson, *U.S.A.*	40 55 N	74 10 W
97	Patna, *India*	25 37 N	85 12 E
85	Pátras, *Greece*	38 15 N	21 45 E
84	Pau, *France*	43 18 N	0 22 W
88	Pavlodar, *Kazakhstan*	52 21 N	76 59 E
52	Peace, *r., Canada*	59 0 N	111 26 W
86	Pechora, *r., Russian Fed.*	68 10 N	54 0 E
61	Pecos, *r., U.S.A.*	29 42 N	101 22 W
83	Pécs, *Hungary*	46 5 N	18 14 E
97	Pegu, *Myanmar*	17 18 N	96 31 E
102	Pekanbaru, *Indonesia*	0 33 N	101 20 E
60	Pekin, *U.S.A.*	40 34 N	89 40 W
74	Pelotas, *Brazil*	31 45 S	52 20 W
102	Pematangsiantar, *Indonesia*	2 59 N	99 1 E
108	Pemba I., *Tanzania*	5 10 S	39 45 E
62	Pendleton, *U.S.A.*	45 40 N	118 47 W
58	Pennsylvania, *d., U.S.A.*	41 0 N	78 0 W
59	Pensacola, *U.S.A.*	30 26 N	87 12 W
86	Penza, *Russian Fed.*	53 11 N	45 0 E
60	Peoria, *U.S.A.*	40 43 N	89 38 W
70	Pereira, *Colombia*	4 47 N	75 46 W
86	Perm, *Russian Fed.*	58 1 N	56 10 E
84	Perpignan, *France*	42 42 N	2 54 E
110	Perth, *Australia*	31 58 S	115 49 E
79	Perth, *U.K.*	56 24 N	3 28 W
59	Perth Amboy, *U.S.A.*	40 31 N	74 16 W
70	Peru, *S. America*	10 0 S	75 0 W
84	Perugia, *Italy*	43 6 N	12 24 E
84	Pescara, *Italy*	42 27 N	14 13 E
96	Peshawar, *Pakistan*	34 1 N	71 40 E
58	Peterborough, *Canada*	44 18 N	78 19 W
59	Petersburg, *U.S.A.*	37 14 N	77 24 W
88	Petropavlovsk, *Kazakhstan*	54 53 N	69 13 E
89	Petropavlovsk Kamchatskiy, *Russian Fed.*	53 3 N	158 43 E
74	Petrópolis, *Brazil*	22 30 S	43 6 W
86	Petrozavodsk, *Russian Fed.*	61 46 N	34 19 E
82	Pforzheim, *Germany*	48 53 N	8 41 E
59	Philadelphia, *U.S.A.*	40 0 N	75 10 W
101	Philippines, *Asia*	12 0 N	122 0 E
102	Phnom Penh, *Cambodia*	11 35 N	104 55 E
63	Phoenix, *U.S.A.*	33 27 N	112 5 W
82	Piacenza, *Italy*	45 3 N	9 42 E
83	Piatra Neamț, *Romania*	46 56 N	26 22 E
80	Picardy, *f., France*	49 47 N	2 45 E
61	Piedras Negras, *Mexico*	28 40 N	100 32 W
108	Pietermaritzburg, *South Africa*	29 36 S	30 24 E
72	Pilcomayo, *r., Argentina/Paraguay*	25 15 S	57 43 W

132

133

PAGE	PLACENAME	LATITUDE	LONGITUDE
102	Sunda Str., *Indonesia*	6 0 S	105 50 E
97	Sundarbans, *f., India/Bangla.*	22 0 N	89 0 E
79	Sunderland, *U.K.*	54 55 N	1 22 W
81	Sundsvall, *Sweden*	62 22 N	17 20 E
60	Superior, *U.S.A.*	46 42 N	92 5 W
60	Superior, L., *Canada/U.S.A.*	48 0 N	88 0 W
102	Surabaya, *Indonesia*	7 14 S	112 45 E
102	Surakarta, *Indonesia*	7 32 S	110 50 E
96	Surat, *India*	21 10 N	72 54 E
88	Surgut, *Russian Fed.*	61 13 N	73 20 E
101	Surigao, *Phil.*	9 47 N	125 30 E
71	Suriname, *S. America*	4 0 N	56 0 W
81	Surtsey, *i., Iceland*	63 18 N	20 37 W
62	Susanville, *U.S.A.*	40 25 N	120 39 W
58	Susquehanna, *r., U.S.A.*	39 33 N	76 5 W
96	Sutlej, *r., Pakistan*	29 26 N	71 9 E
100	Suwon, *S. Korea*	37 16 N	126 59 E
99	Suzhou, *China*	31 21 N	120 40 E
81	Svendborg, *Denmark*	55 4 N	10 38 E
79	Swansea, *U.K.*	51 37 N	3 57 W
108	Swaziland, *Africa*	26 30 S	31 30 E
81	Sweden, *Europe*	63 0 N	16 0 E
61	Sweetwater, *U.S.A.*	32 28 N	100 25 W
60	Swift Current, *town, Canada*	50 17 N	107 49 W
79	Swindon, *U.K.*	51 33 N	1 47 W
82	Switzerland, *Europe*	47 0 N	8 15 E
110	Sydney, *Australia*	33 55 S	151 10 E
53	Sydney, *Canada*	46 10 N	60 10 W
86	Syktyvkar, *Russian Fed.*	61 42 N	50 45 E
88	Syr Darya, *r., Asia*	46 0 N	61 12 E
58	Syracuse, *U.S.A.*	43 3 N	76 10 W
94	Syria, *Asia*	35 0 N	38 0 E
94	Syrian Desert, *Asia*	32 0 N	39 0 E
86	Syzran, *Russian Fed.*	53 10 N	48 29 E
82	Szczecin, *Poland*	53 25 N	14 32 E
83	Szeged, *Hungary*	46 16 N	20 8 E
83	Székesfehérvár, *Hungary*	47 12 N	18 25 E

T

PAGE	PLACENAME	LATITUDE	LONGITUDE
101	Tabaco, *Phil.*	13 21 N	123 44 E
108	Tabora, *Tanzania*	5 2 S	32 50 E
95	Tabriz, *Iran*	38 5 N	46 18 E
94	Tabūk, *Saudi Arabia*	28 25 N	36 35 E
101	Tacloban, *Phil.*	11 14 N	125 1 E
72	Tacna, *Peru*	18 1 S	70 15 W
62	Tacoma, *U.S.A.*	47 15 N	122 27 W
74	Tacuarembó, *Uruguay*	31 42 S	56 0 W
100	Taegu, *S. Korea*	35 52 N	128 36 E
100	Taejon, *S. Korea*	36 20 N	127 26 E
87	Taganrog, *Russian Fed.*	47 14 N	38 55 E
84	Tagus, *r., Portugal/Spain*	39 0 N	8 57 W
113	Tahiti, *i., Îs. de la Société*	17 37 S	149 27 W
62	Tahoe, L., *U.S.A.*	39 7 N	120 3 W
99	Taibei, *Taiwan*	25 5 N	121 32 E
99	Tainan, *Taiwan*	23 1 N	120 14 E
99	Taiwan, *Asia*	23 30 N	121 0 E
99	Taiwan Str., *China/Taiwan*	25 0 N	120 0 E
99	Taiyuan, *China*	37 50 N	112 30 E
99	Taizhong, *Taiwan*	24 9 N	120 40 E
107	Ta'izz, *Yemen*	13 35 N	44 2 E
98	Tajikistan, *Asia*	39 0 N	70 30 E
100	Takamatsu, *Japan*	34 28 N	134 5 E
100	Takaoka, *Japan*	36 47 N	137 0 E
100	Takasaki, *Japan*	36 20 N	139 0 E
98	Taklimakan Shamo, *des., China*	38 10 N	82 0 E
73	Talca, *Chile*	35 26 S	71 40 W
73	Talcahuano, *Chile*	36 43 S	73 7 W
59	Tallahassee, *U.S.A.*	30 26 N	84 19 W
81	Tallinn, *Estonia*	59 22 N	24 48 E
86	Tambov, *Russian Fed.*	52 44 N	41 28 E
59	Tampa, *U.S.A.*	27 58 N	82 38 W
81	Tampere, *Finland*	61 32 N	23 45 E
64	Tampico, *Mexico*	22 18 N	97 52 W
108	Tanga, *Tanzania*	5 7 S	39 5 E
108	Tanganyika, L., *Africa*	5 37 S	29 30 E
84	Tangier, *Morocco*	35 48 N	5 45 W
99	Tangshan, *China*	39 37 N	118 5 E
101	Tanjay, *Phil.*	9 30 N	123 10 E
108	Tanzania, *Africa*	5 0 S	35 0 E
71	Tapajós, *r., Brazil*	2 25 S	54 40 W
85	Taranto, *Italy*	40 28 N	17 14 E
13	Tarim Basin, *f., Asia*	40 0 N	83 0 E
101	Tarlac, *Phil.*	15 29 N	120 37 E
83	Tarnów, *Poland*	50 1 N	20 59 E
84	Tarragona, *Spain*	41 7 N	1 15 E
98	Tashkent, *Uzbekistan*	41 16 N	69 13 E
112	Tasman Sea, *Pacific Oc.*	38 0 S	162 0 E
110	Tasmania, *d., Australia*	42 30 S	147 0 E
94	Taurus Mts., *Turkey*	37 15 N	34 15 E
95	Tbilisi, *Georgia*	41 43 N	44 48 E
65	Tegucigalpa, *Honduras*	14 5 N	87 14 W
95	Tehran, *Iran*	35 40 N	51 26 E
64	Tehuantepec, G. of, *Mexico*	16 0 N	95 0 W
94	Tel-Aviv-Yafo, *Israel*	32 5 N	34 46 E
102	Telukbetung, *Indonesia*	5 28 S	105 16 E
88	Temirtau, *Kazakhstan*	50 5 N	72 55 E
63	Tempe, *U.S.A.*	33 25 N	111 56 W
61	Temple, *U.S.A.*	31 6 N	97 21 W
75	Tenerife, *i., Canary Is.*	28 10 N	16 30 W
110	Tennant Creek, *town, Australia*	19 31 S	134 15 E
59	Tennessee, *d., U.S.A.*	35 50 N	85 30 W
59	Tennessee, *r., U.S.A.*	37 4 N	88 33 W
74	Teófilo Otoni, *Brazil*	17 52 S	41 31 W
64	Tepic, *Mexico*	21 30 N	104 51 W
71	Teresina, *Brazil*	5 9 S	42 46 W
84	Terni, *Italy*	42 34 N	12 44 E
58	Terre Haute, *U.S.A.*	39 27 N	87 24 W
84	Tetuan, *Morocco*	35 34 N	5 22 W
61	Texarkana, *U.S.A.*	33 26 N	94 3 W
61	Texas, *d., U.S.A.*	31 30 N	100 0 W
61	Texas City, *U.S.A.*	29 23 N	94 54 W
102	Thailand, *Asia*	16 0 N	101 0 E
102	Thailand, G. of, *Asia*	11 0 N	101 0 E
79	Thames, *r., U.K.*	51 30 N	0 5 E
96	Thar Desert, *India*	28 0 N	72 0 E
59	The Everglades, *f., U.S.A.*	26 0 N	80 40 W
95	The Gulf, *Asia*	27 0 N	50 0 E
80	The Hague, *Neth.*	52 5 N	4 16 E
79	The Minch, *str., U.K.*	58 10 N	5 50 W
79	The Pennines, *hills, U.K.*	54 40 N	2 20 W
85	Thessaloniki, *Greece*	40 38 N	22 56 E
106	Thiès, *Senegal*	14 48 N	16 56 W
97	Thimbu, *Bhutan*	27 29 N	89 40 E
82	Thionville, *France*	49 22 N	6 11 E
59	Thomasville, *U.S.A.*	30 50 N	83 59 W
102	Thonburi, *Thailand*	13 43 N	100 27 E
53	Thule, *Greenland*	77 30 N	69 29 W
58	Thunder Bay, *town, Canada*	48 25 N	89 14 W
98	Tian Shan, *mts., Asia*	42 0 N	80 30 E
99	Tianjin, *China*	39 8 N	117 12 E
98	Tianshui, *China*	34 25 N	105 58 E
106	Tibesti Mts., *Chad*	21 0 N	17 30 E
98	Tibet, *d., China*	32 20 N	86 0 E
98	Tibetan Plateau, *f., China*	34 0 N	86 15 E
73	Tierra del Fuego, *i., Argentina/Chile*	54 0 S	69 0 W
95	Tigris, *r., Asia*	31 0 N	47 27 E
63	Tijuana, *Mexico*	32 32 N	117 1 W
80	Tilburg, *Neth.*	51 34 N	5 5 E
111	Timaru, *New Zealand*	44 23 S	171 41 E
106	Timbuktu, *Mali*	16 49 N	2 59 W
83	Timişoara, *Romania*	45 47 N	21 15 E
58	Timmins, *Canada*	48 30 N	81 20 W
103	Timor, *i., Indonesia*	9 30 S	125 0 E
56	Tinian, *i., Mariana Is.*	14 58 N	145 38 E
79	Tipperary, *Rep. of Ire.*	52 29 N	8 10 W
85	Tiranë, *Albania*	41 20 N	19 48 E
83	Tîrgu Mureş, *Romania*	46 33 N	24 34 E
97	Tiruchirapalli, *India*	10 50 N	78 43 E
83	Tisa, *r., Yugo.*	45 9 N	20 16 E
72	Titicaca, L., *Bolivia/Peru*	16 0 S	69 0 W
106	Tizi Ouzou, *Algeria*	36 44 N	4 5 E
108	Toamasina, *Madagascar*	18 10 S	49 23 E
88	Tobol, *r., Russian Fed.*	58 15 N	68 12 E
71	Tocantins, *r., Brazil*	1 50 S	49 15 W
106	Togo, *Africa*	8 30 N	1 0 E
112	Tokelau Is., *Pacific Oc.*	9 0 S	171 45 W
100	Tokushima, *Japan*	34 3 N	134 34 E
100	Tokyo, *Japan*	35 40 N	139 45 E
83	Tolbukhin, *Bulgaria*	43 34 N	27 52 E
84	Toledo, *Spain*	39 52 N	4 2 W
58	Toledo, *U.S.A.*	41 40 N	83 35 W
108	Toliara, *Madagascar*	23 20 S	43 41 E
64	Toluca, *Mexico*	19 20 N	99 40 W
86	Tol'yatti, *Russian Fed.*	53 32 N	49 24 E
88	Tomsk, *Russian Fed.*	56 30 N	85 5 E
112	Tonga, *Pacific Oc.*	20 0 S	175 0 W
62	Tongue, *r., U.S.A.*	46 24 N	105 25 W
110	Toowoomba, *Australia*	27 35 S	151 54 E
60	Topeka, *U.S.A.*	39 3 N	95 41 W
81	Torne, *r., Sweden*	67 13 N	23 30 E
58	Toronto, *Canada*	43 42 N	79 25 W
61	Torreón, *Mexico*	25 33 N	103 26 W
67	Tortola, *i., B.V.Is.*	18 28 N	64 40 W
84	Tortosa, *Spain*	40 49 N	0 31 E
83	Toruń, *Poland*	53 1 N	18 35 E
84	Toulon, *France*	43 7 N	5 53 E
84	Toulouse, *France*	43 33 N	1 24 E
80	Tournai, *Belgium*	50 36 N	3 23 E
84	Tours, *France*	47 23 N	0 42 E
110	Townsville, *Australia*	19 13 S	146 48 E
100	Toyama, *Japan*	36 42 N	137 14 E
100	Toyohashi, *Japan*	34 46 N	137 22 E
94	Trabzon, *Turkey*	41 0 N	39 43 E
58	Trenton, *Canada*	44 6 N	77 36 W
80	Trier, *Germany*	49 45 N	6 39 E
82	Trieste, *Italy*	45 40 N	13 47 E
97	Trincomalee, *Sri Lanka*	8 34 N	81 13 E
62	Trinidad, *U.S.A.*	37 10 N	104 31 W
65	Trinidad & Tobago, *S. America*	10 30 N	61 20 W
61	Trinity, *r., U.S.A.*	29 55 N	94 45 W
94	Tripoli, *Lebanon*	34 27 N	35 50 E
84	Tripoli, *Libya*	32 58 N	13 12 E
84	Tripolitania, *f., Libya*	31 0 N	13 30 E
60	Tripp, *U.S.A.*	43 13 N	97 58 W
75	Tristan da Cunha, *i., Atlantic Oc.*	37 50 S	12 30 W
96	Trivandrum, *India*	8 41 N	76 57 E
58	Trois-Rivières, *town, Canada*	46 21 N	72 34 W
81	Tromsö, *Norway*	69 42 N	19 0 E
81	Trondheim, *Norway*	63 36 N	10 23 E
59	Troy, *Ala., U.S.A.*	31 49 N	86 0 W
60	Troy, *Mo., U.S.A.*	38 59 N	90 59 W
82	Troyes, *France*	48 18 N	4 5 E
70	Trujillo, *Peru*	8 6 S	79 0 W
88	Tselinograd, *Kazakhstan*	51 10 N	71 28 E
100	Tsu, *Japan*	34 43 N	136 35 E
113	Tuamotu Archipelago, *is., Pacific Oc.*	17 0 S	142 0 W
63	Tucson, *U.S.A.*	32 13 N	110 58 W
63	Tucumcari, *U.S.A.*	35 10 N	103 44 W
101	Tuguegarao, *Phil.*	17 36 N	121 44 E
98	Tula, *r., Mongolia*	48 53 N	104 35 E
63	Tulare, *U.S.A.*	36 13 N	119 21 W
70	Tulcan, *Ecuador*	0 50 N	77 48 W
61	Tulsa, *U.S.A.*	36 9 N	95 58 W
70	Tuluá, *Colombia*	4 5 N	76 12 W
84	Tunis, *Tunisia*	36 47 N	10 10 E
84	Tunisia, *Africa*	34 0 N	9 0 E
61	Tupelo, *U.S.A.*	34 16 N	88 43 W
82	Turin, *Italy*	45 4 N	7 40 E
107	Turkana, L., *Kenya*	4 0 N	36 0 E
94	Turkey, *Asia*	39 0 N	35 0 E
88	Turkmenistan, *Asia*	40 0 N	60 0 E
65	Turks and Caicos Is., *C. America*	21 30 N	71 50 W
81	Turku, *Finland*	60 27 N	22 15 E
59	Tuscaloosa, *U.S.A.*	33 12 N	87 33 W
97	Tuticorin, *India*	8 48 N	78 10 E
56	Tutuila, *i., Samoa*	14 18 S	170 42 W
112	Tuvalu, *Pacific Oc.*	8 0 S	178 0 E
64	Tuxtla Gutiérrez, *Mexico*	16 45 N	93 9 W
83	Tuzla, *Bosnia.*	44 33 N	18 41 E
86	Tver', *Russian Fed.*	56 47 N	35 57 E
62	Twin Falls, *town, U.S.A.*	42 34 N	114 28 W
61	Tyler, *U.S.A.*	32 21 N	95 18 W
84	Tyrrhenian Sea, *Med. Sea*	39 0 N	12 30 E
88	Tyumen, *Russian Fed.*	57 11 N	65 29 E

U

PAGE	PLACENAME	LATITUDE	LONGITUDE
108	Ubangi, *r., Congo/Zaïre*	0 25 S	17 50 E
100	Ube, *Japan*	34 0 N	131 16 E
74	Uberaba, *Brazil*	19 47 S	47 57 W
74	Uberlândia, *Brazil*	18 57 S	48 17 W
98	Ubsa Nur, *l., Mongolia*	50 30 N	92 30 E
70	Ucayali, *r., Peru*	4 40 S	73 20 W
96	Udaipur, *India*	24 36 N	73 47 E
81	Uddevalla, *Sweden*	58 20 N	11 56 E
82	Udine, *Italy*	46 3 N	13 15 E
86	Ufa, *Russian Fed.*	54 45 N	55 58 E
108	Uganda, *Africa*	1 0 N	33 0 E
62	Uinta Mts., *U.S.A.*	40 45 N	110 5 W
102	Ujung Pandang, *Indonesia*	5 9 S	119 28 E
87	Ukraine, *Europe*	49 30 N	32 4 E
98	Ulan Bator, *Mongolia*	47 54 N	106 52 E
98	Ulan-Ude, *Russian Fed.*	51 55 N	107 40 E
98	Uliastaj, *Mongolia*	47 42 N	96 52 E
82	Ulm, *Germany*	48 24 N	10 0 E
100	Ulsan, *S. Korea*	35 32 N	129 21 E
86	Ul'yanovsk, *Russian Fed.*	54 19 N	48 22 E
81	Umeå, *Sweden*	63 50 N	20 15 E
108	Umtata, *South Africa*	31 35 S	28 47 E
53	Ungava B., *Canada*	59 0 N	67 30 W
95	United Arab Emirates, *Asia*	24 0 N	54 0 E
79	United Kingdom, *Europe*	54 0 N	3 0 W
54	United States of America, *N. America*	39 0 N	100 0 W
81	Uppsala, *Sweden*	59 55 N	17 38 E
86	Ural Mts., *Russian Fed.*	60 0 N	59 0 E
87	Ural'sk, *Kazakhstan*	51 19 N	51 20 E
52	Uranium City, *Canada*	59 32 N	108 43 W
60	Urbana, *U.S.A.*	40 7 N	88 12 W
88	Urgench, *Uzbekistan*	41 35 N	60 41 E
95	Urmia, L., *Iran*	37 40 N	45 28 E
64	Uruapan, *Mexico*	19 26 N	102 4 W
74	Uruguay, *r., Argentina/Uruguay*	34 0 S	58 30 W
74	Uruguay, *S. America*	33 15 S	56 0 W
98	Ürümqi, *China*	43 43 N	87 38 E
87	Ust Urt Plateau, *f., Kazakhstan*	43 30 N	55 0 E
88	Ust-Kamenogorsk, *Kazakhstan*	50 0 N	82 40 E
62	Utah, *d., U.S.A.*	39 37 N	112 28 W
58	Utica, *U.S.A.*	43 6 N	75 5 W
80	Utrecht, *Neth.*	52 4 N	5 7 E
100	Utsunomiya, *Japan*	36 40 N	139 52 E
88	Uzbekistan, *Asia*	42 0 N	63 0 E
83	Uzda, *Belorussia*	53 28 N	27 11 E
83	Uzhgorod, *Ukraine*	48 38 N	22 15 E

V

PAGE	PLACENAME	LATITUDE	LONGITUDE
81	Vaasa, Finland	63 6 N	21 36 E
96	Vadodara, India	22 19 N	73 14 E
82	Vaduz, Liech.	47 8 N	9 32 E
57	Valdez, U.S.A.	61 7 N	146 17 W
73	Valdivia, Chile	39 46 S	73 15 W
59	Valdosta, U.S.A.	30 51 N	83 51 W
82	Valence, France	44 56 N	4 54 E
84	Valencia, Spain	39 29 N	0 24 W
70	Valencia, Venezuela	10 14 N	67 59 W
80	Valenciennes, France	50 22 N	3 32 E
84	Valladolid, Spain	41 39 N	4 45 W
70	Valledupar, Colombia	10 31 N	73 16 W
84	Valletta, Malta	35 53 N	14 31 E
73	Valparaíso, Chile	33 2 S	71 38 W
94	Van, L., Turkey	38 35 N	42 52 E
62	Vancouver, Canada	49 13 N	123 6 W
62	Vancouver, U.S.A.	45 39 N	122 40 W
62	Vancouver I., Canada	50 0 N	126 0 W
81	Vänern, l., Sweden	59 0 N	13 15 E
112	Vanua Levu, i., Fiji	16 33 S	179 15 E
112	Vanuatu, Pacific Oc.	16 0 S	167 0 E
97	Varanasi, India	25 20 N	83 0 E
81	Varangerfjorden, est., Norway	70 0 N	29 30 E
83	Varna, Bulgaria	43 13 N	27 57 E
81	Västerås, Sweden	59 36 N	16 32 E
81	Vatnajökull, mts., Iceland	64 20 N	17 0 W
81	Vättern, l., Sweden	58 30 N	14 30 E
81	Växjö, Sweden	56 52 N	14 50 E
70	Venezuela, S. America	7 0 N	65 20 W
82	Venice, Italy	45 26 N	12 20 E
80	Venlo, Neth.	51 22 N	6 10 E
64	Veracruz, Mexico	19 11 N	96 10 W
108	Vereeniging, South Africa	26 41 S	27 56 E
89	Verkhoyansk, Russian Fed.	67 25 N	133 25 E
89	Verkhoyansk Range, mts., Russian Fed.	66 0 N	130 0 E
58	Vermont, d., U.S.A.	44 0 N	72 30 W
82	Verona, Italy	45 27 N	10 59 E
84	Versailles, France	48 48 N	2 8 E
84	Vesuvius, mtn., Italy	40 48 N	14 25 E
81	Viborg, Denmark	56 28 N	9 25 E
61	Vicksburg, U.S.A.	32 14 N	90 56 W
110	Victoria, d., Australia	37 0 S	145 0 E
62	Victoria, Canada	48 26 N	123 20 W
73	Victoria, Chile	38 13 S	72 20 W
108	Victoria Falls, f., Zimbabwe/Zambia	17 58 S	25 45 E
52	Victoria I., Canada	71 0 N	110 0 W
108	Victoria, L., Africa	1 0 S	33 0 E
82	Vienna, Austria	48 13 N	16 22 E
102	Vientiane, Laos	18 1 N	102 48 E
102	Vietnam, Asia	15 0 N	108 0 E
101	Vigan, Phil.	17 35 N	120 23 E
84	Vigo, Spain	42 15 N	8 44 W
97	Vijayawada, India	16 34 N	80 40 E
64	Villahermosa, Mexico	18 0 N	92 53 W
83	Vilnius, Lithuania	54 40 N	25 19 E
89	Vilyuysk, Russian Fed.	63 46 N	121 35 E
73	Viña del Mar, Chile	33 2 S	71 34 W
59	Vineland, U.S.A.	39 29 N	75 2 W
83	Vinnitsa, Ukraine	49 11 N	28 30 E
101	Virac, Phil.	13 35 N	124 12 E
67	Virgin Gorda, i., B.V.Is.	18 30 N	64 26 W
67	Virgin Is. (British), C. America	18 30 N	64 30 W
67	Virgin Is. (U.S.A.), C. America	18 30 N	65 0 W
59	Virginia, d., U.S.A.	37 30 N	78 45 W
59	Virginia Beach, town, U.S.A.	36 51 N	75 59 W
63	Visalia, U.S.A.	36 20 N	119 18 W
101	Visayan Sea, Phil.	11 40 N	123 40 E
52	Viscount Melville Sd., Canada	74 30 N	104 0 W
97	Vishakhapatnam, India	17 42 N	83 24 E
83	Vistula, r., Poland	54 23 N	18 52 E
86	Vitebsk, Belorussia	55 10 N	30 14 E
112	Viti Levu, i., Fiji	18 0 S	178 0 E
89	Vitim, r., Russian Fed.	59 30 N	112 36 E
74	Vitória, Brazil	20 19 S	40 21 W
84	Vitoria, Spain	42 51 N	2 40 W
71	Vitória da Conquista, Brazil	14 53 S	40 52 W
87	Vladikavkaz, Russian Fed.	43 2 N	44 43 E
86	Vladimir, Russian Fed.	56 8 N	40 25 E
99	Vladivostok, Russian Fed.	43 9 N	131 53 E
85	Vlorë, Albania	40 28 N	19 27 E
87	Volga, r., Russian Fed.	45 45 N	47 50 E
87	Volgograd, Russian Fed.	48 45 N	44 30 E
86	Vologda, Russian Fed.	59 10 N	39 55 E
106	Volta, L., Ghana	7 0 N	0 0 0
74	Volta Redonda, Brazil	22 31 S	44 5 W
87	Volzhskiy, Russian Fed.	48 48 N	44 45 E
86	Vorkuta, Russian Fed.	67 27 N	64 0 E
87	Voronezh, Russian Fed.	51 40 N	39 13 E

W

PAGE	PLACENAME	LATITUDE	LONGITUDE
80	Waal, r., Neth.	51 45 N	4 40 E
60	Wabash, r., U.S.A.	37 46 N	88 2 W
61	Waco, U.S.A.	31 55 N	97 8 W
107	Wad Medani, Sudan	14 24 N	33 30 E
80	Wadden Sea, Neth.	53 15 N	5 5 E
52	Waddington, Mt., Canada	51 30 N	125 0 W
100	Wakayama, Japan	34 12 N	135 10 E
82	Wałbrzych, Poland	50 48 N	16 19 E
79	Wales, d., U.K.	53 0 N	3 30 W
112	Wallis, Îles, is., Pacific Oc.	13 16 S	176 15 W
108	Walvis Bay, town, South Africa	22 50 S	14 31 E
111	Wanganui, New Zealand	39 56 S	175 0 E
83	Warsaw, Poland	52 15 N	21 0 E
82	Warta, r., Poland	52 45 N	15 9 E
59	Washington, U.S.A.	38 55 N	77 0 W
62	Washington, d., U.S.A.	47 43 N	120 0 W
58	Waterbury, U.S.A.	41 33 N	73 2 W
79	Waterford, Rep. of Ire.	52 16 N	7 8 W
58	Waterloo, Canada	43 28 N	80 31 W
58	Watertown, U.S.A.	43 59 N	75 55 W
60	Waukesha, U.S.A.	43 1 N	88 14 W
60	Wausau, U.S.A.	44 58 N	89 40 W
60	Wauwatosa, U.S.A.	43 4 N	88 2 W
114	Weddell Sea, Antarctica	73 0 S	42 0 W
99	Weifang, China	36 44 N	119 10 E
111	Wellington, New Zealand	41 17 S	174 47 E
99	Wenzhou, China	28 2 N	120 40 E
82	Weser, r., Germany	53 15 N	8 30 E
80	West Frisian Is., Neth.	53 20 N	5 0 E
75	West Indies, is., C. America	21 0 N	74 0 W
59	West Palm Beach, town, U.S.A.	26 42 N	80 5 W
80	West Schelde, est., Neth.	51 25 N	3 40 E
88	West Siberian Plain, f., Russian Fed.	60 0 N	75 0 E
58	West Virginia, d., U.S.A.	39 0 N	80 30 W
110	Western Australia, d., Australia	25 0 S	123 0 E
96	Western Ghats, mts., India	15 30 N	74 30 E
106	Western Sahara, Africa	25 0 N	13 30 W
112	Western Samoa, Pacific Oc.	13 55 S	172 0 W
111	Westport, New Zealand	41 46 S	171 38 E
111	Whangarei, New Zealand	35 43 S	174 20 E
58	Wheeling, U.S.A.	40 5 N	80 42 W
61	White, r., U.S.A.	33 53 N	91 10 W
107	White Nile, r., Sudan	15 45 N	32 25 E
86	White Sea, Russian Fed.	65 30 N	38 0 E
52	Whitehorse, Canada	60 41 N	135 8 W
63	Whitney, Mt., U.S.A.	36 35 N	118 18 W
110	Whyalla, Australia	33 4 S	137 34 E
61	Wichita, U.S.A.	37 41 N	97 20 W
61	Wichita Falls, town, U.S.A.	33 54 N	98 30 W
79	Wicklow Mts., Rep. of Ire.	53 6 N	6 20 W
82	Wiesbaden, Germany	50 5 N	8 15 E
79	Wight, Isle of, U.K.	50 40 N	1 17 W
103	Wilhelm, Mt., P.N.G.	6 0 S	144 55 E
80	Wilhelmshaven, Germany	53 32 N	8 7 E
58	Wilkes-Barre, U.S.A.	41 14 N	75 53 W
66	Willemstad, Neth. Antilles	12 12 N	68 56 W
58	Williamsport, U.S.A.	41 16 N	77 3 W
59	Wilmington, Del., U.S.A.	39 46 N	75 31 W
59	Wilmington, N.C., U.S.A.	34 14 N	77 55 W
59	Wilson, U.S.A.	35 43 N	77 56 W
62	Wind River Range, mts., U.S.A.	43 5 N	109 25 W
108	Windhoek, Namibia	22 34 S	17 6 E
58	Windsor, Canada	42 18 N	83 0 W
65	Windward Is., C. America	13 0 N	60 0 W
65	Windward Passage, str., Carib. Sea	20 0 N	74 0 W
60	Winnipeg, Canada	49 53 N	97 10 W
53	Winnipeg, L., Canada	52 45 N	98 0 W
60	Winona, U.S.A.	44 3 N	91 39 W
59	Winston-Salem, U.S.A.	36 5 N	80 18 W
82	Winterthur, Switz.	47 30 N	8 45 E
110	Winton, Australia	22 22 S	143 0 E
60	Wisconsin, d., U.S.A.	44 30 N	90 0 W
80	Witten, Germany	51 26 N	7 19 E
83	Włocławek, Poland	52 39 N	19 1 E
82	Wolfsburg, Germany	52 27 N	10 49 E
110	Wollongong, Australia	34 25 S	150 52 E
79	Wolverhampton, U.K.	52 35 N	2 6 W
100	Wonsan, N. Korea	39 7 N	127 26 E
60	Woods, L. of the, Canada/U.S.A.	49 15 N	94 45 W
108	Worcester, South Africa	33 39 S	19 26 E
79	Worcester, U.K.	52 12 N	2 12 W
58	Worcester, U.S.A.	42 14 N	71 48 W
89	Wrangel I., Russian Fed.	71 0 N	180 0 0
83	Wrocław, Poland	51 5 N	17 0 E
99	Wuhan, China	30 35 N	114 19 E
99	Wuhu, China	31 23 N	118 25 E
80	Wuppertal, Germany	51 15 N	7 10 E
82	Würzburg, Germany	49 48 N	9 57 E
98	Wutongqiao, China	29 21 N	103 48 E
99	Wuxi, China	31 35 N	120 19 E
99	Wuzhou, China	23 30 N	111 21 E
110	Wyndham, Australia	15 29 S	128 5 E
62	Wyoming, d., U.S.A.	43 10 N	107 36 W

X

PAGE	PLACENAME	LATITUDE	LONGITUDE
99	Xi'an, China	34 16 N	108 54 E
99	Xiangfan, China	32 20 N	112 5 E
99	Xiangtan, China	27 55 N	112 47 E
71	Xingu, r., Brazil	1 40 S	52 15 W
98	Xining, China	36 35 N	101 55 E
99	Xuzhou, China	34 17 N	117 18 E

Y

PAGE	PLACENAME	LATITUDE	LONGITUDE
89	Yablonovy Range, mts., Russian Fed.	53 20 N	115 0 E
62	Yakima, U.S.A.	46 36 N	120 31 W
89	Yakutsk, Russian Fed.	62 10 N	129 20 E
100	Yamagata, Japan	38 16 N	140 19 E
88	Yamal Pen., Russian Fed.	70 20 N	70 0 E
97	Yamuna, r., India	25 20 N	81 49 E
97	Yangon, Myanmar	16 45 N	96 20 E
99	Yantai, China	37 30 N	121 22 E
106	Yaoundé, Cameroon	3 51 N	11 31 E
86	Yaroslavl, Russian Fed.	57 34 N	39 52 E
100	Yatsushiro, Japan	32 32 N	130 35 E
95	Yazd, Iran	31 54 N	54 22 E
61	Yazoo, r., U.S.A.	32 22 N	91 0 W
86	Yekaterinburg, Russian Fed.	56 52 N	60 35 E
99	Yellow Sea, Asia	35 0 N	123 0 E
52	Yellowknife, Canada	62 30 N	114 29 W
62	Yellowstone, r., U.S.A.	47 55 N	103 45 W
107	Yemen, Asia	15 55 N	48 30 E
89	Yenisei, r., Russian Fed.	69 0 N	86 0 E
95	Yerevan, Armenia	40 10 N	44 31 E
99	Yichang, China	30 43 N	111 22 E
98	Yining, China	43 57 N	81 23 E
102	Yogyakarta, Indonesia	7 48 S	110 24 E
100	Yokohama, Japan	35 28 N	139 28 E
59	Yonkers, U.S.A.	40 56 N	73 52 W
79	York, U.K.	53 58 N	1 7 W
59	York, U.S.A.	39 58 N	76 44 W
110	York, C., Australia	10 58 S	142 40 E
58	Youngstown, U.S.A.	41 5 N	80 40 W
62	Yuba City, U.S.A.	39 8 N	121 27 W
65	Yucatan Channel, Carib. Sea	21 30 N	86 0 W
85	Yugoslavia, Europe	44 0 N	20 0 E
57	Yukon, r., U.S.A.	62 35 N	164 20 W
52	Yukon Territory, d., Canada	65 0 N	135 0 W
63	Yuma, U.S.A.	32 43 N	114 37 W
99	Yuzhno Sakhalinsk, Russian Fed.	46 58 N	142 45 E

Z

PAGE	PLACENAME	LATITUDE	LONGITUDE
80	Zaandam, Neth.	52 27 N	4 49 E
83	Zabrze, Poland	50 18 N	18 47 E
86	Zagorsk, Russian Fed.	56 20 N	38 10 E
82	Zagreb, Croatia	45 49 N	15 58 E
95	Zagros Mts., Iran	32 0 N	51 0 E
108	Zaïre, Africa	2 0 S	22 0 E
108	Zaïre, r., Zaïre	6 0 S	12 30 E
108	Zambezi, r., Mozambique/Zambia	18 15 S	35 55 E
108	Zambia, Africa	14 0 S	28 0 E
101	Zamboanga, Phil.	6 55 N	122 5 E
58	Zanesville, U.S.A.	39 56 N	82 1 W
108	Zanzibar, Tanzania	6 10 S	39 12 E
87	Zaporozhye, Ukraine	47 50 N	35 10 E
84	Zaragoza, Spain	41 39 N	0 54 W
106	Zaria, Nigeria	11 1 N	7 44 E
94	Zarqa, Jordan	32 4 N	36 5 E
81	Zealand, i., Denmark	55 30 N	12 0 E
80	Zeebrugge, Belgium	51 20 N	3 13 E
99	Zhangjiakou, China	41 0 N	114 50 E
99	Zhangzhou, China	24 57 N	118 36 E
99	Zhanjiang, China	21 5 N	110 12 E
99	Zhejiang, d., China	29 15 N	120 0 E
99	Zhengzhou, China	34 35 N	113 38 E
83	Zhitomir, Ukraine	50 18 N	28 40 E
99	Zibo, China	36 50 N	118 0 E
82	Zielona Góra, Poland	51 57 N	15 30 E
108	Zimbabwe, Africa	18 0 S	30 0 E
86	Zlatoust, Russian Fed.	55 10 N	59 38 E
94	Zonguldak, Turkey	41 26 N	31 47 E
83	Zrenjanin, Yugo.	45 22 N	20 23 E
98	Zunyi, China	27 41 N	106 50 E
82	Zürich, Switz.	47 23 N	8 33 E
82	Zwickau, Germany	50 43 N	12 30 E

Map Projections

Map projections are the means by which the earth's curved surface can be transferred to or projected upon a flat surface, like the pages of this atlas. They are systematic drawings of lines representing parallels or meridians on a flat surface. They show either the whole earth or some portion of it. No single map projection can represent the earth's spherical surface without some distortion or areas, shapes, directions, or distances.

Although in practice nearly all projections are derived mathematically, most are more easily visualized if you think of a light shining through the grid of parallels and meridians on a globe. The shadows these lines would cast on a flat piece of paper would form a projection. The piece of paper could also be rolled into a cylinder or a cone. Thus, there are several kinds of projections. Theses are azimuthal, cylindrical, and conical (*See* diagrams below).

Azimuthal

Cylindrical

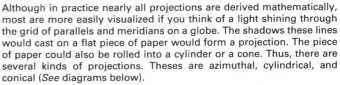

Conical

An Azimuthal projection is constructed by the projection of part of the globe onto a flat surface which touches the globe at only one point. The zenithal gnomonic projection (A) touches the globe at a pole. This is good for showing polar air routes, because the shortest distance between any two points is a straight line. Air-route distances from one point (e.g. Capetown) are best shown by the Oblique Zenithal Equidistant projection (B). Azimuthal projections are best for larger scale maps of small areas so that distortion around the edges is not too great.

Cylindrical projections are constructed by projecting a portion of the globe onto a cylinder which touches the globe only along one line, e.g. the equator. This line is the only one true to scale, with distortion of size and shape increasing towards the top and bottom of the cylinder. The Mercator projection (A) is one kind of cylindrical projection. It avoids distortion of shape by making an increase in scale along the parallels. Although there is still size distortion, the Mercator's best use is for navigation since directions can be plotted as straight lines. The Mollweide projection (B) is a cylindrical projection on which the meridians are no longer parallel. This is an equal-area projection, which is useful for mapping distributions. In this case, it is "interrupted" or cut apart in the oceans. Cylindrical projections are best for mapping the whole world.

Conical projections use the projection of the globe onto a cone which caps the globe and touches it along a parallel. The scale is correct along this line and along the meridians. In the simple conic projection (A), the scale is correct along the heavy parallel and the meridians. Bonne's projection (B) is another conical projection. It is an equal-area projection, but there is shape distortion around its edges. Conical projections cannot cover the entire globe. They are best suited for mid-latitude or temperate regions with large longitudinal extent, e.g. Asia.

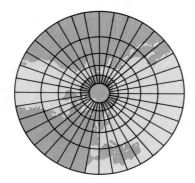

(A) **Zenithal Gnomonic**

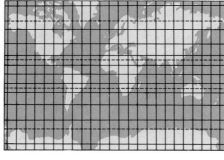

(A) **Mercator**

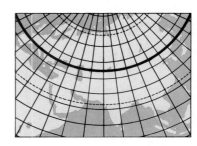

(A) **Simple Conic**

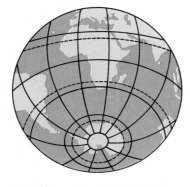

(B) **Oblique Zenithal Equidistant**

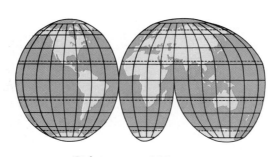

(B) **Interrupted Mollweide**

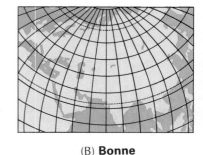

(B) **Bonne**

In this atlas, many projections are used. They have been carefully chosen for their specific advantages. The names of the projections appear below the bar scales on the maps. Almost all of the world and continental maps are equal-area projections. Most of the large-scale maps are conical projections, which have correct shapes and true directions.